Observational Research in U.S. Classroor---
New Approaches for Understanding Cultural and Linguistic Diversity

D1409638

The present national reform agendas stress th
expectations be accessible to all students, including students from groups
whose achievement has traditionally lagged behind that of majority culture
students. Improving achievement in U.S. schools, important for both social
and economic stability, will require that instruction be responsive to our
nation's increasingly diverse student population. This book includes theoretical frameworks as well as substantive research findings and provides
examples of recently developed classroom observation instruments based
on research on effective teaching practices for culturally and linguistically
diverse students. Each chapter presents a new aspect of classroom observation research that will assist educators in their endeavors to improve U.S.
schools.

Hersh C. Waxman is Professor of Educational Leadership and Cultural Studies in the College of Education at the University of Houston; a Principal Researcher in the U.S. Department of Education, National Center for Research
on Education, Diversity, and Excellence; and a Principal Investigator in the
U.S. Department of Education, National Laboratory for Student Success,
the Mid-Atlantic Regional Educational Laboratory. His research focuses on
classroom learning environments, school and teacher effectiveness, urban
education, and students at risk of failure.

Roland G. Tharp is Director of the Center for Research on Education, Diversity, and Excellence (CREDE); Professor of Education and Psychology
at the University of California, Santa Cruz; and recipient of the prestigious
1993 Grawemeyer Award in education for the book *Rousing Minds to Life:
Teaching, Learning, and Schooling in Social Context*. His most recent book is
Teaching Transformed: Achieving Excellence, Fairness, Inclusion, and Harmony.

R. Soleste Hilberg is an Education Research Specialist at the Center for
Research on Education, Diversity, and Excellence (CREDE) at the University
of California, Santa Cruz.

Observational Research in U.S. Classrooms was published in collaboration with
CREDE, a federally funded research and development program focused on
improving the education of students whose ability to reach their potential
is challenged by language or cultural barriers, race, geographic location, or
poverty.

This book is dedicated to the memory of Dr. Margaret Wang,
a wonderful educator, researcher, and mentor
who introduced me to the field of observing classroom behavior
in culturally diverse schools. (HCW)

Observational Research in U.S. Classrooms

New Approaches for Understanding Cultural and Linguistic Diversity

Edited by

HERSH C. WAXMAN
University of Houston

ROLAND G. THARP
University of California, Santa Cruz

R. SOLESTE HILBERG
University of California, Santa Cruz

CAMBRIDGE
UNIVERSITY PRESS

PUBLISHED BY THE PRESS SYNDICATE OF THE UNIVERSITY OF CAMBRIDGE
The Pitt Building, Trumpington Street, Cambridge, United Kingdom

CAMBRIDGE UNIVERSITY PRESS
The Edinburgh Building, Cambridge CB2 2RU, UK
40 West 20th Street, New York, NY 10011-4211, USA
477 Williamstown Road, Port Melbourne, VIC 3207, Australia
Ruiz de Alarcón 13, 28014 Madrid, Spain
Dock House, The Waterfront, Cape Town 8001, South Africa

http://www.cambridge.org

© Cambridge University Press 2004

First published 2004

Printed in the United States of America

Typeface Palatino 10/13 pt.   *System* LATEX 2$_\varepsilon$ [TB]

A catalog record for this book is available from the British Library.

Library of Congress Cataloging in Publication Data
Observational research in U.S. classrooms : new approaches for understanding
cultural and linguistic diversity / edited by Hersh C. Waxman, Roland G. Tharp,
R. Soleste Hilberg.
    p.   cm.
Includes bibliographical references and index.
ISBN 0-521-81453-7 – ISBN 0-521-89142-6 (pb.)
1. Observation (Educational method)   2. Teaching – Social aspects – United States.
I. Waxman, Hersholt C.   II. Tharp, Roland G., 1930–   III. Hilberg, R. Soleste., 1959–
LB1027.28 .O35   2003
371.1'007'2 – dc21   2002031563

ISBN 0 521 81453 7 hardback
ISBN 0 521 89142 6 paperback

Contents

Tables, Figures, and Appendixes

FIGURES

Contributors

Marty Alberg, Center for Research in Educational Policy, University of Memphis

Marisa Castellano, Center for Social Organization of Schools, Johns Hopkins University

Amanda Datnow, Rossier School of Education, University of Southern California

R. William Doherty, Center for Research, Diversity, and Excellence, University of California, Santa Cruz

Jana Echevarria, Department of Educational Psychology, California State University, Long Beach

Georgia Epaloose, Zuni Public School District, Zuni, New Mexico

Peggy Estrada, Center for Research, Diversity, and Excellence, University of California, Santa Cruz

R. Soleste Hilberg, Center for Research, Diversity, and Excellence, University of California, Santa Cruz

Stephanie L. Knight, Department of Educational Psychology, Texas A&M University

Deborah Lowther, College of Education, University of Memphis

Yolanda N. Padrón, College of Education, University of Houston

Héctor H. Rivera, College of Education, University of Houston

Steven M. Ross, Center for Research in Educational Policy, University of Memphis

Deborah J. Short, Center for Applied Linguistics, U.S. Department of Education

Lana J. Smith, Instruction and Curriculum Leadership, University of Memphis

Robert G. Smith, Superintendent, Arlington Public Schools, Arlington, Virginia

Roland G. Tharp, Center for Research, Diversity, and Excellence, University of California, Santa Cruz

Hersh C. Waxman, College of Education, University of Houston

Susan Yonezawa, Center for Research in Educational Equity, Assessment, and Teaching Excellence, University of California, San Diego

1

Introduction

Purposes and Perspectives on Classroom Observation Research

R. Soleste Hilberg, Hersh C. Waxman, and Roland G. Tharp

The purpose of this book is to provide researchers, scholars, and educators with examples of recently developed classroom observation instruments based on current research on effective teaching practices, many developed explicitly for use in today's culturally and linguistically diverse classrooms. The chapters describe several new instruments and include examples of how they have been used to examine effective instruction, schools, and school-based reform models in classrooms and schools with diverse students. Although most observational research in culturally and linguistically diverse settings has been qualitative, systematic classroom observation research has been widely used during the past three decades (Waxman, 1995; Waxman & Huang, 1999). And, although findings from that research have led to a substantive knowledge base on effective teaching practices (Brophy & Good, 1986; Waxman & Walberg, 1982), many critics have argued that systematic observation lacks a theoretical/conceptual framework and merely focuses on discrete categories or small segments of observable teacher behaviors that can be easily measured with observation instruments (Ornstein, 1991). Indeed, most of the early observation instruments focused on direct instruction and easily quantifiable behaviors associated with basic skills instruction, rendering them inappropriate, or when used alone inadequate, for examining today's diverse classrooms. Today, researchers and educators need instruments based on the most recent theoretical/conceptual work and empirical research on effective pedagogy (Tharp, Estrada, Dalton, & Yamauchi, 2000; Waxman & Walberg, 1999). This book presents a rich variety of such instruments.

The editors and authors of this book are all affiliated with the Center for Research on Education, Diversity, and Excellence (CREDE). Most of the instruments and methods in this book were recently presented at CREDE-sponsored symposia at the annual meeting of the American Education Research Association (AERA) or the Invitational Each Teach Classroom Observation Conference held in Santa Cruz, California, in September 1999. Most of the contributors to this book also are prominent educators with major research programs focusing on culturally and linguistically diverse classrooms.

SYSTEMATIC CLASSROOM OBSERVATION

Systematic classroom observation is a quantitative method of measuring classroom behaviors from direct observations that specifies both the events or behaviors that are to be observed and how they are to be recorded (Medley, 1992). Prior to the use of systematic observational methods, research on effective teaching typically consisted of subjective data based on personal and anecdotal accounts of effective teaching (Nuthall & Alton-Lee, 1990). In order to develop a scientific basis to teaching, researchers began to use the more objective and reliable measures of systematic classroom observation. In the past few decades, several hundred different observational systems have been developed and used in classrooms and research studies (Anderson & Burns, 1989).

Generally, data collected through systematic observation focus on the frequency with which specific behaviors or types of behavior occur in the classroom and the length of time they occur. Several elements are common to most observational systems: (a) a purpose for the observation, (b) operational definitions of all observed behaviors, (c) training procedures for observers, (d) a specific observational focus, (e) a setting, (f) a unit of time, (g) an observation schedule, (h) a method to record the data, and (i) methods to process and analyze data (Stallings & Mohlman, 1988).

Although several observational procedures or techniques have been used to examine effective teaching (e.g., charts, rating scales, checklists, and narrative descriptions), the most widely used method has been systematic classroom observation based on interactive coding systems. These interactive coding systems allow the observer to record nearly everything that students and teachers do during a given time interval (Stallings & Mohlman, 1988). These interaction systems are very objective and typically do not require the observer to make strong inferences or judgments about the behaviors they observe in the classroom.

In other words, these low-inference observational systems provide specific and easy identifiable behaviors that observers can easily code (Stodolsky, 1990).

Some of the major advantages of using classroom observation are that they (a) permit researchers to study the processes of education in naturalistic settings, (b) provide more detailed and precise evidence than other data sources, and (c) can be used to stimulate change and verify that the change occurred (Anderson & Burns, 1989). The descriptions of instructional events that are provided by this method have also been found to lead to improved understanding and better models for improving teaching (Copley & Williams, 1993; Good & Biddle, 1988).

Another advantage of systematic observation is that the findings from research studies using them have provided a coherent, well-substantiated knowledge base about effective instruction. Many of the reviews and summaries of the classroom observation research have consistently found that a number of classroom behaviors significantly relate to students' academic achievement (Brophy & Good, 1986; Rosenshine, 1987; Rosenshine & Stevens, 1986; Walberg, 1986, 1991, 1995). Several aspects of classroom instruction such as (a) conducting daily reviews, (b) presenting new material, (c) conducting guided practice, (d) providing feedback and correctives, (e) conducting independent practice, and (f) conducting weekly and monthly reviews have been found to be significantly related to students' academic achievement (Rosenshine, 1987). In other words, research using systematic classroom observation has provided us with a substantial knowledge base that has helped us understand effective teaching.

PURPOSES OF CLASSROOM OBSERVATION

Traditionally, there have been four specific areas in which systematic classroom observation has been found to be especially useful for educational practice: (a) describing instructional practices, (b) investigating instructional inequities for different groups of students, (c) improving teacher education programs, and (d) improving teachers' classroom instruction based on feedback from individual classroom profiles.

Describing Instructional Processes

Two of the fundamental purposes of classroom observation research are describing the current status of instructional practices and identifying instructional problems (Good, 1988; Good & Brophy, 2000; Waxman, 1995; Waxman & Huang, 1999). As Good (1988) puts it, "one role of observational research is to describe what takes place in classrooms in order to delineate the complex practical issues that confront practitioners" (p. 337). Many observational studies have been designed to describe specific educational phenomena. Large-scale observational studies such as those of Sirotnik (1983) and Waxman, Huang, and Padrón (1995), for example, have examined instructional practices in elementary and secondary schools. Sirotnik (1983) examined 1,000 elementary and secondary classrooms and found that there was very little variety in teaching practices across subjects and grades. He found that the majority of class time was spent either with the teacher lecturing to the class or students working on written assignments. Waxman, Huang, and Padrón (1995) observed 90 sixth- and eighth-grade classrooms from 16 inner-city middle level schools and found similar results. Students were typically involved in whole-class instruction and were not interacting with either their teacher or other students. Students rarely selected their own instructional activities and were generally very passive in the classroom, often just watching or listening to the teacher, even though they were on task about 94% of the time. The teacher observation results revealed that teachers typically focused on the content of the task or assignment, responded to students' signals, communicated the task's procedures, and checked students' work. Teachers spent very little time interacting with students regarding personal issues, encouraging students to succeed, showing personal regard for students, and showing interest in students' work.

Another aspect of descriptive observational studies involves the extent to which technology is used in the classroom. Although a large number of studies have examined technology use in schools, most of these studies have relied on self-report data from administrators, teachers, or students. These types of data are often unreliable and tend to be upwardly biased in the direction of overreporting actual technology use. Therefore, it is important to observe and record the extent to which technology is used in classrooms and used by individual students. In one such study, Waxman and Huang (1995) used systematic classroom observation to examine the extent to which computer technology was integrated into the curriculum of 200 elementary and secondary school inner-city classrooms. They found that there was no integration (i.e., use) of computer technology in the elementary school classrooms, and students were observed working with computers only 2% of the time in middle school classrooms. Huang and Waxman (1996) also conducted systematic observations of 1,315 middle school students in 220 mathematics classrooms to examine technology use. Results revealed that students were observed using calculators about 25% of the time, but they used computers less than 1% of the time in their mathematics classes.

Other work in the area of instructional technology has focused on how technology use impacts instructional behaviors and students' motivation, anxiety, and perceptions of their classroom learning environment (Waxman & Huang, 1996, 1996–1997). In a study involving classroom observations of over 2,000 middle school students, Waxman and Huang (1996) found significant differences in classroom instruction, depending upon the amount of technology used by the teacher. Instruction in classroom settings where technology was not often used tended to involve whole-class approaches in which students generally listened or watched the teacher. Instruction in classroom settings where technology was moderately used had much less whole-class instruction and much more independent work. These findings are quite similar to those of previous research that supports the notion that technology use may change teaching from the traditional teacher-centered model to a more student-centered instructional approach. Another important finding from this study was that students in classrooms where technology was moderately used were also found to be on task significantly more than students who were in settings where technology was not widely used.

Some other uses of descriptive observational studies have been to (a) evaluate programs and, more specifically, evaluate the fidelity or degree of implementation of programs (Stallings & Freiberg, 1991), (b) examine the extent to which higher-level thought processes are emphasized in schools (Padrón & Waxman, 1993), and (c) investigate the extent to which multicultural education is emphasized in urban classrooms (Saldana & Waxman, 1996, 1997). A final important use involves school effectiveness studies in which classroom observation data have been used to investigate observable differences between effective and ineffective schools (Stringfield & Teddlie, 1991; Teddlie, Kirby, & Stringfield, 1989; Teddlie & Stringfield, 1993; Waxman & Huang, 1997; Waxman, Huang, Anderson, & Weinstein, 1997). Waxman and Huang (1997), for example, observed over 700 students from four effective and four ineffective urban elementary schools that served predominantly African American students and found that students from the effective schools were observed significantly more (a) working in an individualized setting, (b) interacting with their teacher, and (c) working on written assignments. On the other hand, students from the ineffective schools were observed in (a) whole-class settings, (b) not interacting with their teacher, (c) interacting with others, (d) reading, and (e) working with manipulative materials significantly more than students from the effective schools.

Identifying Instructional Inequities

A second area in which systematic classroom observation has been found to be beneficial is in investigating instructional inequities for different groups of students. Classroom observation can answer some important questions, such as "Are some students being treated differently in the classroom, and does that explain why some students learn more than others?" Often this issue has been defined as differences in opportunity to learn or inequitable allocation of instruction. Another way of asking this question is "To what extent is there variation in the quality and quantity of instruction that students experience in school, and does that variation explain inequality in educational outcomes?"

Several studies have found that some groups or types of students are treated differently by teachers in classrooms and that these inequitable patterns of teacher–student interaction in classrooms result in differential learning outcomes for students (Fennema & Peterson, 1987). Many studies, for example, have found gender imbalances in teachers' interaction patterns in the classroom. Brophy and Good's (1974) review of the research found that consistent sex-related differences exist in the classroom in teachers' interaction patterns. Boys, for example, typically have been found to receive more praise and criticism in the classroom than girls. Brophy and Good also found that teachers have more behavioral, procedural, and academic interactions with boys than with girls. Boys have also been found to ask more questions in the classroom, and teachers have been found to ask boys more questions. Good and his colleagues (Good, Slavings, Harel, & Emerson, 1987; Good, Slavings, & Mason, 1988) have also conducted several observational studies that examined why low-achieving students in secondary schools asked fewer questions than high-achieving students. They found that students from an upper-middle-class elementary school asked more questions than students from lower-middle-class schools.

Other studies have looked at both sex- and ethnic-related differences in the classroom. Hart (1989) examined the relationship between teacher–student interaction and mathematics achievement by race and sex. She found that (a) White and Black male students had more classroom interactions than students from other groups, (b) there was a disparity in the type of interaction between White and Black students, and (c) boys were involved in more public interactions with teachers than girls. In other words, it appears that patterns of teacher–student interaction may be influenced not only by the sex of the student, but also by the ethnicity of the student.

Padrón, Waxman, and Huang (1999) observed behavior differences between resilient (i.e., successful) and nonresilient (i.e., less successful) elementary school students from low socioeconomic backgrounds. They found that resilient students spent significantly more time interacting with teachers for instructional purposes, whereas nonresilient students spent more time interacting with other students for social or personal purposes. Resilient students were also observed watching or listening significantly more often than nonresilient students, whereas nonresilient students were observed more often not attending to the task. The percentage of time that resilient students were observed on task (85%) was much higher than that of nonresilient students (61%). The magnitude of these differences was both statistically and educationally significant and illustrated the instructional inequities that exist within classrooms.

The findings from these classroom observational studies have important policy implications for schools. If differential classroom behaviors by sex and ethnicity are found to exist, policymakers may need to examine the quality and quantity of classroom instruction for some groups of students and determine if instructional interventions are needed. In future studies, researchers may also want to examine teachers' expectations and/or the classroom behavior of teachers to see if they impact the classroom behavior of individual students.

Improving Teacher Education Programs

Although there are conflicting findings regarding the research on the effects of early field experiences (Waxman & Walberg, 1986), there is some evidence that systematic classroom observation is an effective component of preservice teacher education programs (Freiberg & Waxman, 1988; Merkley & Hoy, 1992–1993; Timm & Marchant, 1992; Waxman, Rodriguez, Padrón, & Knight, 1988). Systematic observation of classroom teachers provides prospective teachers with the opportunity to actually observe specific teaching behaviors emphasized in teacher education courses. It allows prospective teachers the opportunity to integrate what they are learning in their teacher education courses with the realities of the classroom. Furthermore, such focused observations allow prospective teachers to see how classroom instruction can differentially influence student behavioral and affective outcomes.

Waxman et al. (1988) illustrated how the use of systematic classroom observation can be an important component of teacher education programs. Not only did the prospective teachers in the study observe some of the teaching skills that were emphasized in their teacher education courses, but they also observed how those instructional behaviors differentially affected student outcomes. Merkley and Hoy (1992–1993) found that observation improved preservice teachers' ability to describe selected classroom teaching behaviors and cite significantly more examples than students in the control group, who received the more typical written material and lecture on a classroom lesson. Systematic classroom observation can provide a common language for describing effective teaching. Such observation enables prospective teachers to focus on specific teaching skills that they have been learning about in their pedagogy courses. Many of the prospective teachers in the Waxman et al. (1988) study, for example, indicated that the systematic observations were the most beneficial aspect of the course for them. They also reported that their observations helped them become more aware of the social reality of teaching from the teacher's perspective.

Another area in which systematic classroom observation can help prospective teachers is during the student teaching phase. Freiberg, Waxman, and Houston (1987), for example, used systematic classroom observation to provide feedback to student teachers. In their experimental study, one group of student teachers received traditional supervision from a university supervisor, the second group of student teachers received traditional supervision and systematic feedback about their classroom instruction from the Stallings Observational System (SOS), and the third group of student teachers received systematic feedback, engaged in self-analysis, and received feedback from their peers. At the end of one semester, student teachers who had engaged in self-analysis and collegial feedback significantly improved their classroom instruction in desired directions, whereas student teachers in the other two groups did not. This study clearly suggests that when student teachers receive systematic feedback on their classroom instruction, engage in discussions about their instruction with their peers and supervisor, and conduct self-analyses of their teaching, they are likely to improve their instruction. The findings from this study also suggest that systematic feedback alone may not be sufficient to improve the instruction of student teachers.

A final area in which observation may be especially useful is during the induction phase or first few years of teaching. Schaffer, Stringfield, and Wolfe (1992), for example, used classroom observation data collected from a university-based, collaborative 2-year teacher induction program to improve beginning teachers' classroom instruction. For each year of the project, individualized feedback on classroom instruction was provided to teachers near the beginning of the school year. These teachers also received a 3-hour feedback/instruction session each week in which their classroom profiles were discussed along with other instructional and organizational classroom issues. Classroom observation data were similarly collected on each teacher near the end of the school year. During the first year of the program, these beginning teachers improved their instruction in classroom organizational and management skills. During the second year, the improvement was found to be in the more intellectually complex areas of teaching.

Improving Teaching Practices

Research using observational methods has yielded important information that has practical implications for the improvement of teaching practices. One of the traditional problems hindering teachers' classroom instruction has been the lack of valid and accurate information that teachers could use to facilitate their professional growth (Johnson, 1974). Many teachers, even experienced ones, are not always aware of the nature of their interactions with individual students (Doyle, 1979). Consequently, one of the most important purposes of systematic classroom observation is to improve teachers' classroom instruction (Stallings & Freiberg, 1991; Stallings, Needels, & Stayrook, 1979). Feedback from individual classroom profiles derived from systematic observations has been found to help teachers understand their own strengths and weaknesses and has consequently enabled them to improve their instruction significantly. Using feedback, teachers become aware of how their classroom functions and thus can modify their teaching behaviors (Brophy, 1979; Stallings, Needels, & Sparks, 1987). This process typically involves having trained observers systematically observe teachers and students in their classrooms and later providing teachers with information about the observation in clinical sessions. This approach is based on the assumption that teachers value accurate information that can be useful in improving their instruction.

There is growing evidence that feedback from systematic observations can be used to improve teaching (Stallings & Freiberg, 1991). Several studies have found that teachers positively changed their attitude and behaviors toward pupils after receiving feedback from classroom observations (Ebmeier & Good, 1979; Good & Brophy, 1974; Good & Grouws, 1979; Stallings, 1980). Good and Brophy's (1974) *treatment study* exemplifies this type of research. In that study, teachers were given feedback based on 40 hours of classroom observation. As a result of this "one-shot" interview in which feedback was given, teachers' interaction patterns changed, and their attitudes toward individual students changed, too. Stallings (1980), Ebmeier and Good (1979), and Good and Grouws (1979) have utilized similar strategies. Teachers were given individual feedback regarding their classroom instruction and then were found to change their behavior in desirable ways. All these studies have found that teachers can improve their classroom instruction given appropriate feedback and suggestions for improvement.

The overall findings from these studies suggest that feedback from classroom observations is a viable and effective mechanism for providing teachers with the information they need about their classroom behavior. This feedback is intended to create an *imbalance* in teachers' perceptions of their own behaviors. This imbalance exists whenever teachers find out that their attitudes or perceptions of their teaching differ from those of trained observers. Teachers in such a state of imbalance are motivated to do something about their behavior in order to restore their balanced condition (Gage, 1972). A similar notion is that self-awareness increases teachers' control of their actions and the possibility that they will modify them (Feiman, 1981). More recently, Waxman et al. (1995) provided schoolwide feedback to middle school teachers that compared their school profile on classroom instructional behaviors to an overall districtwide average of these same behaviors. Feedback from these profiles was used to stimulate dialogue and discussion about instructional strengths and weaknesses in the school. The profiles also helped initiate discussion about specific instructional areas that needed to be improved in the school. It should be pointed out again that these profiles provided some guidelines for practice; they were not attempts to tell teachers what to do. These profiles provide teachers with concepts and criteria that they can use to reflect about their own teaching

(Nuthall & Alton-Lee, 1990). The feedback session was not viewed as one in which research findings should be applied to specific rules or guidelines for teachers to follow. Rather, the observational feedback was intended to be used as a guide for teachers so that they could reflect on their practices and decide what action to take. In-services, workshops, formalized staff development programs, and university courses were some of the possibilities that teachers could choose if they wanted to continue to collaborate with researchers in order to help them improve their instruction. In summary, the use of feedback from classroom observations appears to be a potent strategy that can improve instructional behaviors in specific classrooms and schools.

OVERVIEW OF BOOK

This book provides a unique contribution to the field of school and classroom research and practice. At present there is growing interest in systematic classroom observation, as evidenced by the large number of recent studies in the United States and other countries that have used such methods (Waxman, 1995; Waxman & Huang, 1999). The Classroom Observation Special Interest Group of AERA has also seen a large increase in the number of U.S. and international educators who have attended their sessions at AERA annual meetings.

Although the primary focus of the chapters in this book is either (a) newly developed instruments based on research on teacher and school effectiveness in diverse classrooms and their theoretical and conceptual frameworks or (b) descriptions of empirical findings from recent studies in diverse classroom settings, using new instruments or combined methodologies, each chapter describes the development, the theoretical/conceptual background, methods, reliability, and validity data, and appropriate uses of the instruments used, as well as substantive research findings obtained from use of the instrument(s).

In chapter 2, "Using Multiple Perspectives in Observations of Diverse Classrooms: The Sheltered Instruction Observation Protocol (SIOP)," Jana Echevarria and Deborah J. Short present the SIOP, a 30-item instrument based on effective sheltered instruction (SI) for English language learners, developed through CREDE research to help schools meet the challenge of educating our nation's increasingly linguistically and culturally diverse students. Principles from English as a second language and bilingual education research contributed to the theoretical rationale. The SI model is grounded in the understanding that English language learners can acquire content knowledge while they develop and improve their academic English language skills. Each item of the SIOP specifies a feature of effective sheltered instruction. The SIOP offers an innovative approach for observing and measuring the effectiveness of sheltered lessons and provides university faculty, teachers, and principals with explicit information on what constitutes good sheltered instruction. It has been used in classroom-based research to observe and rate sheltered lessons and in professional development to help teachers plan and implement high-quality lessons.

In chapter 3, R. Soleste Hilberg, R. William Doherty, Georgia Epaloose, and Roland G. Tharp present "The Standards Performance Continuum" (SPC), a 5-point rubric for assessing teacher performance of the Standards for Effective Pedagogy, instructional strategies advocated by Tharp, Estrada, Dalton, and Yamauchi (2000) for teaching linguistically and culturally diverse students. These standards are drawn from sociocultural and cognitive theories of teaching and learning. Their effectiveness is explained in terms of how each standard increases the likelihood that learners will elaborate and, consequently, learn instructional content. This chapter describes the measure and includes information relevant to its use as a research instrument, and it discusses statistical methods appropriate for SPC data. This chapter also presents studies that used the SPC to (a) examine the relationship between teacher performance of the Standards for Effective Pedagogy and student achievement, (b) determine the extent to which the standards were used at a school site, and (c) use the SPC to facilitate change in teaching and document the progress of reforms that address improved teaching practice.

In chapter 4, "The Uses of the Classroom Observation Schedule to Improve Classroom Instruction," Hersh C. Waxman and Yolanda N. Padrón present the development and uses of the Classroom Observation Schedule (COS), a unique classroom observation instrument that focuses on student behavior rather than on teaching. This systematic instrument documents individual student behaviors with reference to (a) interactions with teachers and/or peers and the purpose of those interactions, (b) settings in which observed behaviors occur, (c) types of material with which students are working, and (d) specific types of activities in which they engage. The COS was originally developed at the Learning Development and Research Center (University of Pittsburgh) and has been slightly modified and used in two other federally funded national research centers: the Center for Education in the Inner Cities and CREDE. It also has been used in a number of recent studies examining effective instruction in multiethnic settings. Data from the COS can be used as process data (i.e., independent variables) that directly or indirectly affect student outcomes. Data may also serve as dependent variables that are associated with contextual conditions, teacher attitudes or behaviors, and the degree of program implementation variables or to assess changes in aspects of student behavior and classroom instruction.

Chapter 5, by Stephanie L. Knight and Robert G. Smith, "Development and Use of a Classroom Observation Instrument to Investigate Teaching for Meaning in Diverse Classrooms," describes a classroom observation instrument based on the Teaching for Meaning (TFM) instructional model, developed for students placed at risk of school failure as a counter to programs for at-risk students that focus on basic skills instruction. Knight and Smith posit that the recent emphasis on high-stakes testing may lead to an even greater push for basic skills instruction for low-performing students, often students who live in poverty or are linguistically or culturally diverse. TFM is characterized by instruction that embeds skill learning in activities that feature conceptually challenging content and draw on students' prior knowledge to make the content meaningful. This instructional model was found to increase student learning in areas requiring advanced thinking skills. The TFM instrument includes three components: (a) determination of student engagement rates, (b) a log to record qualitative data on classroom processes and events related to TFM behaviors, and (c) indicators of seven target behaviors representing teaching for meaning rated using a Likert-type scale. The authors effectively illustrate the utility of measures that combine both qualitative and quantitative components. This chapter summarizes the use of the instrument in two studies that examined the implementation and quality of teaching for meaning behaviors and their relationship to other outcome measures.

In chapter 6, "Patterns of Language Arts Instructional Activity and Excellence in First- and Fourth-Grade Culturally and Linguistically Diverse Classrooms," Peggy Estrada presents a study in which she examined pedagogy and classroom organization in culturally and linguistically diverse classrooms using the Activity Settings Observation System (ASOS) (Chapter 9). Her study provides a quantitative overview of instructional patterns found in first- and fourth-grade language arts classrooms. She documented teachers' use of effective classroom organization and pedagogy, and found that teachers who use more effective pedagogy also tend to use multiple simultaneous diverse activities, and that students whose teachers used more of the effective pedagogy features measured with the ASOS demonstrated higher achievement on both teacher ratings of student performance and norm-referenced tests. These findings are representative of the types of findings that can be obtained using systematic classroom observation instrumentation.

In chapter 7, "Using Classroom Observation as a Research and Formative Evaluation Tool in Educational Reform: The School Observation Measure," Steven M. Ross, Lana J. Smith, Marty Alberg, and Deborah Lowther present a classroom observation instrument developed at the Center for Research in Educational Policy at the University of Memphis to provide a "snapshot" of the teaching and learning activities *throughout a school*. The School Observation Measure (SOM) was developed so that key stakeholders can receive immediate information about the effects of reforms and to justify efforts and expenditure of resources because the ultimate goal of reforms, improved student learning, is typically not evidenced for 5 or more years. The SOM focuses on classroom teaching as the factor most likely to affect student achievement. During the past several years, SOM has formed the cornerstone of both research and formative evaluation studies in over 300 schools to determine how educational reform efforts are impacting changes in teaching consonant with instructional goals. This chapter describes the development, content, validation, and application of SOM to research on teaching and learning, with emphasis on recent uses in culturally diverse settings.

In chapter 8, "Observing School Restructuring in Multilingual, Multicultural Classrooms: Balancing Ethnographic and Evaluative Approaches," Amanda Datnow and Susan Yonezawa present their *eclectic* methodology for conducting classroom observations in culturally and linguistically diverse schools. Their methodology is four-pronged, covering the range of observational methods from ethnographic to low-inference, and was designed to gather a variety of data to illuminate the complexities inherent in schoolwide reform. Data collected by this methodology were used to evaluate school implementations of externally developed reform models. To date, little attention has been given to how the promoted reform models suit schools serving linguistically and culturally diverse student populations. The rich and varied information on the effects of restructuring models that can be obtained from using this methodology is highly relevant to the policy community. This becomes increasingly important as districts, states, and the U.S.

government begin to embrace external reform models with a fervor heretofore unseen.

Chapter 9, "Sociocultural Activity Settings in the Classroom: A Study of a Classroom Observation System," by Héctor H. Rivera and Roland G. Tharp, presents the theoretical conceptualization, development, and measurement properties of an observational measure used for coding features of effective instruction for diverse students. This instrument is based on CREDE's Standards for Effective Pedagogy and is unique in that it uses the *activity setting* as the unit for analysis. The Activity Setting Observation System (ASOS) provides a "thin," quantitative description of classroom activity by recording the presence or absence of the following aspects of activity settings: Product of Activity, Student Initiative or Choice, Joint Productive Activity, Modeling and Demonstration, Teacher/Student Dialogue, and Responsive Assistance. All ASOS categories are discussed in the language of sociocultural theory. The study presented in this chapter yielded significant levels of observer reliability, and it outlines the steps necessary to achieve successful observer training and reliability.

Chapter 10, "The Influence of School Reform on Classroom Instruction in Diverse Schools: Findings from an Observational Study of *Success for All*," by Marisa Castellano and Amanda Datnow, presents a study in which the authors examine the effectiveness of a comprehensive school reform for culturally and linguistically diverse students. Castellano and Datnow maintain that educators know what is needed to improve education for all students, and that the present task is to create the conditions in schools under which all children can succeed. The authors posit that reforms must affect the classroom if they are to be successful, and yet little is known about what occurs at the classroom level. In their study, they used both quantitative and qualitative methods to examine *Success for All* (SFA), a reform emphasizing reading success in elementary school featuring highly specified materials and teaching methods. SFA reorganizes instructional time and resources to provide a rich reading curriculum. The authors explore the effects of that reorganization on both teachers and students in schools serving diverse students, and whether those changes result in improved student engagement and learning.

The final chapter, "Future Directions for Classroom Observation Research," by Hersh C. Waxman, R. Soleste Hilberg, and Roland G. Tharp, summarizes the work presented in the book, reviews some of the ways classroom observation has contributed to the research knowledge in the field of teacher effectiveness, and discusses some of the important implications of the book for the improvement of teaching and student learning in culturally diverse settings. Some of the criticisms and cautions related to the use of structured observation and techniques are also summarized. Finally, some new directions for observational research are reported and three specific views are described: (a) using instruments that reflect best practices or educational standards, (b) instruments that focus on student behaviors as well as teachers, and (c) combining qualitative and quantitative methods in observation instruments.

SUMMARY

Research on systematic classroom observation has been conducted for nearly four decades, but for the most part, this work has not had a substantive impact on the basic instruction approaches that exist today. Despite the growing evidence that students from culturally and linguistically diverse settings do not respond to traditional instruction approaches, this direct instructional model of teaching still persists (Waxman & Padrón, 2002; Waxman, Padrón, & Arnold, 2001). Although there have been slight shifts of focus in some content areas, such as science and mathematics, from the traditional lecture and drill approaches to a slightly greater emphasis on teaching for understanding and teaching in investigative ways (McKinney, 1992), these shifts of emphasis will have no long-term effects unless there are mechanisms to foster their development and use. There needs to be a strong commitment on the part of teachers to change their traditional teaching practices. To build this commitment, teachers need to believe that these practices will make a difference, and they also need administrative support and training.

In conclusion, the observational instruments and instructional behaviors described in this book provide promising new directions in the education of students from linguistically and culturally diverse settings. The book will be of interest to researchers, scholars, and educators who teach about or conduct classroom research in culturally diverse settings. The theoretical/conceptual frameworks of the instruments and the substantive findings from the studies will also be of great interest to educators.

References

Anderson, L. W., & Burns, R. B. (1989). *Research in classrooms: The study of teachers, teaching, and instruction.* Oxford: Pergamon Press.

Brophy, J. E. (1979). *Using observation to improve your teaching* (Occasional Paper No. 21). East Lansing: Institute for Research on Teaching, Michigan State University.

Brophy, J. E., & Good, T. L. (1974). *Teacher–student relationships: Causes and consequences.* New York: Holt, Rinehart, & Winston.

Brophy, J. E., & Good, T. L. (1986). Teacher behavior and student achievement. In M. C. Wittrock (Ed.), *Handbook of research on teaching* (3rd ed., pp. 328–375). New York: Macmillan.

Copley, J. V., & Williams, S. E. (1993). Systematic classroom observations of technology use. In H. C. Waxman & G. W. Bright (Eds.), *Approaches to research on teacher education and technology* (pp. 113–122). Charlottesville, VA: Association for the Advancement of Computing in Education.

Doyle, W. (1979). Making managerial decisions in classrooms. In D. L. Duke (Ed.), *Classroom management* (pp. 42–74). Chicago: National Society for the Study of Education.

Ebmeier, H., & Good, T. L. (1979). The effects of instructing teachers about good teaching on the mathematics achievement of fourth-grade students. *American Educational Research Journal, 16,* 1–16.

Feiman, S. (1981). Exploring connections between different kinds of educational research and different conceptions of inservice education. *Journal of Research and Development in Education, 14*(2), 11–21.

Fennema, E., & Peterson, P. L. (1987). Effective teaching for girls and boys: The same or different? In D. C. Berliner & B. V. Rosenshine (Eds.), *Talks to teachers* (pp. 111–125). New York: Random House.

Freiberg, H. J., & Waxman, H. C. (1988). Alternative feedback approaches for improving student teachers' classroom instruction. *Journal of Teacher Education, 39*(4), 8–14.

Freiberg, H. J., Waxman, H. C., & Houston, W. R. (1987). Enriching feedback to student-teachers through small group discussion. *Teacher Education Quarterly, 14*(3), 71–82.

Gage, N. L. (1972). *Teacher effectiveness and teacher education.* Palo Alto, CA: Pacific.

Good, T. L. (1988). Observational research . . . grounding theory in classrooms. *Educational Psychologist, 25,* 375–379.

Good, T. L., & Biddle, B. (1988). Research and the improvement of mathematics instruction: The need for observational resources. In D. Grouws & T. Cooney (Eds.), *Research agenda for mathematics education: Effective mathematics teaching* (pp. 114–142). Reston, VA: National Council of Teachers of Mathematics.

Good, T. L., & Brophy, J. E. (1974). Changing teacher and student behavior: An empirical investigation. *Journal of Educational Psychology, 66,* 390–405.

Good, T. L., & Brophy, J. E. (2000). *Looking in classrooms* (8th ed.). New York: Longman.

Good, T. L., & Grouws, D. (1979). The Missouri Mathematics Effectiveness Project: An experimental study in fourth-grade classrooms. *Journal of Educational Psychology, 71,* 355–362.

Good, T. L., Slavings, R. L., Harel, K., & Emerson, H. (1987). Student passivity: A study of questioning-asking in K–12 classrooms. *Sociology of Education, 60,* 181–199.

Good, T. L., Slavings, R. L., & Mason, D. A. (1988). Learning to ask questions: Grade and school effects. *Teaching and Teacher Education, 4,* 363–378.

Hart, L. E. (1989). Classroom processes, sex of students, and confidence in learning mathematics. *Journal for Research in Mathematics Education, 20,* 242–260.

Huang, S. L., & Waxman, H. C. (1996). Classroom observations of middle school students' technology use in mathematics. *School Science and Mathematics, 96*(1), 28–34.

Johnson, D. W. (1974). Affective outcomes. In H. J. Walberg (Ed.), *Evaluating educational performance* (pp. 99–112). Berkeley, CA: McCutchan.

McKinney, K. (1992). *Improving math and science teaching.* Washington, DC: Office of Educational Research and Improvement, U. S. Department of Education.

Medley, D. M. (1992). Structured observation. In M. C. Alkin (Ed.), *Encyclopedia of educational research* (6th ed., pp. 1310–1315). New York: Macmillan.

Merkley, D. M., & Hoy, M. P. (1992–1993). Observation as a component in teacher preparation. *National Forum of Teacher Education Journal, 2,* 15–21.

Nuthall, G., & Alton-Lee, A. (1990). Research on teaching and learning: Thirty years of change. *The Elementary School Journal, 90,* 546–570.

Ornstein, A. C. (1991). Teacher effectiveness research: Theoretical consideration. In H. C. Waxman & H. J. Walberg (Eds.), *Effective teaching: Current research* (pp. 63–80). Berkeley, CA: McCutchan.

Padrón, Y. N., & Waxman, H. C. (1993). Teaching and learning risks associated with limited cognitive mastery in science and mathematics for limited proficient students. In Office of Bilingual Education and Minority Language Affairs (Ed.), *Proceedings of the third national research symposium on limited English proficient students: Focus on middle and high school issues* (Vol. 2, pp. 511–547). Washington, DC: National Clearinghouse for Bilingual Education.

Padrón, Y. N., Waxman, H. C., & Huang, S. L. (1999). Classroom and instructional learning environment differences between resilient and non-resilient elementary school students. *Journal of Education for Students Placed at Risk of Failure, 4*(1), 63–81.

Rosenshine, B. V. (1987). Explicit teaching. In D. C. Berliner & B. V. Rosenshine (Eds.), *Talks to teachers* (pp. 75–92). New York: Random House.

Rosenshine, B. V., & Stevens, R. (1986). Teaching functions. In M. C. Wittrock (Ed.), *Handbook of research on teaching* (3rd ed., pp. 376–391). New York: Macmillan.

Saldana, D. C., & Waxman, H. C. (1996). The interrogation of multicultural education in urban middle level schools. *Issues in Middle Level Education, 5*(2), 9–29.

Saldana, D. C., & Waxman, H. C. (1997). An observational study of multicultural teaching in urban middle level schools. *Equity and Excellence in Education, 30*(1), 40–46.

Schaffer, E., Stringfield, S., & Wolfe, D. (1992). An innovative beginning teacher induction program: A two-year analysis of classroom interactions. *Journal of Teacher Education, 43,* 181–192.

Sirotnik, K. A. (1983). What you see is what you get – Consistency, persistency, and mediocrity in classrooms. *Harvard Educational Review, 53,* 16–31.

Stallings, J. A. (1980). Allocated academic learning time revisited, or beyond time on task. *Educational Researcher, 9*(11), 11–16.

Stallings, J. A., & Freiberg, H. J. (1991). Observation for the improvement of teaching. In H. C. Waxman & H. J. Walberg (Eds.), *Effective teaching: Current research* (pp. 107–133). Berkeley, CA: McCutchan.

Stallings, J. A., & Mohlman, G. G. (1988). Classroom observation techniques. In J. P. Keeves (Ed.), *Educational research, methodology, and measurement: An international handbook* (pp. 469–474). Oxford: Pergamon Press.

Stallings, J. A., Needels, M. C., & Sparks, G. M. (1987). Observation for the improvement of student learning. In D. C. Berliner & B. V. Rosenshine (Eds.), *Talks to teachers* (pp. 129–158). New York: Random House.

Stallings, J. A., Needels, M. C., & Stayrook, N. (1979). *How to change the process of teaching basic reading skills at the secondary school level*. Menlo Park, CA: SRI International.

Stodolsky, S. S. (1990). Classroom observation. In J. Milllman & L. Darling-Hammond (Eds.), *The new handbook of teacher evaluation: Assessing elementary and secondary school teachers* (pp. 175–190). Newbury Park, CA: Sage.

Stringfield, S., & Teddlie, C. (1991). Observers as predictors of schools' multi-year outlier status on achievement tests. *The Elementary School Journal, 91*(4), 357–376.

Teddlie, C., Kirby, P., & Stringfield, S. (1989). Effective vs. ineffective schools: Observable differences in the classroom. *American Journal of Education, 97*(3), 221–236.

Teddlie, C., & Stringfield, S. (1993). *Schools make a difference: Lessons learned from a 10-year study of school effects*. New York: Teachers College Press.

Tharp, R. G., Estrada, P., Dalton, S. S., & Yamauchi, L. (2000). *Teaching transformed: Achieving excellence, fairness, inclusion, and harmony*. Boulder, CO: Westview Press.

Timm, J. T., & Marchant, G. J. (1992). Using a structured observational instrument in observational settings in teacher education. *Teaching Education, 5*, 65–70.

Walberg, H. J. (1986). Synthesis of research on teaching. In M. C. Wittrock (Ed.), *Handbook of research on teaching* (3rd ed., pp. 214–229). New York: Macmillan.

Walberg, H. J. (1991). Productive teaching and instruction: Assessing the knowledge base. In H. C. Waxman & H. J. Walberg (Eds.), *Effective teaching: Current research* (pp. 33–62). Berkeley, CA: McCutchan.

Walberg, H. J. (1995). Generic practices. In G. Cawelti (Ed.), *Handbook of research on improving student achievement* (pp. 7–19). Arlington, VA: Educational Research Services.

Waxman, H. C. (1995). Classroom observations of effective teaching. In A. C. Ornstein (Ed.), *Teaching: Theory into practice* (pp. 76–93). Needham Heights, MA: Allyn & Bacon.

Waxman, H. C., & Huang, S. L. (1995). An observational study of technology integration in urban elementary and middle schools. *International Journal of Instructional Media, 22*, 329–339.

Waxman, H. C., & Huang, S. L. (1996). Classroom instruction differences by level of technology use in middle school mathematics. *Journal of Educational Computing Research, 14*, 147–159.

Waxman, H. C., & Huang, S. L. (1996–1997). Differences by level of technology use on students' motivation, anxiety, and classroom learning environment in mathematics. *Journal of Educational Technology Systems, 25*(1), 67–77.

Waxman, H. C., & Huang, S. L. (1997). Classroom instruction and learning environment differences between effective and ineffective urban elementary schools for African American students. *Urban Education, 32,* 7–44.

Waxman, H. C., & Huang, S. L. (1999). Classroom observation research and the improvement of teaching. In H. C. Waxman & H. J. Walberg (Eds.), *New directions for teaching practice and research* (pp. 107–129). Berkeley, CA: McCutchan.

Waxman, H. C., Huang, S. L., Anderson, L. W., & Weinstein, T. (1997). Classroom process differences in inner-city elementary schools. *Journal of Educational Research, 91,* 49–59.

Waxman, H. C., Huang, S. L., & Padrón, Y. N. (1995). Investigating the pedagogy of poverty in inner-city middle level schools. *Research in Middle Level Education, 18*(2), 1–22.

Waxman, H. C., & Padrón, Y. N. (2002). Research-based teaching practices that improve the education of English language learners. In L. Minaya-Rowe (Ed.), *Teacher training and effective pedagogy in the context of student diversity* (pp. 3–38). Greenwich, CT: Information Age.

Waxman, H. C., Padrón, Y. N., & Arnold, K. A. (2001). Effective instructional practices for students placed at risk of failure. In G. D. Borman, S. C. Stringfield, & R. E. Slavin (Eds.), *Title I: Compensatory education at the crossroads* (pp. 137–170). Mahwah, NJ: Erlbaum.

Waxman, H. C., Rodriguez, J., Padrón, Y. N., & Knight, S. L. (1988). The use of systematic classroom observations during field experience components of teacher education programs. *The College Student Journal, 22,* 199–202.

Waxman, H. C., & Walberg, H. J. (1982). The relation of teaching and learning: A review of reviews of process-product research. *Contemporary Education Review, 1,* 103–120.

Waxman, H. C., & Walberg, H. J. (1986). Effects of early field experiences. In J. D. Raths & L. G. Katz (Eds.), *Advances in teacher education* (Vol. 2, pp. 165–184). Norwood, NJ: Ablex.

Waxman, H. C., & Walberg, H. J. (Eds.). (1999). *New directions for teaching practice and research.* Berkeley, CA: McCutchan.

2

Using Multiple Perspectives in Observations of Diverse Classrooms

The Sheltered Instruction Observation Protocol (SIOP)

Jana Echevarria and Deborah J. Short

Mai knew that the teacher wanted her to become a good writer. And the teacher, Mrs. Galinski, had the students write every day in this 2-hour summer school class. For a half hour each morning, they would read a newspaper article individually and then discuss it as a class. Next, they had 30 minutes to write about the topic in their journals. Sometimes Mai understood the topic, like the article about teenagers getting drunk and crashing a car, but at other times she didn't, like the article on global warming, which had a lot of unfamiliar science words. For 20 minutes (after a 10-minute break), students would then volunteer to read their story or essay aloud, but Mai was too nervous about her English skills and her writing ability to speak up. The American students read aloud, and once in a while one of her fellow English as a Second Language (ESL) classmates took the chance too. Mrs. Galinski would comment on the students' texts, but Mai and the other students didn't. The class ended with 30 minutes of sustained silent reading, which Mai enjoyed because she could read what she wanted to and never had to talk about it. At the end of the class, the teacher would collect their journals and mark them in the evening, returning them the next day. Mai would try to understand the teacher's comments, but she wasn't sure her writing was improving. The teacher would write "Awkward phrasing," "Verb tenses don't match," "No clear antecedent," and "Use more descriptive words," but Mai didn't know what to do. She asked the teacher for some help a few times, but Mrs. Galinski would just write a substitution on the entry – an adjective, a proper noun, sometimes a sentence – then move on to the next student or activity. The summer school day was so short that there wasn't time after class or after school to get together.

Across town in another Building Writing Skills class with a similar curriculum, Aziza was having a different experience. Each day, when she entered Mr. Walker's class, she would see objectives listed on the board related to the writing genre the students would practice, the skill they would look for when peer editing, and the language function or grammar feature of the day.

Mr. Walker would explain these to the class. Before reading a newspaper article, Mr. Walker and the class did an activity. Sometimes they looked at photographs and described what they saw, and Mr. Walker would list their words and later suggest how they might use those words in their writing. Sometimes he acted out a scenario with student volunteers, like a reporter interviewing witnesses to a crime. Then, after they read an article, they would act out their own group scenario and write it up. Before they read about the teenagers who crashed their car, student groups made a word web about peer pressure – what it leads to and how to resist it. Mr. Walker modeled how they could complete their web on the board before they got to work. After reading the article, they discussed it with a partner to form an opinion on whether peer pressure led to the crash or not and then wrote an opinion essay. Each day after writing, Mr. Walker introduced the skill of the day – capitalization, subject–verb agreement, topic sentences, and the like. The students met in small groups to read and comment on one another's work, paying attention to the writing skill and the language or grammar feature (e.g., asking clarification questions, using passive voice). Two of the five writing pieces each week had to be rewritten using the peer edits and turned in for Mr. Walker's feedback. During the 30-minute sustained silent reading that followed the peer editing, Mr. Walker would have a 5-minute conference with each student twice a week. They would discuss a writing piece one time and the book used for silent reading the other. Aziza was pleased that Mr. Walker felt her writing was improving and gave her advice on what features to work on in future assignments. He also suggested stories for her to read from the class library that modeled some of his advice, like stories with good dialogue or vivid descriptions.

Mai and Aziza experienced different teaching styles in their summer school writing classes. Both had been in the United States for 1 year and were able to converse in English with classmates. They had been in self-contained ESL classes for three periods a day the past school year. Two periods focused on language arts and one on U.S. history. Their math and science classes held a mix of ESL and native English-speaking students and were harder to understand. They went to summer school to accelerate their English language learning, but only Aziza ended the program feeling that she had achieved significant growth in her writing ability.

This chapter introduces a research-based model of sheltered instruction that promotes the kinds of teaching practices that make Aziza's teacher more effective than Mai's in promoting learning. The model is instantiated in an observation instrument, the Sheltered Instruction Observation Protocol (SIOP) (Echevarria, Vogt, & Short, 2000). The SIOP may be used as part of a program for preservice and inservice professional development, as a guide for planning sheltered content lessons, as a training resource for faculty, and as an observation and evaluation measure for site-based administrators and researchers who evaluate teachers.

The advantage of the SIOP model is that it contains current best practice for English language learners (ELLs) and effective instruction organized in one easy-to-use instrument. The model is broad enough so that it doesn't preclude teachers from using a variety of instructional approaches from directed instruction to cooperative learning. Rather than a step-by-step technique, the SIOP provides a framework for practice that enables teachers to draw from their own repertoire. Another advantage is that the SIOP is an effective coaching tool providing concrete examples of the features of high-quality sheltered instruction. It also provides a means for monitoring teacher progress over time. However, one disadvantage is that the 30-item instrument may be overwhelming initially and cumbersome to score while doing an observation. This chapter will present ways in which the SIOP was used to observe and document teachers' implementation of the model in diverse classrooms.

Sheltered instruction (SI) is an approach for teaching content to ELLs in strategic ways that make the subject matter concepts comprehensible while promoting the students' English language development. (It may be referred to as SDAIE, specially designed academic instruction in English.) Although there is an increasing number of ELLs in classrooms across the United States and an increasing number of sheltered classes being offered – particularly as teachers prepare ELLs to meet high academic standards – the training of teachers and principals for working effectively with this population has not kept pace. The use of SI techniques is inconsistent from class to class, school to school, and district to district. The model of SI presented here is intended to reduce this variability and provide guidance in the best practices for SI grounded in two decades of classroom-based research, experiences of competent teachers, and findings from the professional literature.

The SIOP offers an innovative approach for observing and measuring the effectiveness of sheltered lessons, providing a tool that allows teachers and principals to know what good SI is and how to evaluate it. The presence of the identified SI features in a lesson indicates that the lesson meshes with the effective SI model, yet it is the rating of the teacher's instruction that determines how well the model is implemented.

BACKGROUND

Each year, the United States becomes more ethnically and linguistically diverse, with over 90% of recent immigrants from non-English-speaking countries. From 1989–1990 to 1996–1997, the number of limited-English-proficient (LEP) students in public schools grew by 70%, whereas total enrollment increased by only 14% (National Clearinghouse for Bilingual Education, 1999). It is projected that for the 1999–2000 school year, LEP enrollment will have grown 104% of the 1989–1990 level, whereas total enrollment will have grown less than 14% (National Clearinghouse for Bilingual Education, 1999). In 1996–1997, over 3.4 million school-age children were identified as LEP, approximately 7.4% of the K–12 public school student population (Macias, 1998). Although the number of LEP students has grown exponentially across the United States, these students have higher dropout rates and their level of academic achievement has lagged significantly behind that of their language majority peers (Bennici & Strang, 1995; Moss & Puma, 1995).

These findings reflect growing evidence that most schools are not meeting the challenge of educating linguistically and culturally diverse students well. This is quite problematic because federal and state governments are calling for *all* students to meet high standards and are adjusting national and state assessments as well as state graduation requirements to reflect these new levels of achievement. In order for students whose first language is not English to succeed in school and become productive citizens in our society, they need to receive better educational opportunities in U.S. schools.

All ELLs in U.S. schools today are not alike. They enter U.S. schools with a wide range of language proficiencies (in English and in their native languages) and of subject matter knowledge. Some ELL immigrant students had strong academic backgrounds before they came to the United States and entered our schools. They were literate in their native language and may have begun the study of a second language. For these students, much of what they need is English language development so that as they become more proficient in English, they can transfer the knowledge they have already learned to the courses they are taking in the United States. A few subjects, such as U.S. history, may need special attention because these students may not have studied them before.

Other immigrant students have very limited formal schooling – perhaps due to war in their native countries or the remote rural location of their homes. They are not literate in their native language, and they have not had schooling experiences such as changing teachers and classrooms for each subject. They have significant gaps in their educational backgrounds, lack knowledge in specific subject areas, and often need time to become accustomed to school routines and expectations.

Some ELLs have grown up in the United States but speak a language other than English at home. Some of these students are literate in their home language, such as Chinese, Arabic, or Spanish, and need to add English to their knowledge base in school. Others are not literate in any language. They have never mastered English or their home language and may be caught in a state of semiliteracy that is hard to escape.

Given the variability in these students' backgrounds, they often need different pathways for academic success. To meet this challenge, fundamental shifts need to occur in teacher development, program design, curricula and materials, and instructional and assessment practices. The SIOP model promotes, in particular, strategies for improved teacher development and instructional practice.

THE SI APPROACH

This chapter focuses specifically on SI, an approach that can extend the time students have for getting language support services while giving them a jump start on the content subjects they will need for graduation. The SI approach draws from and complements effective methods advocated for mainstream classrooms but adds specific strategies for developing English language skills at the same time that students are learning the subject matter. In SI classes, ELLs become familiar with the academic tasks and routine activities they will face in mainstream classrooms.

For ELLs to succeed in school, they must master not only English vocabulary and grammar, but also the way English is used in core content classes. This academic English includes semantic and syntactic knowledge along with functional language use. Using English, students must be able to read and understand expository text, write persuasively, argue points of view, and take notes from teachers' lectures. They must articulate their thinking skills in English – make hypotheses, express analyses, and draw conclusions. ELLs must pull together their emerging knowledge of the English language with the content knowledge they are studying to complete the academic tasks assigned. They must also learn *how* to do these tasks – generate an outline, negotiate roles in cooperative groups, interpret charts and maps, and so forth. The combination of these three knowledge bases – knowledge of English, knowledge of the content topic, and knowledge of how the tasks are to be accomplished – constitutes the major components of academic literacy needed for school success (Short, 1998).

Another consideration for school success is the explicit socialization of ELLs to the implicit cultural expectations of the classroom, such as turn taking, participation rules, interaction styles, and established routines. Student comfort with the social participation structure of an academic task can vary according to culturally learned assumptions about appropriateness in communication and in social relationships, individual personality, and power relations in the classroom social system and in society (Erickson & Shultz, 1991). Teachers need to engage in culturally responsive teaching that is sensitive to and builds upon culturally different ways of learning, behaving, and using language (Bartolome, 1994).

Students' language learning is promoted through social interaction and contextualized communication (Tharp & Gallimore, 1988; Vygotsky, 1978), which can be readily generated in the SI classroom. Teachers guide students to construct meaning and to understand complex content concepts by scaffolding instruction. Teachers pay attention to students' capacity for working in English, beginning instruction at the current level of understanding and moving students to higher levels. They adjust their speech (e.g., paraphrase, provide analogies, elaborate students' responses) to facilitate student comprehension and participation where otherwise the discourse might be beyond their proficiency level (Bruner, 1978). They also adjust instructional tasks to be incrementally challenging (e.g., preteach vocabulary before a reading assignment) so that students learn the skills necessary to complete tasks on their own (Applebee & Langer, 1983).

SI plays a major role in several educational program designs. It may be part of an ESL program, a late-exit bilingual program, a two-way bilingual immersion program, a newcomer program, or a foreign language immersion program. Any program in which students are learning content in a nonnative language should utilize the SI approach. In some schools, SI is provided to classes composed entirely of ELLs. In others, a mix of native and nonnative English speakers may be present. Bilingual, ESL, and content teachers may be the instructors for these classes (Sheppard, 1995). Yet, all content teachers should be trained in second language acquisition and ESL methodology.

Research has shown, however, that great variability exists in the design of SI courses and the delivery of SI lessons, even among trained teachers (August & Hakuta, 1997; Berman, McLaughlin, Minicucci, Nelson, & Woodworth, 1995; Kauffman et al., 1994; Sheppard, 1995; Short, 1998). It is our experience as well after two decades of observations that one SI classroom rarely resembles the next in terms of the teacher's instructional language; the tasks the students have to accomplish; the degree of interaction between teacher and student, student and student, and student and text; the amount of time devoted to language development versus content knowledge; the learning strategies taught to and utilized by the students; the availability of appropriate materials; and more. Therefore, we set out to develop a model of effective SI and a tool to measure its implementation in the classroom.

A MODEL FOR SI

The development of an SI model is one key to improving the academic success of ELLs: Preservice teachers need it to develop a strong foundation in SI; university field supervisors need it to observe, evaluate, and provide systematic feedback to teachers in training; practicing teachers need it to strengthen their lesson planning and delivery and to provide students with more consistent instruction; principals and other site-based supervisors need it to train and evaluate teachers.

The model described in this chapter is the product of several research studies conducted by the authors over the past decade. It is grounded in the professional literature and in the experiences and best practice of the researchers and participating teachers who worked collaboratively to develop the observation instrument that codifies it. The theoretical underpinning of the model is that language acquisition is enhanced through meaningful use and interaction. Through SI, students interact in English with meaningful content material relevant to their schooling. Because language processes such as listening, speaking, reading, and writing develop interdependently, SI lessons incorporate activities that integrate those skills.

In model SI classes, language and content objectives are systematically woven into the curriculum of one particular subject area, such as fourth-grade language arts, U.S. history, algebra, or life science. Teachers present the regular grade-level subject curriculum to students through modified instruction in English, although some special curricula may be designed for students with significant gaps in their educational backgrounds or very low literacy skills. Teachers must develop students' academic language proficiency consistently and regularly as part of the lessons and units that they plan and deliver (Crandall, 1993; Echevarria & Graves, 1998; Short, 1991). Our SI model shares many of the strategies found in high-quality nonsheltered teaching for native English speakers, but it is characterized by careful attention to the ELLs' second-language development needs.

Accomplished SI teachers modulate the level of English used with and among students and make the content comprehensible through techniques such as the use of visual aids, modeling, demonstrations, graphic organizers, vocabulary previews, adapted texts, cooperative learning, peer tutoring, multicultural content, and native-language support. They strive to create a nonthreatening environment where students feel comfortable taking risks with language. They also make specific connections between the content being taught and students' experiences and prior knowledge, and they focus on expanding students' vocabulary base. Effective SI lessons generate a high level of student engagement and interaction with the teacher, with each other, and with text that leads to elaborated discourse and higher-order thinking. Students are explicitly taught functional language skills, such as how to negotiate meaning, ask for clarification, confirm information, argue, and persuade. Through instructional conversations and meaningful activities, students practice and apply their new language and content knowledge.

Depending on student proficiency levels, SI teachers offer multiple pathways for students to demonstrate their understanding of the content. They may plan pictorial, hands-on, or performance-based assessments for individual students, group tasks or projects, informal class discussions, oral reports, written assignments, portfolios, and more common measures such as paper-and-pencil tests to check on student comprehension of the subject matter and language growth. Besides increasing students' declarative knowledge (i.e., factual information), teachers highlight and model procedural knowledge (i.e., how to complete an academic task such as organizing a science laboratory report) along with study skills and learning strategies (e.g., note taking).

The SI model is also distinguished by the use of supplementary materials that support the academic text. These may include related reading texts (e.g., trade books), graphs and other illustrations, models and other realia, audiovisual and computer-based resources, adapted text, and more. The purpose of these materials is to enhance student understanding of key topics, issues, and details in the content concepts being taught through alternative means, not teacher lectures or dense textbook prose. Supplementary materials also aid teachers in providing information to students with mixed proficiency levels of English. Some students in a mixed class may be able to utilize the textbook, whereas others may need adapted text.

The SI model was designed for flexibility and tested in a wide range of classroom situations: those with all ELLs and those with a mix of native and nonnative English speakers; those with students who have strong academic backgrounds and those with students who have had limited formal schooling; those with students who are recent arrivals and those who have been in U.S. schools for several years; those with students at beginning levels of English proficiency and those with students at advanced levels. In a preliminary study of student writing (using pre- and posttest measures), students who participated in classes taught by teachers trained in the SI model improved their writing skills significantly more than students in classes with non-SI-trained teachers (Echevarria & Short, 2001).

It is important to recognize that the SI model does not require teachers to discard their favored techniques or add many new elements to a lesson. Rather, the SI model brings together *what to teach* by providing an approach for *how to teach* it. The model offers a framework for selecting and organizing strategies and facilitates the integration of district or state standards for ESL and for specific content areas.

DEVELOPMENT OF THE SIOP

The SIOP was designed as an instrument for educators to use in a number of ways. First, we found that school personnel wanted and needed an objective measure of high-quality sheltered lessons, and the SIOP operationalizes a model of effective SI. Principals and other school site administrators use the SIOP to provide clear, concrete feedback to the teachers they observe. The SIOP is also useful to university faculty who teach SI strategies, as well as those faculty who supervise field experience. Although the SIOP was developed as an observational instrument, teachers use the features of this protocol as a planning guide. Finally, the SIOP is a tool for researchers to use in determining the extent to which SI is implemented in a given classroom and in documenting the fidelity of implementation.

The first version of the SIOP was drafted in 1995 to exemplify the SI model that we were developing. The preliminary instrument was field-tested with SI teachers and refined according to teacher feedback and our observations in the classrooms. This early draft, like subsequent ones, pulled together findings and recommendations from the research literature with our professional experiences and those of our collaborating teachers on effective classroom-based practices from the areas of ESL, bilingual education, reading, language and literacy acquisition, discourse studies, special education, and classroom management.

In 1996, the National Center for Research on Education, Diversity, and Excellence (CREDE) was funded by the Office of Educational Research and Improvement, U.S. Department of Education, and included a study on SI in its research program. The purpose of the research project was to develop an explicit model of SI that could be implemented by teachers of students with LEP to improve their students' academic success.

The project built on preliminary versions of the SIOP as a small cohort of teachers worked with the researchers to refine the SIOP further in 1997. This effort included distinguishing between effective strategies for beginning, intermediate, and advanced English language learners; determining "critical" versus "unique" SI strategies, the latter being language modification or support oriented (e.g., slower speech, use of bilingual dictionaries); and making the SIOP more user friendly. One way to make the instrument more user friendly was to organize its features into three main categories: *Preparation*, or what the teacher needs to do before the lesson; *Instruction*, or what happens during the lesson; and *Review/Assessment*, or how the teacher evaluates student understanding at the conclusion of the lesson. The items under Instruction were further organized into six subcategories: Building Background, Comprehensible Input, Strategies, Interaction, Practice/Application, and Lesson Delivery.

Over the next 3 years (1998–2000), the model was used and refined in four large urban school districts (two on the West Coast and two on the East Coast) to train an expanded team of middle school teachers in implementing effective SI strategies in their classes. Project teachers use SI in a variety of settings, including traditional ESL classes, content-based ESL classes, and sheltered content classes. Some teachers were trained content specialists, and others were trained ESL specialists. The proficiency levels of the ELLs ranged from beginning to advanced. The SIOP was utilized both as an observation instrument for researchers and teachers to match the implementation of lesson delivery to the model of instruction and as a tool for teachers to plan and deliver lessons.

As part of the professional development aspect of the project, teachers participated in 3-day professional development institutes in the summers (one on the East Coast, another on the West Coast) to explore the project's goals and the observation instrument with the researchers. The institutes also provided practice in implementing the project's model of SI using the SIOP through demonstration lessons and discussion and analysis of videotaped classroom scenes. Then, for each school year, we observed classroom instruction and videotaped three classes of each participating teacher, one each in the fall, winter, and spring. Control teachers on each coast who did not participate in the training were videotaped in the fall and spring. After each observation, a SIOP was completed and scored for the teacher. The researchers shared these analyses with teachers on an ongoing basis as a means of facilitating teacher growth and validating the research interpretations. SIOP data collected throughout the project will be analyzed to determine overall teacher change and significant development in specific areas of instructional practice.

In addition, during each year, the teachers and researchers met periodically to discuss topics related to the research agenda, refine the SI model, review and discuss videotaped lessons, and provide constructive feedback to help improve instruction (for further details on the professional development aspects of the project, see Short & Echevarria, 1999).

VALIDITY AND RELIABILITY OF THE SIOP

After several years of field-testing and refining of the SIOP, a study was conducted (Guarino et al., 2001) to establish the validity and reliability of the instrument. A single-blind design was employed. Three videos were judged by the principal investigator (PI) to be highly representative of the tenets of SI, whereas three others were not. The raters were four experts in SI (or SDAIE) from three major universities in southern California. Three held doctorates in education, and the fourth was earning a second master's degree (in education). The raters observed all six videos (each video was approximately 45 minutes long) and scored the teacher on a Likert-type scale ranging from 1 (no evidence) to 7 (clearly evident) on the 31^2 items that comprised the eight subscales: Preparation, Building Background, Comprehensible Input, Strategies, Interaction, Practice/Application, Lesson Delivery, and Review/Evaluation. Cronbach's alpha was calculated for all eight subscales. All but one subscale (Comprehensible Input; alpha $= .8727$) achieved an a priori level of

acceptance. Alphas for the other subscales ranged from .9589 (Preparation) to .9138 (Lesson Delivery). A principal component analysis (PCA)
with varimax rotation was then performed on the 31 items to assess the
instrument's discriminate validity among the subscales. Three factors
were extracted accounting for 98.4% of the variance, as indicated by the
eigenvalues of the factors that accounted for variances greater than 1.

A discriminant functional analysis (DFA) using the eight subscales as predictors of membership in the two groups (performing or
nonperforming SI) was utilized to measure the instrument's concurrent validity (the PI's assessment of the videotapes). One discriminant
function was calculated, with a chi-square $(17) = 24.07, p < .01$. The univariate tests suggest that the best predictors for distinguishing between
SI and non-SI educators are Preparation, Lesson Delivery, Comprehensible Input, Building Background, Strategies, Practice/Application, and
Review/Evaluation. Only Interaction failed to discriminate between SI
and non-SI environments. The stability of the classification procedure
was checked by a cross-validation run, and there was an 81.25% correct classification rate. This indicates a high degree of consistency in the
classification scheme.

The study on the psychometric properties of the SIOP confirmed that
the SIOP is a highly reliable and valid measure of SI. Further, the findings suggested (a) that the instrument could be modified by reducing the
factor structure from eight to three and (b) that Interaction failed to dif-
ferentiate between SI and non-SI teachers. Based on these findings, we
modified the SIOP to a three-factor structure (Preparation, Instruction,
Review/Evaluation) and modified the Interaction items to strengthen
their distinction from non-SI (e.g., we eliminated the item "Pronunci-
ation and intonation easily understandable"). Further, we changed the
scoring to a 5-point scale, using the range 0–4.

THE SIOP

The SIOP provides concrete examples of the features of SI that can enhance and expand teachers' instructional practice (see the appendix
for an abbreviated version). The protocol is composed of 30 items
grouped into three main sections: Preparation, Instruction, and Review/
Assessment. The six items under Preparation examine the lesson-
planning process, including the language and content objectives, the
use of supplementary materials, and the meaningfulness of the activities. Instruction is subdivided into six categories: Building Background,

TABLE 2.1. *SIOP Sample*

Preparation			
4	**2**	**0**	**NA**
4. Supplementary materials used to a high degree, making the lesson clear and meaningful (graphs, models, visuals)	Some use of supplementary materials	No use of supplementary materials	
Comments:			

Comprehensible Input, Strategies, Interaction, Practice/Application, and Lesson delivery. The 20 items in these six categories emphasize the instructional practices that are critical for ELLs, such as making connections with students' background experiences and prior learning, adjusting teacher speech, emphasizing vocabulary development, using multimodal techniques, promoting higher-order thinking skills, grouping students appropriately for language and content development, and providing hands-on materials. As part of the Review/Assessment section, four items consider whether the teacher reviewed the key vocabulary and content concepts, assessed student learning, and provided feedback to students on their output.

Each individual item is scored using a 5-point Likert scale with scores ranging from 0 to 4. For example, in Table 2.1, under Preparation item 4 (use of supplemental materials), a teacher would receive a score of 4 if he used supplementary materials (e.g., graphic organizers, visual aids, trade books) to a high degree throughout his lesson, making the lesson clear and meaningful for the ELLs. Another teacher would receive a score of 2 if she only made some use of supplementary materials. A third might receive a 0 if no supplementary materials were used at all. N/A (not applicable) is also available if a lesson does not warrant the presence of a particular item (see the later discussion of N/A). It is not expected that each item would be present in every daily lesson, but it is expected that effective SI teachers would address each item several times over the course of a week.

In addition to the 5-point rating scale, the SIOP provides space for qualitative data. It is recommended that the observer use the "comments" section to record examples of the presence or absence of each feature. That way, both the observer and the teacher have specific information, in addition to a score, to use in their postlesson discussion. More information may be added to the comments section during the postlesson discussion, documenting the content of the discussion for future reference, which is particularly useful as subsequent lessons are planned.

Teaching Scenarios

The following teaching scenarios demonstrate how the SIOP may be utilized by a researcher, administrator, or teacher education supervisor to observe and rate SI. The focus of these scenarios is on three teachers' implementations of SIOP item 10 under the Comprehensible Input section. The scenarios represent ninth-grade science classrooms with students ranging in ESL proficiency from beginning to advanced (see Colburn & Echevarria, 1999, for a complete sheltered science lesson). An example of how this science lesson would be scored using the SIOP follows each scenario.

Example 1. As Mr. Tai began the lesson, he drew students' attention to the objective written on the board and told students that the purpose of the unit was to understand why some objects float and others sink. As he said the word *float*, he pointed at an orange floating in the aquarium at the front of the room, and as he said the word *sink*, he dropped a peeled orange into the water, which sank to the bottom. Then he repeated while pointing at the corresponding object, "Some things float and others sink." He went on to tell the students that at the end of the unit they would be able to calculate and predict whether something is buoyant enough to float. The words *float, sink, calculate, predict*, and *buoyant* were written on a wall chart for students to see. The word list included content vocabulary (*buoyant, float,* and *sink*) as well as functional language (*calculate* and *predict*). Because many of his students were recent immigrants and had gaps in their educational backgrounds, Mr. Tai was careful to make sure that the students not only knew the meaning of the content vocabulary, but also knew the meaning of words associated with academic tasks, such as *predict* and *calculate*.

Throughout the lesson, Mr. Tai used language structures and vocabulary that he believed the students could understand at their level of proficiency. He slowed his normal rate of speech to make himself better

TABLE 2.2. *SIOP Sample*

Comprehensible Input			
4	2	0	NA
10. Speech appropriate for students' proficiency level (e.g., slower rate, enunciation, and simple sentence structure for beginners)	Speech sometimes inappropriate for students' proficiency level	Speech inappropriate for students' proficiency level	

Comments:

understood by the students, and he enunciated clearly. Also, he avoided the use of idioms, and when he sensed that students did not understand him, he paraphrased to convey the meaning more clearly. He repeated important words frequently and wrote them for students to see.

SIOP EVALUATION. Mr. Tai receives a score of 4 on this item (Comprehensible Input, Table 2.2). He slowed his rate of speech and enunciated clearly when he addressed beginning speakers; he adjusted his speech for the other, more proficient speakers of English. He used a natural speaking voice but paid attention to his rate of speed and enunciation.

Further, Mr. Tai adjusted the level of vocabulary and complexity of the sentences he used so that students could understand. Because most students were beginning English speakers, he selected words that were appropriate to his students' proficiency levels. Although the science book highlighted nearly 15 terms for the unit on buoyancy, Mr. Tai had learned from experience that it was better for his students to learn a smaller number of vocabulary words thoroughly than to give superficial treatment to dozens of content-associated words. His students would be able to use and apply the selected words and their concepts because they would have a complete understanding of their meaning.

Example 2. As is her practice, Mrs. Castillo wrote the objective, "Find the mass/volume ratio for objects that float," on the board. She began the lesson by discussing the fact that some things float and others sink, giving examples of objects that float, such as a large ship, and others that sink, such as a small coin. Then she asked the class if they knew what makes some objects float and others sink. A few students guessed, but nobody was able to give an accurate explanation. During the discussion, Mrs. Castillo paid attention to her rate of speech, and she tried to use sentences that were less complex than those she would normally use, but some of the students still seemed confused while she was talking.

Mrs. Castillo told the students to read the first three pages of their book to themselves and said that they would discuss it when they'd finished. After the students indicated that they were finished reading, Mrs. Castillo asked them if there were any words in the book that they did not know. Several students called out unfamiliar words, and the teacher wrote them on the overhead. Then she assigned students at each table a word to look up in the glossary. After several minutes, she asked the students what they had found. Only about half of the words were included in the glossary because the other words were not science terms per se, such as *therefore* and *principle*. Mrs. Castillo orally gave students the definitions of those words that were not in the glossary and then summarized the information the students had read in the book for 10 minutes. As she talked, she occasionally spoke too fast for many of the students to understand, and she used long, detail-laden sentences in her summary. When she noticed that students were not paying attention, she slowed her rate of speech to make it understandable and to regain students' interest.

SIOP EVALUATION. Mrs. Castillo received a score of 2 for Comprehensible Input. Her rate of speech and enunciation vacillated between that used with native speakers and a rate that her students could understand. She didn't consistently adjust her speech (rate or complexity) to the variety of proficiency levels in the class. She was aware that her ELL students needed extra attention in understanding the language, but she only addressed their needs by asking for unfamiliar vocabulary. She could have paraphrased, using simpler sentence structure, and she could have used synonyms for words that appeared to be too difficult for students to understand.

Example 3. Mr. Gibson began the lesson by having students open their science books to the chapter on buoyancy. He told them that in this unit they would learn what makes objects buoyant. He gave a 5-minute oral introduction to the concepts behind buoyancy, discussing the fact that if the object's mass exceeds its volume, it will sink. Mr. Gibson used a rate and speaking style that was appropriate for fluent English speakers but not for the beginning English speakers in his class. He then directed the students' attention to 15 vocabulary terms written on the board and told them to copy each word, look up the definition in the glossary, and copy the definition onto their paper. After students looked up the vocabulary words in the glossary, Mr. Gibson asked them to put the paper in their homework folders. He told them that they needed to take the words home and that their homework assignment was to use each word in a sentence. He emphasized that students needed to complete their homework because he had been frustrated by the low homework response rate in this class.

Then Mr. Gibson turned to the science book, telling students to open their books to the beginning of the chapter. He proceeded to lecture from the book, asking students questions to stimulate a class discussion. Most students were reluctant to speak up. After lecturing on the material from the first five pages of the book, Mr. Gibson gave the students a worksheet about buoyancy. He told them that they could work in pairs or alone, calculating the mass/volume ratio of the objects shown on the worksheet. He said, "You remember how to calculate mass/volume ratios? First, you determine the volume of the object, and then you take the mass and divide it by the volume. Okay, just calculate the ratios for each object shown on the worksheet, and when you finish, you may begin doing your homework."

SIOP EVALUATION. Mr. Gibson received a 0 on the SIOP for Comprehensible Input. He made no effort to adjust his oral presentation to the needs of the ELLs in his class. He lectured about new, complex concepts without regard to his rate of speech or complexity of speech, variables that impact ELLs' ability to comprehend information in class. Also, copying the definitions of new terms and requiring students to create original sentences is an inordinately difficult task for ELLs. Unwittingly, Mr. Gibson set the students up for failure and then was frustrated by the low number of completed homework assignments. Although he believed that students chose not to complete assignments, in reality they *could not* independently complete the type of assignment he gave.

Further, Mr. Gibson did not discuss the lesson content, class assignment, or homework assignment in any meaningful or understandable way for ELLs. He thought that discussing the material in the chapter would make the concepts clear for his students, and he asked them questions during his lecture. Unfortunately, his efforts were lost on the ELLs, who needed richer, scaffolded development of the lesson's concepts to understand the text or lecture. Also, the few students who participated in the discussion gave the teacher the inaccurate impression that the class was following in the discussion.

Using the SIOP

When observing a lesson with the SIOP, scoring may take place in a number of ways: (a) during the observation itself as individual features are recognized; (b) after the observation, as the observer reflects on the entire lesson, referring to observational field notes; or (c) after the lesson while watching a videotape of the lesson. In using the SIOP over the past several years, we have found that it is most useful to videotape a lesson and analyze it later. Teachers, principals, supervisors, and researchers alike have found this to be an effective way of recording and measuring growth in teaching over time. The videotape may be scored by the observer alone, but it is also a good idea to involve the teacher in the scoring. The teacher and observer can watch the videotape together while scoring, then share the same points of reference when discussing the lesson. We suggest that, to assist in more accurate scoring, the observer ask the teacher for a copy of the lesson plan before observing the lesson. That way, the observer is better able to score the Preparation section as well as recognize N/A items.

We understand that an observation at one point in time does not always accurately represent the teacher's implementation of SI strategies and techniques. Therefore, there is a place for the observer to indicate if the lesson is part of a multiday unit or is a single-day lesson.

How to Score the SIOP

It is important to stress that not all items on the SIOP will be present in every lesson. However, some items are essential for each lesson, such as items under Preparation, Comprehensible Input, Interaction, and Review and Assessment. Over the course of time (several lessons, a week), all items should be represented in one's teaching.

Assigning Scores. The observer determines the level of implementation, guided by the descriptors on the instrument (see Tables 2.1 and 2.2 for sample descriptors). The SIOP provides a 5-point scale as well as space for qualitative data. It is recommended that the observer use the comments section to record examples of the presence or absence of each feature. That way, both the observer and the teacher have specific information, besides a score, to use in their postlesson discussion. More information may be added to the comments section during the postlesson discussion, documenting the content of the discussion for future reference, which is particularly useful as subsequent lessons are planned.

Naturally, there is an element of subjectivity to interpreting the items and assigning scores. For example, one observer may think that on item 3 (Content concepts appropriate for the age and educational background level of students), only grade-level materials are appropriate, whereas another observer may feel that the same content found in materials for lower grade levels may be used because of the students' low reading levels or because students have interrupted educational backgrounds. In either case, observers must be consistent in their interpretation and scoring across settings. Raters can achieve consistency by undergoing joint training in which they can raise questions about different interpretations, seek clarifications, and make decisions about how to score.

Not Applicable (N/A) Category. The scoring option of N/A is important because it distinguishes a feature that is not applicable to the observed lesson from a score of 0, which indicates that the feature should have been present but wasn't. For example, Mr. Leung taught a 5-day unit on the solar system. During the first few lessons of the unit, Mr. Leung concentrated on making the rather dense information accessible to his students. He adapted the text to make it understandable for students and provided ample opportunities for students to use strategies. On the final day of the unit, an observer was present. Mr. Leung wrapped up the unit by having the students complete an enjoyable hands-on activity wherein they applied the concepts they had learned. It was obvious that the students had learned the content and were able to use it in the activity. However, because of the nature of that particular lesson, there was no observed adaptation of content (item 5). Because the lesson did not lend itself to that item and Mr. Leung had covered the item on another day, a score of N/A would be correct in this case.

In the case of Mrs. Nash, however, it would be appropriate to score this feature as 0. Mrs. Nash also taught a unit on the solar system. On the first day of the unit, she showed a video about the solar system followed by a brief oral discussion. The next day, an observer was present as she read from the book and then had students answer chapter questions. There was no evidence that any of the content had been adapted to the variety of student proficiency levels in her class. In fact, many students appeared to be confused as they tried to answer questions based on readings from the grade-level textbook.

The distinction between a 0 and N/A is important because a score of 0 adversely affects the overall score of the lesson, whereas a score of N/A does not because a percentage total is used.

Calculating Scores. The 30 items on the SIOP have a range of possible scores from 0 to 4 or N/A. After scoring each item, the observer tallies all the numeric scores and creates a ratio with the total possible score. The total is usually 120 (30 items × a score of 4), except when N/A items are involved. For each N/A item, 4 points are subtracted from the total score. Mr. Leung's lesson provides an example. He received a score of 4 on 20 items, a score of 3 on 5 items, a score of 2 on 4 items, and 1 N/A. The sum of those scores is 103. One item was rated N/A, so the total possible score was 116. His ratio score was 103/116, or 89%. This is a fairly high level of implementation.

DISCUSSION

We have found that the most appropriate applications of the SIOP are (a) part of a program for preservice and inservice professional development, (b) a guide for planning sheltered content lessons, (c) a training resource for faculty, and (d) an observation and evaluation measure for site-based administrators and researchers who evaluate teachers. For professional development purposes, SIOP ratings are a useful starting point for a collaborative discussion between a teacher and a supervisor or among a group of teachers who might want to meet on a regular basis. In our experience, videotaping a lesson, rating it, and discussing it with the teacher provides an effective forum for professional growth. The discussion can offer constructive feedback and assistance in refining instruction. Observers also gather valuable information from teachers who can explain a student's behavior or why something in the lesson plan did not take place.

Scores may be documented over time to show growth. Using percentages, teachers can see how their implementation of the SIOP features improves. This type of information is also useful for research purposes, to document systematic implementation of the SIOP and the fidelity of the implementation. Plotting scores on a graph illustrates effectively a teacher's areas of strength, as well as areas that require attention or areas teachers have highlighted as important for their own growth. If a teacher consistently shows low scores on certain items, the graph provides the teacher with clear feedback.

Finally, although the SIOP is a useful tool for professional development, the scores should be used with caution. Evaluating a teacher's performance based on one observation using the SIOP would be a misuse of the instrument and its intent. Many variables impact the success or failure of a given lesson such as time of day, time of year, dynamics among students, and the like. Rather than conducting one observation and scoring of a teacher, the observer should rate several lessons over time to achieve a fuller picture of the teacher's implementation of SI. The intent of the SIOP is to improve the academic success of ELLs through a number of constituencies: Preservice teachers need it to develop a strong foundation in SI; university field supervisors need it to observe, evaluate, and provide systematic feedback to teachers in training; practicing teachers need it to strengthen their lesson planning and delivery and to provide students with more consistent instruction; principals and other site-based supervisors need it to train and evaluate teachers.

IMPLICATIONS FOR FUTURE RESEARCH

In developing the SIOP, we conducted our research in sheltered content classes that were part of ESL programs. In the future, it would be useful to examine how SI is implemented in classrooms with ELLs across a variety of program designs, such as transitional bilingual education, developmental bilingual education, two-way immersion, and, for native English speakers, foreign language immersion. This research could identify variations and constraints on the SI model given the program type, language of instruction, and student population. The applicability of the model to any setting where students are learning content through their second language would be a valuable addition to the work already undertaken.

In several of the districts where we conducted our work, ELLs were in classrooms with native English speakers. Although we have some evidence that the SI model has been successful with ELLs, the impact of SI instruction on native English speakers has not yet been studied. Many of the features of the SIOP match features of exemplary teaching for all students, so the SI model's influence on non-ELLs is worth pursuing.

In a related manner, the applicability of the SIOP to special education classes should be explored. Many elements of the SIOP reflect best practices for students with learning challenges such as scaffolding instruction, adapting curriculum, and focusing instruction on key vocabulary and concepts. In a study of student performance in classes whose teachers were SIOP trained, students with learning disabilities made significant improvement in their writing over the course of a year (Echevarria, 1998). Further research is warranted using the SIOP with this population.

A fourth area of investigation is related to student achievement. In the CREDE study, we were restricted by the types of assessments given to the ELLs – more accurately, by the lack of standardized assessment that took place due to student exemptions. However, as more and more districts move to include ELLs in their assessment programs, more data will become available on how ELLs in SI classes perform compared to other ELLs and to non-ELLs. Therefore, the achievement of students in classes with SIOP-trained teachers can be examined through multiple sources of data.

Note

This chapter is adapted with permission from J. Echevarria, M. Vogt, and D. Short, *Making content comprehensible for English language learners: The SIOP Model* (Boston: Allyn & Bacon, 2000).

References

Applebee, A., & Langer, J. (1983). Instructional scaffolding: Reading and writing as natural language activities. *Language Arts, 60*(2), 168–175.

August, D., & Hakuta, K. (Eds.). (1997). *Improving schooling for language minority children: A research agenda.* Washington, DC: National Academy Press.

Bartolome, L. I. (1994). Beyond the methods fetish: Toward a humanizing pedagogy. *Harvard Educational Review, 64*(2), 173–194.

Bennici, F. J., & Strang, E. W. (1995). *An analysis of language minority and limited English proficient students from NELS 1988* (Report to the Office of Bilingual Education and Minority Languages Affairs). Washington, DC: U.S. Department of Education.

Berman, P., McLaughlin, B., Minicucci, C., Nelson, B., & Woodworth, K. (1995). *School reform and student diversity: Case studies of exemplary practices for LEP students.* Washington, DC: National Clearinghouse for Bilingual Education.

Bruner, J. (1978). The role of dialogue in language acquisition. In A. Sinclair, R. Javella, & W. Levelt (Eds.), *The child's conception of language* (pp. 241–256). New York: Springer-Verlag.

Colburn, A., & Echevarria, J. (1999). Meaningful lessons. *The Science Teacher, 66*(2), 36–39.

Crandall, J. A. (1993). Content-centered learning in the United States. *Annual Review of Applied Linguistics, 13*, 111–126.

Echevarria, J. (1998, April). *A model of effective sheltered content instruction*. Paper presented at the Council for Exceptional Children, Division of Diverse Exceptional Learners Conference, Minneapolis.

Echevarria, J., & Graves, A. (1998). *Sheltered content instruction: Teaching English-language learners with diverse abilities*. Boston: Allyn & Bacon.

Echevarria, J., & Short, D. (2001, April). *The Sheltered Instruction Observation Protocol and the achievement of English language learners*. Paper presented at the annual meeting of the American Educational Research Association, Seattle.

Echevarria, J., Vogt, M. E., & Short, D. (2000). *Making content comprehensible for English language learners: The SIOP Model*. Boston: Allyn & Bacon.

Erickson, F., & Shultz, J. (1991). Students' experience of the curriculum. In P. W. Jackson (Ed.), *Handbook of research on curriculum* (pp. 465–485). New York: Macmillan.

Guarino, A. J., Echevarria, J., Short, D., Schick, J. E., Forbes, S., & Rueda, R. (2001). The Sheltered Instruction Observation: Reliability and validity assessment. *Journal of Research in Education, 11*(1), 138–140.

Kauffman, D., Burkart, G., Crandall, J., Johnson, D., Peyton, J., Sheppard, K., & Short, D. (1994). *Content-ESL across the USA*. Washington, DC: ERIC Clearinghouse on Languages and Linguistics.

Macías, R. F. (1998). *Summary report of the survey of the states' limited English proficient students and available educational programs and services, 1996–97*. Washington, DC: National Clearinghouse for Bilingual Education.

Moss, M., & Puma, M. (1995). *Prospects: The congressionally mandated study of educational growth and opportunity* (First year report on language minority and limited English proficient students). Washington, DC: U.S. Department of Education.

National Clearinghouse for Bilingual Education. (1999). *K–12 and LEP enrollment trends*. Available at http://www.ncbe.gwu.edu/ncbepubs/reports/state-data/index.htm

Sheppard, K. (1995). *Content-ESL across the USA* (Technical report, vol. 1). Washington, DC: National Clearinghouse for Bilingual Education.

Short, D. (1991). *How to integrate language and content instruction: A training manual*. Washington, DC: Center for Applied Linguistics.

Short, D. (1998). Social studies and assessment: Meeting the needs of students learning English. In S. Fradd & O. Lee (Eds.), *Creating Florida's multilingual global work force* (Section VI, pp. 1–12). Tallahassee: Florida Department of Education.

Short, D., & Echevarria, J. (1999). *The Sheltered Instruction Observation Protocol: A tool for teacher-researcher collaboration and professional development* (Educational Practice Report No. 3). Santa Cruz, CA, and Washington, DC: Center for Research on Education, Diversity, and Excellence, University of California.

Tharp, R. G., & Gallimore, R. (1988). *Rousing minds to life: Teaching, learning, and schooling in social context*. Cambridge, MA: Harvard University Press.

Vygotsky, L. S. (1978). *Mind and society: The development of higher psychological processes* (M. Cole, V. John-Steiner, S. Scribner, & E. Souberman, Trans.). Cambridge, MA: Harvard University Press.

APPENDIX: The Sheltered Instruction Observation Protocol (SIOP)

Observer: _____   Teacher: _____
Date: _____   School: _____
Grade: _____   ESL level: _____
Class: _____   Lesson: Multi-day   Single-day   (circle one)

Directions:
Circle the number that best reflects what you observe in a sheltered lesson. You may give
a score from 0–4.
Cite under "Comments"   Total Score: ☐   %Score ☐   Type #:_____
specific examples of the
behaviors observed.

I. Preparation

	Highly Evident	Somewhat Evident		Not Evident	NA
	4	3	2	1	0	NA
1. Clearly defined *content objectives* for students	☐	☐	☐	☐	☐	☐
2. Clearly defined *language objectives* for students	☐	☐	☐	☐	☐	☐
3. *Content concepts* appropriate for age and educational background level of students	☐	☐	☐	☐	☐	☐
4. *Supplementary materials* used to a high degree, making the lesson clear and meaningful (graphs, models, visuals)	☐	☐	☐	☐	☐	☐
5. *Adaptation of content* (e.g., text, assignment) to all levels of student proficiency	☐	☐	☐	☐	☐	☐
6. *Meaningful activities* that integrate lesson concepts (e.g., surveys, letter writing, simulations, constructing models) with language practice opportunities for reading, writing, listening, and/or speaking	☐	☐	☐	☐	☐	☐

Comments:

II. Instruction

• 1) Building Background

	4	3	2	1	0	NA
7. *Concepts explicitly linked* to students' background experiences	❏	❏	❏	❏	❏	❏
8. *Links explicitly made* between past learning and new concepts	❏	❏	❏	❏	❏	❏
9. *Key vocabulary emphasized* (e.g., introduced, written, repeated, and highlighted for students to see)	❏	❏	❏	❏	❏	❏

Comments:

• 2) Comprehensible Input

	4	3	2	1	0	NA
10. *Speech* appropriate for students' proficiency level (e.g., slower rate, enunciation, and simple sentence structure for beginners)	❏	❏	❏	❏	❏	❏
11. *Explanation* of academic tasks clear	❏	❏	❏	❏	❏	❏
12. Uses a variety of *techniques* to make content concepts clear (e.g., modeling, visuals, hands-on activities, demonstrations, gestures, body language)	❏	❏	❏	❏	❏	❏

Comments:

• 3) Strategies

	4	3	2	1	0	NA
13. Provides ample opportunities for student to use *strategies* (see Glossary)	❏	❏	❏	❏	❏	❏
14. Consistent use of *scaffolding* techniques throughout lesson, assisting and supporting student understanding such as think-alouds (see Glossary)	❏	❏	❏	❏	❏	❏
15. Teacher uses a variety of *question types throughout the lesson, including those that promote higher-order thinking skills* throughout the lesson (e.g., literal, analytical, and interpretive questions).	❏	❏	❏	❏	❏	❏

Comments:

• **4) Interaction**

	4	3	2	1	0	NA
16. Frequent opportunities for *interactions* and discussion between teacher/student and among students, which encourage elaborated responses about lesson concepts	❏	❏	❏	❏	❏	❏
17. *Grouping configurations* support language and content objectives of the lesson (see Glossary)	❏	❏	❏	❏	❏	❏
18. Consistently provides sufficient *wait time for student response*	❏	❏	❏	❏	❏	❏
19. Ample opportunities for students to *clarify key concepts in L1* (see Glossary)	❏	❏	❏	❏	❏	❏

Comments:

• **5) Practice/Application**

	4	3	2	1	0	NA
20. Provides *hands-on* materials and/or manipulatives for students to practice using new content knowledge	❏	❏	❏	❏	❏	❏
21. Provides activities for students to *apply content and language knowledge* in the classroom	❏	❏	❏	❏	❏	❏
22. Uses activities that integrate all *language skills* (i.e., reading, writing, listening, and speaking)	❏	❏	❏	❏	❏	❏

Comments:

• **6) Lesson Delivery**

	4	3	2	1	0	NA
23. *Content objectives* clearly supported by lesson delivery	❏	❏	❏	❏	❏	❏
24. *Language objectives* clearly supported by lesson delivery	❏	❏	❏	❏	❏	❏
25. *Students engaged* approximately 90–100% of the period (see Glossary)	❏	❏	❏	❏	❏	❏
26. *Pacing* of the lesson appropriate to the students' ability level	❏	❏	❏	❏	❏	❏

Comments:

III. Review/Assessment

	4	3	2	1	0	NA
27. Comprehensive *review* of key vocabulary	❏	❏	❏	❏	❏	❏
28. Comprehensive *review* of key content concepts	❏	❏	❏	❏	❏	❏
29. Regularly provides *feedback* to students on their output (e.g., language, content, work)	❏	❏	❏	❏	❏	❏
30. Conducts *assessment* of student comprehension and learning of all lesson objectives (e.g., spot checking, group response) throughout the lesson (see Glossary)	❏	❏	❏	❏	❏	❏

Comments:

3

The Standards Performance Continuum

A Performance-Based Measure of the Standards for Effective Pedagogy

R. Soleste Hilberg, R. William Doherty,
Georgia Epaloose, and Roland G. Tharp

The Standards Performance Continuum (SPC) is a 5-point rubric that provides a quantitative measure of classroom enactments of the *Standards for Effective Pedagogy*. The first standard, *Joint Productive Activity*, involves teachers and students working together on a common product or goal, with opportunities to converse about their work. The second standard, *Language and Literacy Development*, involves developing competence in the language and literacy of instruction and in the academic disciplines throughout all instructional activities. The third standard, *Contextualization*, situates new academic content in contexts familiar to students to connect it to prior knowledge or experience from the home, school, or community. The fourth standard, *Challenging Activities*, uses complex tasks requiring the application or use of content knowledge to achieve an academic goal. The fifth standard, *Instructional Conversation*, is a planned, goal-directed conversation between a teacher and a small group of students. Tharp, Estrada, Dalton, and Yamauchi (2000) proposed these standards as the most effective strategies for teaching culturally, linguistically, and economically diverse students who are less successful in school, but they also stress their importance for *all* learners.

There is growing evidence of the effectiveness of classroom implementations of these standards. For example, Padrón and Waxman (1999) found that in fourth- and fifth-grade classrooms with largely Latino English language learners (ELLs) where the standards were used to a moderate degree, students perceived themselves as more capable readers, perceived more cohesion in the classroom, and spent slightly to moderately more time on task. Students were also observed to be on task significantly more (86%) than students in classrooms where the standards were not used (62%). In studies of classrooms with predominantly Latino ELLs, Estrada (this volume) found that teachers' use of the standards in literacy instruction was related to higher reading and language scores on the Spanish Assessment of Basic Education (SABE) for first graders, and Stanford Achievement Test-9 (SAT-9) language scores for fourth graders. Hilberg, Tharp, and DeGeest (2000) randomly assigned classes of eighth-grade Native American students to either treatment (Five Standards) or control (Traditional) mathematics instruction and found that students in the Five Standards condition evidenced more conceptual learning on tests at the end of the math unit and higher retention of unit content 2 weeks later. Doherty and Pinal (2002) found that teachers' use of joint productive activity (JPA) during language arts instruction for primarily Latino ELLs reliably predicted students' self-reported use of effective comprehension strategies, and students' self-reported use of effective comprehension strategies reliably predicted their achievement gains on standardized comprehension tests (SAT-9). Students' use of ineffective comprehension strategies, unrelated to teachers' use of JPA, predicted declines in comprehension achievement. Doherty and Pinal (2002) also found a direct link between teachers' use of JPA and gains in students' comprehension achievement when students' ability to read in English was held constant. Saunders and Goldenberg (1999) found that instructional conversation and contextualization greatly assisted the reading comprehension and thematic understanding of students with varying levels of English proficiency.

The SPC is an important tool for researchers and educators working to improve education for diverse students for several reasons. First, though systematic classroom observation has been used extensively in education research over the past three decades, research in classrooms with linguistically and culturally diverse students has been predominantly qualitative. The SPC is a quantitative measure of performance of teaching strategies that are effective for diverse students. The data generated can be used as either dependent or independent variables in experimental and quasi-experimental studies, allowing the analysis of *causal* relationships that are not open to qualitative or correlational methods. Second, many of the measures developed and used widely in the past three decades were designed to meet an investigator's specific research needs. As such, a theoretical basis is often not well articulated, and the measures focus more on description than explanation, thus making conclusions or inferences problematic. The SPC, however, is based on a coherent, comprehensive theory of diversity education derived from over 2 decades of research utilizing a broad range of research methodologies and an equally broad range of samples and settings, with contributions from anthropologists, ethnographers, linguists, psychologists, sociologists, teachers, teacher educators, and education researchers. The theory has been published and is available to all who consider using the SPC and want to know more about its theoretical basis (Tharp & Gallimore, 1988; Tharp et al., 2000). Third, although many measures rate phenomena in terms of their *frequencies*, the SPC measures theoretically meaningful differences in the *quality* of observed behaviors, thus providing explanatory power to analyses of the relationship between the quality of teaching performance and student outcomes. Finally, because SPC data are generated by a single rating rather than multiple time-based ratings, multiple measures can easily be used concurrently. The primary disadvantage of the SPC is that it provides information on a limited set of teacher behaviors. However, the information provided can be useful for assessing the effectiveness of instruction, professional development activities, or school reform efforts. A second disadvantage of the SPC is that it typically requires more training to obtain adequate reliability than the other measures presented in this volume. Although an understanding of the theory underlying the Standards for Effective Pedagogy is recommended, we have found that the cell criteria are specific enough to achieve high intercoder agreement between observers with little or no prior understanding of sociocultural theory.

THEORETICAL FOUNDATION OF THE SPC

The SPC is founded on the sociocultural tenet that learning occurs best when novices collaborate and converse with more experienced and more knowledgeable others on a shared task (Vygotsky, 1978). From this perspective, learning and development are inherently social, and the construction of knowledge and meaning is situated within a socially created context. *Teaching* is assisting students' performance, with the goal of increasing that which students can do unassisted by the teacher; *learning* represents movement through an individual's zone of proximal development (ZPD), the difference between independent and assisted performance, in the direction of increased competence and autonomy (Tharp & Gallimore, 1988; Tharp et al., 2000).

From a cognitive perspective, learning is the process of associating new information with prior knowledge (Baddeley, 1990). For this to occur, and for new information to be retained in memory, learners must engage in some sort of elaboration of the new information (Dansereau, 1988; Slavin, 1996; Wittrock, 1986). *Elaboration* refers to the internal process of associating new and prior knowledge in a meaningful context (Baddeley, 1990; Craik & Lockhart, 1972; Craik & Tulving, 1975). Furthermore, elaborative strategies that focus on the conceptual characteristics of new information (i.e., its meaning, personal and social relevance, and relationship to prior knowledge and experience) result in better learning and recall than strategies focused on more superficial characteristics (Baddeley, 1990; Craik & Lockhart, 1972). More importantly, a small amount of conceptual processing produces more learning than a large amount of more superficial processing (Craik & Tulving, 1975). Each of the pedagogy standards proposed by Tharp and his colleagues promotes conceptual elaboration and, consequently, assists learning.

THE DIMENSIONS AND DISTINCTIONS OF THE SPC

Table 3.1 presents the dimensions underlying each of the Five Standards. Each cell defines theoretically equivalent changes in teaching performance along each dimension. The following discussion describes the rationale for defining the highest end of each dimension.

Joint Productive Activity (JPA)

In JPAs, participants collaborate to generate a product or achieve a common goal. During such goal-directed collaboration, participants with varying levels of skill and expertise interact, exchange information, and share their views, perceptions, rationales, and problem-solving or thinking strategies. The dimension underlying JPA is *collaboration*, and the continuum ranges from students working on individual products to students and teacher collaborating on a joint product (see Table 3.1). The teacher's role in JPA is to participate as a full collaborator; model language, skills, and problem-solving strategies; and assess and responsively assist student performance.

Although JPA is similar in many respects to some cooperative learning strategies, not all cooperative learning rises to the level of JPA. The teacher's role in many forms of cooperative learning is to move from group to group, checking student work and providing advice and assistance (Cohen & Lotan, 1997; Davidson, 1997; Heller, Keith, & Anderson, 1997). According to Tharp et al. (2000), however, to assist student performance most effectively, the teacher must be a full collaborator

TABLE 3.1. *The Dimensions Underlying the Standards*

Standard	Dimension	Not Enacted	Partially Enacted	Fully Enacted
JPA[a]	Collaboration	Students work on individual product	Students collaborate on a joint product	The teacher and a small group of students collaborate on a joint product
LLD[b]	Language use	Instruction is dominated by teacher talk	Activities provide opportunities for students' sustained reading, writing, or speaking	The teacher provides systematic assistance in activities that *generate* extended language use and development of content vocabulary
CTX[c]	Connected learning	New information is provided in an abstract, disconnected manner	Activities are incidentally connected to students' prior knowledge and experience	The teacher integrates new information with what students already know from their home, school, or community
CA[d]	Cognitive complexity	Activities rely on repetition, recall, and convergent thinking to generate declarative or procedural knowledge	Activities are connected to academic concepts	The teacher uses challenging standards and feedback to advance student understanding to more complex levels
IC[e]	Student–teacher dialogue	Recitation script, lecture, or whole-class instruction predominates	The teacher and a small group of students converse on an academic topic	The teacher and a small group of students converse about their views, judgments, and rationales in relation to an academic topic to achieve an instructional goal

[a] Joint productive activity
[b] Language and literacy development
[c] Contextualization
[d] Challenging activities
[e] Instructional conversation

with students in the activity. For assistance to be effective, it must be understandable to the student, responsive to the student's needs, correct, and sufficiently elaborated to allow the student an opportunity to correct misconceptions (Webb, Troper, & Fall, 1995). In addition, the student must have and use the opportunity to apply the assistance in solving problems (Vedder, 1988).

Language and Literacy Development (LLD)

Language proficiency is highly correlated with overall school achievement. The development of effective and appropriate language use is fundamental to learning, thinking, problem solving (Ashworth, 1979; Collier, 1995), and the co-construction of knowledge (Wells & Chang-Wells, 1992). The dimension underlying the development of language and literacy is *language use,* and the continuum ranges from instruction dominated by teacher talk to instruction in which academic language use by students predominates. The critical role of the teacher is to assist student language development through questioning, rephrasing, and modeling.

Language provides the raw material for cognition and is the interface through which prior knowledge and experience, the foundation for new learning, are accessed (Rueda, 1999). Purposeful discourse influences such mental functions as attention, logical memory, and the formation of concepts (Wertsch, 1985) and helps learners reorganize material in new ways, resolve inconsistencies, and fill in gaps in understandings (Webb et al., 1995). Discourse generates more elaborate conceptualizations and strengthens connections between new information and prior learning (Wittrock, 1990). Most importantly, language is best learned through meaningful use and purposeful conversation (Tharp et al., 2000). The most effective instruction, therefore, is that which generates language use and requires that students gain sufficient mastery of language to complete the learning task.

Contextualization

Connecting educational content to students' personal lives and providing instruction in familiar, everyday contexts about which students have prior knowledge enable students to make sense of new information and construct new knowledge. The dimension underlying contextualization is *connected learning,* and the continuum ranges from instruction in which new information is presented in an abstract, atomistic, decontextualized manner to instruction that is *integrated* with prior knowledge and experience. The teacher's task is to build upon what students already know. Instruction that is situated in problems and issues from familiar contexts provides opportunities for connecting students' informal understandings to more abstract levels of understanding. Even incidental connections between the formal concepts of the learning situation and everyday concepts can make the new information more relevant and meaningful and, consequently, more likely to be attended to (Cacioppo & Petty, 1982). Integrating new information into familiar contexts facilitates the organization of the new information into long-term memory by *priming*, or making more available, associated knowledge (Collins & Loftus, 1975). The increased availability of associated knowledge results in a more conceptual form of processing (Craik & Lockhart, 1972; Craik & Tulving, 1975), which, in turn, improves retention and facilitates recall (Baddeley, 1990).

Challenging Activities

In addition to teaching course content, challenging activities teach higher-order thinking skills such as analyzing, categorizing, evaluating, generalizing, synthesizing and summarizing, exploring patterns, determining causal relationships, or problem solving (Tharp & Gallimore, 1988). Challenging activities require (a) appropriate leveling of tasks so that all students are stretched to grow within their ZPDs, (b) opportunities to use and apply new information, and (c) a balance between challenge and assistance to advance student understanding to more complex levels (Tharp et al., 2000). The dimension underlying challenging activities is *cognitive complexity*. The critical role of the teacher is to assess and assist student understanding.

Challenging standards and feedback on performance are essential elements of challenging activities. Standards or goals enhance motivation (Locke, Shaw, Saari, & Latham, 1981), and when both standards and feedback are present, self-evaluative mechanisms motivate learners to modify their performance to achieve greater accordance with the standards (Bandura & Cervone, 1983; Bandura & Schunk, 1981). Self-evaluation, according to Schraw and Sperling-Dennison (1994), involves planning (goal setting and the allocation of resources prior to learning), information management strategies (organizing, elaborating, summarizing), comprehension monitoring (assessment of one's learning or use of strategies), and evaluation (analyzing learning and strategies after the learning episode). This regulation of cognition typifies metacognition (Brown, 1987; Flavell, 1987), not only generating declarative knowledge (knowledge about self and strategies) and procedural knowledge (knowledge of how to use strategies), but also promoting the development of conditional knowledge – knowledge of when and why to use strategies (Schraw & Sperling-Dennison, 1994).

Instructional Conversation

The amount and quality of teacher–student academic interactions are two of the most important factors in student learning (Wang, Haertel, & Walberg, 1994). The dimension underlying instructional conversation (IC) is *student–teacher dialogue*, and the dimension ranges from informal, nonacademic discourse in whole-class settings to a goal-directed, fully inclusive conversation between the teacher and a small group of students. The critical task of the teacher is to elicit and extend student talk on academic, personal, social, and cultural experience in relation to an academic topic (Tharp & Gallimore, 1988, 1991; Yamauchi & Tharp, 1995).

According to Tharp and his colleagues (Tharp & Gallimore, 1991; Tharp & Yamauchi, 1994), student–teacher dialogue is the most effective means for assisting the development of basic thinking skills and the ability to form, express, and exchange ideas. Fully inclusive small-group ICs are stressed because they increase the participation of all students, including the more passive learners (Menke & Pressley, 1994). As such, ICs enable the teacher to (a) assist all students' conceptual elaboration of new content, (b) contextualize instruction in the learner's experience base (Ochs, 1982), (c) individualize instruction to match students' varied ability levels, (d) assess and assist learning, and (e) maintain appropriate cognitive challenge (Goldenberg, 1991; Tharp & Gallimore, 1988; Tharp et al., 2000).

LEVELS OF THE SPC

The SPC defines five levels of enactment for each standard (values range from 0 to 4): (a) *Not Observed* – the standard is not present; (b) *Emerging* – elements of the standard are implemented; (c) *Developing* – the standard is partially implemented; (d) *Enacting* – the standard is fully implemented; and (e) *Integrating* – at least three standards are fully implemented simultaneously in an instructional activity. SPC subscale scores are summed to form an SPC total score for each observation. The SPC is presented in Table 3.2, with cell criteria defining enactment of each standard at each of these five levels. The instructional model represented by the highest level of enactment of all of the standards requires a classroom organization composed of multiple, simultaneous, diversified small-group activities, with the teacher as a full collaborating member of one group.

OBSERVER TRAINING

As with most criterion-based measures, adequate training of observers is essential (Frick & Semmel, 1978). Training (10 to 20 hours, depending on trainees' expertise) includes instruction on the bases and definitions of the standards and trainer and trainee jointly rating videotapes of classroom instruction. Training *requires* the *SPC Manual*. Interrater reliability should be assessed as part of the training, which, of course, should occur prior to data collection. Periodic retraining is recommended to maintain accuracy and to minimize deterioration of observer skill when observations are performed intermittently over an extended period of time (Frick & Semmel, 1978).

CLASSROOM OBSERVATION PROCEDURES

Prior to conducting observations, teachers must receive adequate information regarding the purpose of the observations. Minimally, this information should include (a) the goals of the research, (b) the role of observers, (c) ethical issues such as confidentiality and treatment of research participants, and (d) when and how research results will be made available. Observers will need the following:

- school visitation regulations;
- proper identification such as a badge or name tag;
- school schedule(s);
- faculty list with grade level(s) taught, subject area, room number, and preparation periods;
- school map;
- schedule of classes to observe;
- a copy of the SPC measure and either paper or electronic observation forms;

	Not Observed	Emerging	Developing	Enacting	Integrating
General Definition:	*The standard is not observed.*	*One or more elements of the standard are enacted.*	*The teacher designs and enacts activities that demonstrate a partial enactment of the standard.*	*The teacher designs, enacts, and assists in activities that demonstrate a complete enactment of the standard.*	*The teacher designs, enacts, and assists in activities that demonstrate skillful integration of multiple standards simultaneously.*
Joint Productive Activity *Teacher and Students Producing Together*	*Joint Productive Activity* is not observed.	Students are seated with a partner or group, AND (a) collaborate or assist one another, OR (b) are instructed in how to work in groups, OR (c) contribute individual work, not requiring collaboration, to a joint product.	The teacher and students collaborate on a joint product in a whole-class setting, OR students collaborate on a joint product in pairs or small groups.	The teacher and a small group of students collaborate on a joint product.	The teacher designs, enacts, and collaborates in joint productive activities that demonstrate skillful integration of multiple standards simultaneously.
Language & Literacy Development *Developing Language and Literacy Across the Curriculum*	*Language & Literacy Development* is not observed.	(a) The teacher explicitly models appropriate language; OR (b) students engage in brief, repetitive, or drill-like reading, writing, or speaking activities; OR (c) students engage in social talk while working.	The teacher provides structured opportunities for academic language development in sustained reading, writing, or speaking activities.	The teacher designs and enacts instructional activities that *generate* language expression and development of content vocabulary AND *assists* student language use or literacy development through questioning, rephrasing, or modeling.	The teacher designs, enacts, and assists in language development activities that demonstrate skillful integration of multiple standards simultaneously.

(continued)

TABLE 3.2. (*continued*)

	Not Observed	Emerging	Developing	Enacting	Integrating
Contextualization *Making Meaning – Connecting School to Students' Lives*	*Contextualization* is not observed.	The teacher (a) includes some aspect of students' everyday experience in instruction, OR (b) connects classroom activities by theme or builds on the current unit of instruction, OR (c) includes parents or community members in activities or instruction.	The teacher makes incidental connections between students' prior experience/ knowledge from home, school, or community and the new activity/ information.	The teacher integrates the new activity/ information with what students already know from home, school, or community.	The teacher designs, enacts, and assists in contextualized activities that demonstrate skillful integration of multiple standards simultaneously.
Challenging Activities *Teaching Complex Thinking*	*Challenging Activity* is not observed.	The teacher (a) accommodates students' varied ability levels, OR (b) connects student comments to content concepts, OR (c) sets and presents standards for student performance, OR (d) provides students with feedback on their performance.	The teacher designs and enacts activities that connect instructional elements to academic content OR advance student understanding to more complex levels.	The teacher designs and enacts activities that are connected to academic content; assists and uses challenging standards to advance student understanding to more complex levels; AND provides students with feedback on their performance.	The teacher designs, enacts, and assists in challenging activities that demonstrate skillful integration of multiple standards simultaneously.

Instructional Conversation *Teaching Through Conversation*	*Instructional Conversation* is not observed.	The teacher (a) responds to student talk in ways that are comfortable for students, OR (b) uses questioning, listening, *or rephrasing to elicit student talk,* OR (c) converses with students on a nonacademic topic.	The teacher converses with a small group of students on an academic topic AND *elicits student talk* with questioning, listening, rephrasing, or modeling.	The teacher designs and enacts an instructional conversation (IC) with a clear academic goal; listens carefully to assess and assist student understanding; AND questions students on their views, judgments, or rationales. All students are included in the IC, AND student talk occurs at higher rates than teacher talk.	The teacher designs, enacts, and assists in instructional conversations that demonstrate skillful integration of multiple standards simultaneously.

- a brief written explanation of the research available to provide to teachers if requested; and
- protocols for dealing with substitute or student teachers, cancellations, or unanticipated events such as school functions, field trips, or testing.

Upon entering a classroom, observers offer their name and affiliation to the teacher if possible, then find a location on the perimeter of the classroom from which to observe as unobtrusively as possible. Observers may ask questions for clarification, if necessary, but should not participate in classroom activities. Observers should also be prepared to respond briefly and adequately to questions or concerns from teachers. When leaving, observers thank the teacher if appropriate.

DATA-RECORDING PROCEDURES

At the beginning of the observation, observers record the teacher's name, date, school, observer's name, observation beginning and ending times, subject, grade, and number of students. Throughout the observational period, a running description of classroom events should be recorded in the "notes" field of either the electronic or hard copy version of the SPC observation form. The content of the notes should provide sufficient justification for the SPC ratings made, as well as relevant information such as classroom interactions, teaching strategies, assessments used, or any other supplementary information useful to or required by the study. During the observation, it may be useful to move about the room or to change locations to examine the materials, content, goals and assessments in instructional activities, and the nature of interactions and communications among students and between the teacher and students.

SPC RATINGS

The primary purpose of the SPC is to gather data on a teacher's use of the standards during a specified period of time. One SPC rating is made for each classroom observation, which typically lasts for 45 to 90 minutes. However, the duration of the observational period is specified by the researcher and may last an entire morning or entire day of a single teacher. Often the duration will be based on the school schedule: In secondary schools in which students move from class to class, the duration of the observation will coincide with the length of each class;

in elementary schools, the duration is determined by the portion of the day the subject areas of interest are taught. What is most important is that the duration of the observational period be held constant across all observations.

If an observation contains multiple activities, either sequential or simultaneous, the rating for the observation is based on the highest level observed for each standard. For example, in a classroom some students work individually, and some collaborate with peers in small groups. The activity in which students work individually would be rated as Not Observed for JPA, whereas the small-group activity would be rated as Developing. Thus the JPA rating for the observation period would be Developing (2). However, an activity that is brief or insignificant in light of the entire observation does not influence the observation rating. For example, if a teacher provides brief assistance to one child and together they solve a single math problem, an Enacting level JPA, in a class that primarily involves lecture and individual student work, that brief JPA would not affect the rating of the observation.

There are two approaches to making SPC ratings. One approach is to make initial ratings early in the observation period, then modify them upward throughout the observation when new activities or information warranting higher ratings are encountered. This approach is useful when activities or interactions vary during the observation. Adjustments will be made to ratings only to note increases in use of the standards. For example, the observer may note that students are making individual contributions to a joint product and score JPA as Emerging. Later, the observer may notice student collaboration and modify the initial score upward to Developing. A second approach is to make ratings only at the end of the observation, based primarily on the recorded notes. Whatever approach is used, SPC ratings should be completed prior to leaving the classroom.

STATISTICAL ISSUES

Although the SPC is strictly speaking an ordinal scale, SPC data are generated by ratings rather than rankings. As such, SPC data fall into the gray area between ordinal and interval data like those of many measures commonly used in research in education and psychology. There are two primary statistical considerations regarding the analysis and interpretation of ordinal data such as those generated by the SPC. First, although the distances between SPC values may represent theoretically equivalent intervals, the actual distances are unknown. No assumptions can be made about equal differences between scores at different points along the continuum. For example, a difference between a score of 1 and a score of 2 may not be the same as the difference between a score of 2 and a score of 3. Nor can it be assumed that a score of 4 is twice that of a score of 2. Therefore interpretations of ordinal data are best discussed in relative rather than absolute terms. The second issue is that ordinal data are unlikely to be normally distributed (Harwell & Gatti, 2001). This can be problematic with SPC data. When a small subset of ratings is at the Integrating level, data are likely to be positively skewed. The distribution of SPC data should always be inspected and, if necessary, one-stretch transformations performed to make scores more normally distributed.

The measurement scale has important implications for the meaning embodied by the data, but the issues of scales, statistical testing, and interpretation have been controversial for decades. Sometimes interpretations are based on ignorance of the level of the data, but often they are simply pragmatic: The interpretations are meaningful and add to our understanding.

In most cases, it is more reasonable to interpret SPC data according to the rules for rating data than to have analyses and interpretations restricted by the rules for rank data. Our decisions are based on the nature of the variable rather than strictly on the nature of the data. When SPC data are used as a predictor variable, our choice between parametric or nonparametric tests is based more on (a) the degree to which the assumptions underlying parametric tests are satisfied; (b) the permissible transformations that the data undergo in testing; (c) questions of power, sensitivity, and flexibility (Boneau, 1961; Gaito, 1960, 1980; Townsend & Ashby, 1984); and (d) the research question than on issues of scaling.

If the underlying assumptions of parametric tests are reasonably satisfied and the research goal is to compare samples or to discover what other variables contribute to changes in the criterion variable, or if there are significant interactions between predictors, then parametric tests are a reasonable choice. Regression analysis for estimating parameters, multivariate models to estimate effects on correlated outcome measures, and cluster analyses to derive groupings of cases or variables all have practical applications with SPC data. When SPC scores are used as the criterion variable, for comparisons between sets of SPC scores, or when the assumptions underlying parametric tests are not met, nonparametric, or distribution-free, tests such as the Mann–Whitney U test or sign tests for comparing samples, the Kruskal–Wallis analysis of variance, or the Friedman two-way analysis of variance are recommended.

Researchers have a choice other than being conservative or liberal on issues of the proper handling of ordinal data: They can treat the data separately according to both sets of assumptions and make sure that both analyses lead to the same conclusions (Fraenkel & Wallen, 1993; Wright, 1997). Multiple methods add confidence to our choice of tests as well as to the reliability of our results.

SUBSTANTIVE FINDINGS

To illustrate some of the uses of the SPC, we present examples from three of our research projects, highlighting applications in (a) the examination of the relationship between the use of the standards and student achievement, (b) professional development to assist teachers increase the use of the standards, and (c) assessing schoolwide use of the standards.

SPC Ratings and Student Achievement

In our first example, in a school serving largely low-income Latinos with varying levels of English proficiency, we examined the relationship between teachers' use of the Standards for Effective Pedagogy during language arts instruction and gains in student achievement on year-end standardized tests (SAT-9). The findings of this study, reported in Table 3.3, indicate a relationship between the standards and student performance. After accounting for the effects of teachers' years of experience and students' grade level and English proficiency, higher SPC total scores, found by summing individual subscale scores, predicted greater achievement gains than would be predicted by students' SAT-9 scores from the previous year. This relationship was found on the comprehension, reading, spelling, and vocabulary SAT-9 subtests. There was no effect on the language subtest, and the relationship was only marginally significant for vocabulary. Further analyses found that teachers' use of the standards when English was the language of instruction reliably predicted English language and vocabulary achievement, whereas, as might be predicted, in classes where instruction was in Spanish, teachers' use of the standards was unrelated to student gains in English language and vocabulary.

TABLE 3.3. *Hierarchical Analysis of SAT-9 Subtests*

Variable	ß	t^a	R	R^2	df	F
Overall NCE						
Teacher Experience	−.010	−.16	.01	.00	1, 264	.03
Grade	−.025	−.36	–	–	–	–
Mode	−.143	−2.32*	.15	.02	3, 262	1.87
SPC Total Scores	.286	3.17*	.24	.06	4, 261	3.97*
Comprehension						
Teacher Experience	−.006	−.10	.01	.00	1, 264	.01
Grade	−.030	−.44	–	–	–	–
Mode	−.134	−2.17*	.14	.02	3, 262	1.66
SPC Total	.223	2.45*	.20	.04	4, 261	2.77*
Language						
Teacher Experience	−.046	−.75	.05	.00	1, 264	.57
Grade	−.214	−3.12*	–	–	–	–
Mode	−.070	−1.14	.21	.04	3, 262	3.93*
SPC Total	.050	.56	.21	.04	4, 261	3.02*
Reading						
Teacher Experience	−.059	−.95	.06	.00	1, 264	.91
Grade	.054	.77	–	–	–	–
Mode	−.099	−1.60	.12	.02	3, 262	1.34
SPC Total	.258	2.85*	.21	.05	4, 261	3.06*
Spelling						
Teacher Experience	.069	1.13	.07	.01	1, 264	1.28
Grade	−.008	−.11	–	–	–	–
Mode	−.151	−2.47*	.17	.03	3, 262	2.47
SPC Total	.290	3.24*	.26	.07	4, 261	4.54*
Vocabulary						
Teacher Experience	−.001	−.01	.00	.00	1, 264	.00
Grade	.126	1.81	–	–	–	–
Mode	−.045	−.73	.12	.01	3, 262	1.25
SPC Total	.177	1.94*	.17	.03	4, 261	1.89
Instruction in English Language						
Teacher Experience	.121	1.34	.12	.02	1, 120	1.80
Grade	−.249	−2.53*	.26	.07	2, 119	4.15*
SPC Total	.208	2.29*	.32	.11	3, 118	4.62*
Vocabulary						
Teacher Experience	.114	1.25	.11	.01	1, 120	1.57
Grade	−.012	−.12	.11	.01	2, 119	.79
SPC Total	.243	2.61*	.26	.07	3, 118	2.82*
Instruction in Spanish Language						
Teacher Experience	−.069	−.82	.07	.01	1, 141	.68
Grade	−.171	−1.75	.16	.03	2, 140	1.87
SPC Total	−.136	−.87	.18	.03	3, 139	1.50
Vocabulary						
Teacher Experience	−.019	−.22	.02	.00	1, 141	.05
Grade	.285	2.97*	.24	.06	2, 140	4.43*
SPC Total	.045	.29	.24	.06	3, 139	2.96*

[a] * = $p < .05$.

These findings should not be construed as providing support for English-only instruction for all ELLs. With no outcome measures of Spanish language and vocabulary achievement for this sample, the relationship between teachers' use of the standards and students' Spanish vocabulary and language development when Spanish is the language of instruction remains a question for further study.

In this study, the SPC allowed a quantitative assessment of teacher performance of the standards, which in turn allowed the relationship between use of the standards and student achievement to be examined. The SPC will allow hypothesis testing in experimental designs, which is currently extremely limited in education research.

SPC Ratings for Professional Development of Teachers

In our next example, a teacher on a Native American reservation in the Southwest was observed in his first year of teaching, and his performance of the standards was rated using the SPC. Over the year, the teacher received inservice training on the standards and was then observed again. As can be seen in Figure 3.1, this teacher improved on four of the five standards. Used this way, the SPC can provide useful feedback for both the teacher and professional developers.

SPC Ratings and the Effectiveness of Professional Development

In our final example, in a research project at a public elementary school in central California serving predominantly ELLs, we assessed the

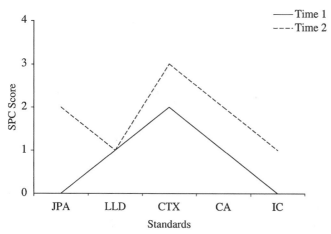

FIGURE 3.1. Increase in the use of the standards by an individual teacher.

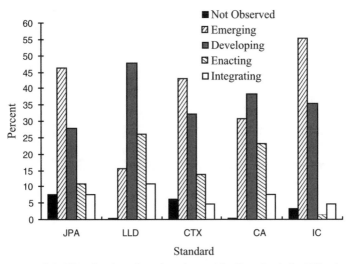

FIGURE 3.2. Distribution of teachers' use of the Standards for Effective Pedagogy.

effectiveness of our professional development activities at the school level. We made two observations of each teacher with the SPC over the course of the spring semester. Figure 3.2 presents the distribution of sub-scale scores for each standard for all teachers combined. As can be seen, teachers were at the Enacting level for Language and Literacy Development and Challenging Activities. We used this information to target our future professional development activities to increase teachers' use of JPA and instructional conversation. We also examined teachers' sub-scale scores to identify individual teachers who most needed assistance.

DISCUSSION

This chapter presented the Standards Performance Continuum (SPC), a rubric for assessing teaching performance of the Standards for Effective Pedagogy and procedures for its systematic use. The SPC is appropriate for many roles in meeting the challenges of improving education: as an instrument for research on effective instruction, a guide for professional development, and a tool for education reform. As a research instrument, the SPC is being used in a multisite research and development project to extend the research on the efficacy of the standards in culturally and linguistically diverse educational settings as a predictor variable. The SPC is also being used as an outcome variable to assess the effectiveness of the professional development activities at the core of this project.

The SPC also provides developmental guidelines useful for teacher professional development. Tharp and Gallimore (1988) have long maintained that education reform must focus on improving teaching. However, for teachers to be successful in taking on new roles and changing practices that have withstood decades of reform efforts, they will need a clear articulation of the role of the teacher and clear standards for teaching performance. The SPC provides such standards, as well as developmental guidelines for teachers learning to enact them. According to Putnam and Borko (2000), teachers' interactions with colleagues are primary determinants of what is learned and how it is learned. Discourse among educators provides such cognitive tools as language, ways of interacting, ideas, theories, and concepts. For teachers to be successful in taking on new roles and changing their practices, they need opportunities to participate "in a professional community that discusses new teacher materials and strategies and that supports the risk taking and struggle entailed in transforming practice" (McLaughlin & Talbert, 1993, p. 15, as cited in Putnam & Borko, 2000). It is hoped that the SPC will serve as a useful tool in such discourse and facilitate changes in practice.

The SPC is a useful tool in school reform because it provides a common language to facilitate and frame communications between groups from different discourse communities whose perceptions, interpretations, experiences, and priorities often differ. Substantive, enduring school reform requires a common vision and collaborative effort between the researchers, teachers, professional developers, administrators, and communities involved. The SPC has already proven useful in meeting the needs of each of these groups in our school/community co-constructed education reform project. Researchers assisting the district used the SPC to document the progress of the reform efforts and to determine the relationship between use of the strategies and student outcomes. The SPC can also allow comparisons between classrooms, schools, and districts. Teachers used the SPC to facilitate self-reflection and peer dialogue concerning pedagogy and unit planning. Professional development specialists used the SPC to guide and assess their efforts, to facilitate individual and group consultations, and as a framework for planning inservices and summer institutes. Administrators incorporated the SPC with a teacher professional development portfolio evaluation and the district curriculum. The immediate benefits of all participants in the reform project using the SPC to meet their varying needs were clear and immediate: The SPC provided specific information about teaching practice that was readily available and easily interpretable.

Although there are many uses for the SPC, we would like to point out three cautions pertaining to its appropriate use. First, observers must receive adequate training and periodic retraining to maintain accuracy and interrater reliability. Second, prior to conducting observations, teachers need a clear understanding of the purpose of the observation, how data will be used, and what information they can expect to receive from researchers or observers. Finally, although the SPC is a useful tool for professional development and research on pedagogy, it is not appropriate for teacher evaluations. Information gained from SPC data relates exclusively to specific aspects of pedagogy. Teaching, however, is a highly complex activity, composed of additional important features such as curriculum, classroom management, and classroom climate, as well as a broad array of knowledge and skills not measured by the SPC. Teaching cannot be identified as good or bad, effective or ineffective, master or novice based solely on SPC ratings. The SPC measures only a teacher's performance of the Standards for Effective Pedagogy, and the link between use of the standards and teacher effectiveness is an open question awaiting future research utilizing controlled studies.

It is hoped that the SPC can serve a useful role in such controlled studies addressing important questions. For example, does the use of the standards improve student learning and, if so, are some standards more important than others? Are the standards effective only for linguistically and culturally diverse students, or are they equally effective for all students? Is their effectiveness limited by subject area or grade level or is it consistent across domains and grades? These questions merely scratch the surface of the rich body of research engendered by the Center for Research on Education, Diversity & Excellence and facilitated by the SPC in its mission to transform pedagogy and improve learning for all students.

Note

This work was supported under the Education Research and Development Program, PR/Award No. R306A60001, the Center for Research on Education, Diversity & Excellence (CREDE), as administered by the Office of Educational Research and Improvement (OERI), National Institute on the Education of At-Risk Students (NIEARS), U.S. Department of Education (USDOE). The contents, findings, and opinions expressed here are those of the author and do not necessarily represent the positions or policies of OERI, NIEARS, or the USDOE.

References

Ashworth, D. P. (1979). *Social interaction and consciousness.* New York: Wiley.

Baddeley, A. D. (1990). *Human memory: Theory and practice.* Boston: Allyn & Bacon.

Bandura, A., & Cervone, D. (1983). Self-evaluative and self-efficacy mechanisms governing the motivational effects of goal systems. *Journal of Personality and Social Psychology, 45,* 1017–1028.

Bandura, A., & Schunk, D. H. (1981). Cultivating competence, self-efficacy, and intrinsic interest through proximal self-motivation. *Journal of Personality and Social Psychology, 41,* 586–598.

Boneau, C. A. (1961). A note on measurement scales and statistical tests. *American Psychologist, 16,* 260–261.

Brown, A. L. (1987). Metacognition, executive control, self-regulation, and other more mysterious mechanisms. In F. E. Weinert & R. H. Kluew (Eds.), *Metacognition, motivation, and understanding* (pp. 65–116). Hillsdale, NJ: Erlbaum.

Cacioppo, J. T., & Petty, R. E. (1982). The need for cognition. *Journal of Personality and Social Psychology, 42,* 116–131.

Cohen, E. G., & Lotan, R. A. (1997). *Working for equity in heterogeneous classrooms.* New York: Teachers College Press.

Cohen, J., & Cohen, P. (1983). *Applied multiple regression/correlation analysis for the behavioral sciences* (2nd ed.). Hillsdale, NJ: Erlbaum.

Collier, V. P. (1995). *Promoting academic success for ESL students: Understanding second language acquisition for school.* Elizabeth, NJ: New Jersey Teachers of English to Speakers of Other Languages-Bilingual Educators.

Collins, A. M., & Loftus, E. F. (1975). A spreading activation theory of semantic processing. *Psychological Review, 82,* 407–428.

Craik, F. I., & Lockhart, R. S. (1972). Levels of processing: A framework for memory research. *Journal of Verbal Learning and Verbal Behavior, 11,* 671–684.

Craik, F. I., & Tulving, E. (1975). Depth of processing and the retention of words in episodic memory. *Journal of Experimental Psychology: General, 104,* 268–294.

Dansereau, D. F. (1988). Cooperative learning strategies. In C. E. Weinstein, E. T. Goetz, & P. A. Alexander (Eds.), *Learning and study strategies: Issues in assessment, instruction, and evaluation* (pp. 103–120). Orlando, FL: Academic Press.

Davidson, N. (1997). Small-group learning and teaching in mathematics: A selective review of the research. In E. Dubinski, D. Matthews, & B. E. Reynolds (Eds.), *Readings in cooperative learning for undergraduate mathematics.* (pp. 59–68). Washington, DC: Mathematical Association of America.

Doherty, R. W., Hilberg, R. S., Pinal, A. & Tharp, R. G. (2003). *Five standards and student achievement. NABE Journal of Research and Practice.* 1(1), 1–24.

Doherty, R. W., & Pinal, A. (2002, November). *Joint productive activity, cognitive reading strategies, and achievement.* Paper presented at the annual Conference of the National Council of Teachers of English, Atlanta.

Flavell, J. H. (1987). Speculations about the nature and development of metacognition. In F. E. Weinert & R. H. Kluew (Eds.), *Metacognition, motivation, and understanding* (pp. 21–29). Hillsdale, NJ: Erlbaum.

Fraenkel, J. R., & Wallen, N. E. (1993). *How to design and evaluate research in education.* New York: McGraw-Hill.

Frick, T., & Semmel, M. I. (1978). Observer agreement and reliabilities of classroom observational measures. *American Educational Research 48*(1), 157–184.

Gaito, J. (1960). Scale classification and statistics. *Psychological Review 67*, 277–278.

Gaito, J. (1980). Measurement scales and statistics: Resurgence of an old misconception. *Psychological Bulletin, 87*(3), 564–567.

Goldenberg, C. (1991). *Instructional Conversations and their classroom applications* (Research Report No. 2). Washington, DC: National Center for Research on Cultural Diversity and Second Language Learning.

Harwell, M. R., & Gatti, G. G. (2001). Rescaling ordinal data to interval data in educational research. *Review of Educational Research, 71*(1), 105–131.

Heller, P., Keith, R., & Anderson, S. (1997). Teaching problem solving through cooperative grouping, Part 1: Group versus individual problem solving. In E. Dubinski, D. Matthews, & B. E. Reynolds (Eds.), *Readings in cooperative learning for undergraduate mathematics* (pp. 159–171). Washington, DC: Mathematical Association of America.

Hilberg, R. S., Tharp, R. G., & DeGeest, L. (2000). The efficacy of CREDE's standards-based instruction in American Indian mathematics classes. *Equity and Excellence in Education, 33*(2), 32–39.

Locke, G. J., Shaw, K. N., Saari, L. M., & Latham, G. P. (1981). Goal setting and task performance: 1969–1980. *Psychological Bulletin, 90*, 125–152.

McLaughlin, M. W., & Talbert, J. E. (1993). *Contexts that matter for teaching and learning: Strategic opportunities for meeting the nation's educational goals.* Stanford, CA: Center for Research on the Context of Secondary School Teaching, Stanford University.

Menke, D. J., & Pressley, M. (1994). Elaborative interrogation: Using "why" questions to enhance the learning from text. *Journal of Reading, 37*(8), 642–645.

Ochs, E. (1982). Talking to children in Western Samoa. *Language in Society, 11*, 77–104.

Padrón, Y. N., & Waxman, H. C. (1999). Classroom observations of the Five Standards of Effective Teaching in urban classrooms with English language learners. *Teaching and Change, 7*(1), 79–100.

Putnam, R. T., & Borko, H. (2000). What do new views of knowledge and thinking have to say about research on teacher learning? *Educational Researcher, 29*(1), 4–15.

Rueda, R. (1999, April). *Hart and Risley's research on everyday childhood experiences: Implications for English-language learners.* Paper presented at the annual meeting of the American Education Research Association, Montreal, Canada.

Saunders, W. M., & Goldenberg, C. (1999). *The effects of instructional conversations and literature logs on the story comprehension and thematic understanding of English proficient and limited English proficient students.* Santa Cruz, CA: Center for Research on Education, Diversity & Excellence, University of California.

Schraw, G., & Sperling-Dennison, R. (1994). Assessing metacognitive awareness. *Contemporary Educational Psychology, 19*, 460–475.

Slavin, R. E. (1996). Research on cooperative learning and achievement: What we know, what we need to know. *Contemporary Educational Psychology, 21*(1), 43–69.

Tharp, R. G., Estrada, P., Dalton, S. S., & Yamauchi, L. (2000). *Teaching transformed: Achieving excellence, fairness, inclusion, and harmony.* Boulder, CO: Westview Press.

Tharp, R. G., & Gallimore, R. (1988). *Rousing minds to life: Teaching, learning, and schooling in social context.* New York: Cambridge University Press.

Tharp, R. G., & Gallimore, R. (1991). *The Instructional Conversation: Teaching and learning in social activity* (Research Report No. 2). Santa Cruz, CA: National Center for Research in Cultural Diversity and Second Language Learning.

Tharp, R. G., & Yamauchi, L. A. (1994). *Effective instructional conversations in Native American classrooms* (Research Report No. 10). Washington, DC: National Center for Research on Cultural Diversity and Second Language Learning.

Townsend, J. T., & Ashby, F. G. (1984). Measurement scales and statistics: The misconception misconceived. *Psychological Bulletin, 46*(2), 394–401.

Vedder, P. (1988). *Cooperative learning: A study on processes and effects of cooperation between primary school children.* Westerhaven Groningen, the Netherlands: Rijkuniversiteit Groningen.

Vygotsky, L. S. (1978). *Mind in society: The development of higher psychological processes.* In (M. Cole, V. John-Steiner, S. Scribner, & E. Souberman, Eds.). Cambridge, MA: Harvard University Press.

Wang, M. C., Haertel, G. D., & Walberg, H. J. (1994). Educational resilience in inner cities. In M. C. Wang & E. W. Gorden (Eds.), *Educational resilience in inner-city America: Challenges and prospects* (pp. 45–72). Hillsdale, NJ: Erlbaum.

Webb, N. M., Troper, J. D., & Fall, R. (1995). Constructive activity and learning in collaborative small groups. *Journal of Educational Psychology, 87*(3), 406–423.

Wells, C. G., & Chang-Wells, G. L. (1992). *Constructing knowledge together: Classrooms as centers of inquiry and literacy.* Portsmouth, NH: Heinemann.

Wertsch, J. V. (1985). *Culture, communication, and cognition: Vygotskian perspectives.* New York: Cambridge University Press.

Wittrock, M. C. (1986). Students' thought processes. In M. C. Wittrock (Ed.), *Handbook of research on teaching* (3rd ed., pp. 297–314). New York: Macmillan.

Wittrock, M. C. (1990). Generative processes of comprehension. *Educational Psychologist, 24*, 345–376.

Wright, D. B. (1997). *Understanding statistics: An introduction for the social sciences.* London: Sage.

Yamauchi, L. A., & Tharp, R. G. (1995). Culturally compatible conversations in Native American classrooms. *Linguistics and Education, 7*, 349–367.

4

The Uses of the Classroom Observation Schedule to Improve Classroom Instruction

Hersh C. Waxman and Yolanda N. Padrón

Systematic classroom observation methods have been widely used in the past several decades to investigate effective teaching practices (Brophy & Good, 1986; Stallings & Mohlman, 1988; Waxman, 1995; Waxman & Huang, 1999). One of the most important uses of the method has been to determine which teaching practices improve student learning (Waxman & Huang, 1999). Most classroom observation instruments typically focus on the teacher as the unit of measurement or observation, and thus they describe a variety of instructional behaviors in which teachers engage. There are limitations, however, with teacher-based classroom observation instruments. First, teacher-focused instruments suggest that teaching practices directly impact student outcomes, without acknowledging that student behaviors impact teacher behaviors as well. Another concern with teacher-focused observation systems is that they often ignore student behaviors that have a greater impact on student outcomes than teacher behaviors.

Another limitation of teacher-based observation instruments is that they generally do not allow researchers to examine individual student behaviors, particularly differences by critical attributes such as student sex, ethnicity, or grouping classification (e.g., gifted/nongifted, resilient/nonresilient, monolingual/bilingual). A final concern with teacher-centered observation systems is that they are often very threatening to classroom teachers. Many teachers are reluctant to volunteer to participate in classroom observation research because they know the focus of attention is on the teachers and their instructional practices.

This chapter describes the uses of a systematic classroom observation instrument, the Classroom Observation Schedule (COS), that was designed to address some of the previous concerns of classroom observation by specifically focusing on individual students rather than the teacher (Waxman, Wang, Lindvall, & Anderson, 1990a, 1990b). The theoretical and conceptual framework for this instrument is the student-mediating paradigm, which maintains that students actively process information and interpret classroom reality (Schunk, 1992; Weinstein, 1989). From this perspective, students are not viewed as passive recipients of instruction; rather, it is believed that classroom activities and instruction are mediated by the attitudes and perceptions of students (Anderson, 1987; Doyle, 1977). The emphasis in this cognitive mediational view of teaching is on students' cognitive interactions with teaching (Winne, 1985). Thus, the focus of teaching shifts from a particular approach or style of teaching to the ways students think about content so that it promotes academic achievement (Winne, 1985). In other words, teaching provides conditions that encourage students to apply cognitive processes to content during instruction. Students' perceptions of the teacher's intended behavior and the students' responses to this behavior are important mediators of teachers' influence. The chapter discusses (a) the development of the instrument, (b) some advantages and disadvantages of the instrument, and (c) how it has been used in several studies.

DESCRIPTION OF THE CLASSROOM OBSERVATION SCHEDULE

The COS is used for collecting student classroom process data. It is a systematic observation schedule designed to document observed student behaviors in the context of ongoing classroom instructional learning processes. In the COS, individual students are observed with reference to (a) their interactions with teachers and/or peers and the purpose of such interactions, (b) the settings in which observed behaviors occur, (c) the types of material with which they are working, (d) the specific types of activities in which they engage, (e) student classroom manner, and (f) language used. Approximately six students from each class are randomly selected to be observed. Often the selection is stratified by important student attributes such as sex, ethnicity, or classification by grouping variables such as gifted/nongifted, regular/mainstreamed, monolingual/bilingual, or resilient/nonresilient. For example, three male and three female students are chosen in each classroom. Each student is observed for ten 30-second intervals during the data collection period. The COS has been used in a number of recent studies that examine effective instruction in multiethnic settings, and its interrater reliability was found to be very high ($r > .95$) in most studies (Padrón & Waxman, 1999; Padrón, Waxman, & Huang, 1999; Waxman & Huang, 1997; Waxman, Huang, & Padrón, 1995).

Data obtained from the COS can be used for several purposes. They can be used as process data (i.e., independent variables) that directly or indirectly affect student outcomes. They may also serve as dependent variables that are associated with contextual conditions, teacher attitudes or behaviors, or degree of program implementation variables. One of the major differences between the COS and other classroom observation instruments is that the COS focuses on individual students or groups of students (e.g., students' sex and/or ethnicity), rather than the teacher or the class, as the unit of analysis.

The instrument was originally developed for a federally funded research project at the Learning Research and Development Center at the University of Pittsburgh that examined similarities and differences across several effective instructional programs such as Mastery Learning, Behavior Analysis, Direct Instruction, the Adaptive Learning Environments Model, and the Bank Street Model of Education. The COS was designed to be a generic instrument that focused on student behaviors found to be related to students' academic achievement. Most of the student behaviors included in the instrument (e.g., students' engaged time, students' instructional interactions with teachers) have been found to be significantly related to students' academic achievement (Brophy & Good, 1986; Walberg, 1986). Second, the instrument was specifically designed to focus on individual students in order to address potential inequities in the classroom such as differences between male and female students' behavior and between minority and White students. The COS also has been used in projects at two other federally funded national research centers: the Center for Education in the Inner Cities and the Center for Research on Education, Diversity & Excellence. Some of the research applications of the instrument are discussed later in the chapter.

Procedures for Observing and Recording

The COS is used to record observations of a student's classroom behavior in 30-second intervals. Space for 10 intervals is provided on the form. The observer watches the student for a 30-second interval and records the types of behaviors that occurred in the various categories. After the 30-second interval, the observer records the appropriate categories that indicate the predominant type of interaction, selection of activity, activity types, setting, manner, and language used that occurred during the interval. Only one category per heading should be recorded for all categories except activity types. If the student works in two or more settings, the one that predominates or occupies the student for the greatest amount of time should be recorded. For the heading of Activity Types, the observer should record or check all the activity types that occurred during that interval. In other words, the categories for activity types are not mutually exclusive, and the observer should check as many categories as he or she observed.

Classroom Observation Procedures

Each observation period is defined as a 60-minute session. During this session, the following cycle will be followed. The coder observes the first student for a 30-second interval and records the first sweep for that student for about 30 seconds, then moves on to observe the second student. When the observation and record of the sixth student are completed, the observer begins the second interval, starting again with an observation of the first student and then repeating the previous procedures with the rest of the students.

In some classrooms, it may not be possible to observe for the full 60-minute period. In such cases, the observer records as many teacher and student intervals as possible and makes sure that the overall assessment instrument is completed at the end of the observation. Observations are not conducted in classrooms where special activities (e.g., standardized testing, guest speakers, films) are being conducted.

Operational Definitions

This section provides operational definitions of the categories listed under each of the six main variables or headings used in the COS.

A. *Interactions* – This variable describes the type and purpose of any interaction a student may have with other students, the teacher, or the support staff. Eight types of interactions are operationalized as follows:
   1. No interaction/independence – This category includes students who are observed to be working alone and not interacting

with others (e.g., a student reads a textbook silently at his or her desk).

2. With teacher–Instructional – An interaction with the teacher for a purpose related to either prescriptive or exploratory activities. Examples include (a) checking the student's work, (b) asking questions about the student's learning, (c) tutoring, (d) demonstrating, and (e) explaining.

3. With teacher–Managerial – The purpose of the interaction deals with noninstructional aspects such as asking and answering routine management questions. Interactions related to management include (a) questions about classroom routines, (b) questions about bathroom privileges, (c) the teacher's reaction to disruptive behavior, and (d) the teacher telling a student to get to work after the student has been off task for an extended period of time.

4. With teacher–Social, Personal – An interaction with the teacher for a purpose related to noninstructional aspects such as (a) comments by the teacher relating to personal matters of a student and vice versa (e.g., "How do you feel? You look very nice today.").

5. With support staff – An interaction with another adult such as a school administrator, teacher aide, or room mother.

6. With other students–Instructional – Students interact with their peers for the purpose of sharing ideas or activities related to the task at hand, helping other students, sharing materials, or providing advice on instructional or managerial activities.

7. With other students–Social, Personal – Students interact with their peers for other than an instructional or managerial purpose, such as being distracted, being disruptive, or interfering with ongoing activities in the classroom (e.g., fighting, arguing, talking, joking, throwing objects, banging furniture, or shouting).

8. Other (specify) – This category includes other interactions that cannot be recorded under the previous categories.

B. *Selection of Activity* – This variable describes whether the activity the students are working on is student selected or teacher assigned. These two types of selections are operationalized as follows:

1. Teacher-assigned activity – This category includes the task or activity that the teacher initiates or assigns to students (e.g.,

teacher lectures, asks questions, etc.). If the student is not on self-scheduling, the teacher is generally assigning learning activities. The teacher has told the student to do something or to start to work, regardless of whether the student is on self-scheduling. This includes a specific instruction from the teacher for the student to do a specific task. The student cannot choose learning activities in order to score "teacher assigned." Examples: (a) The teacher directs a student to start his spelling assignment, (b) the teacher calls five students to start their reading group, (c) the teacher decides to make a change in the schedule for the day and tells the student to work on a learning activity not originally scheduled, and (d) the teacher redirects a student to start his or her reading assignment and put aside another activity currently in progress.

2. Student-selected activity – This category includes the task or activity that students themselves can choose to do (e.g., library search, working on computer games). If the student is on self-scheduling, the student is generally responsible for initiating learning activities. Students may choose to work on a prescriptive or exploratory task and are checked into that task by the teacher on his or her self-schedule sheet. The student must choose the learning activities to work on and when to work on each in order to score "student-selected activity." Examples: (a) The student decided to complete the reading assignment that he or she couldn't finish earlier, and (b) the student decides to complete an art exploratory as one of his or her exploratory activity options.

C. *Activity Types* – This variable describes the types of activities that the students are doing. Sixteen types of activities are operationalized as follows:

   1. Working on written assignments – This category includes all types of written assignments (e.g., writing a composition, answering reading comprehension questions, completing a worksheet).

   2. Interacting–Instructional – This category includes any discussion or dialogue with the teacher, another adult, or another student(s) related to the classroom task.

   3. Interacting–Social – This category includes any dialogue with the teacher, another adult, or another student(s) not related to classroom tasks, such as talking or greeting.

4. Watching or Listening – This category includes watching a presentation, movie, or other visual activities or listening, *but not responding*, to the teacher or the presentation.

5. Reading – This category includes all types of reading activities (e.g., reading a textbook or library book).

6. Getting/returning materials – This category includes interludes or transition periods during which students get or return materials or switch from one subject area to another (e.g., obtaining a piece of paper, sharpening a pencil, or turning in work).

7. Painting, drawing, creating graphics, etc. – This category includes all types of art activities such as cutting, pasting, and constructing.

8. Working with technology – This category includes working on computers, using calculators, and using multimedia equipment.

9. Working with manipulative materials/equipment – This category includes work that involves all kinds of manipulative materials, including games, science equipment, building blocks, and puppets.

10. Viewing videos/slides – This category includes watching films, videos, or slides as classroom activities.

11. Playing games – This category includes all kinds of learning games.

12. Presenting/acting – This category includes all types of activities that are performed or presented to a group of students.

13. Tutoring peers – This category includes all types of peer tutoring.

14. Not attending to task – This category applies to students who may be staring into space for the majority of the observed interval.

15. No activity/transition – This category applies to situations in which no activity is undertaken during the transition from one task to another.

16. Other – These are activities unrelated to the instructional program. Examples: (a) going to the bathroom, (b) washing one's face and hands, (c) eating, (d) getting in line, and (e) cleaning up.

D. *Setting* – This variable describes the location or setting in which students are situated. Four types of settings are operationalized as follows:

1. Whole class – This category includes all students working on the same activity, sharing a common goal(s) and/or idea(s).

2. Small group – This category includes a student who is working in a group with more than two persons (e.g., in a reading group, working on a mural for a social studies project).

3. Pairs – This category includes a student who is working with another student as a pair.

4. Individual – This category includes a student who is working alone (e.g., the student is alone at his or her desk).

E. *Manner* – This variable describes how students are using their time. Five types of manners are operationalized as follows:

1. On task – The student is clearly working at a specific task/ learning activity. If the student was working for the majority of the interval but was off task for about 10 seconds (e.g., staring into space), the student should be scored as being on task. Examples: (a) writing, (b) helping another student, (c) reading, (d) plugging in a tape recorder, (e) putting on headphones, (f) sharpening pencils when the child is not distracted during the process, (g) being checked by the teacher, and (h) being questioned by the teacher in relation to the task.

2. Waiting for teacher – The student has signaled that he or she needs the teacher's help in order to continue working on the specific learning activity and is now waiting for the teacher's assistance. The student must stay physically close to the work. Examples: (a) The student tries to get the teacher's attention in order to check an assignment, ask questions, and so on, and (b) the student raises his or her hand to get the teacher's attention.

3. Distracted – The student is not working on a specific learning task and has not signaled for the teacher's help. Examples: (a) The student is staring into space for the majority of the observed interval, (b) the student is discussing a recent television show with another student that is not related to the specific learning activity, and (c) the student is wandering aimlessly around the room.

4. Disruptive – The student interferes with or disrupts ongoing activities in the classroom. Examples: (a) The student is wandering aimlessly around the room and interferes with another student's learning task, (b) the student is fighting or arguing

with another child, and (c) the student is yelling, banging furniture, or shouting.

5. Other – None of the preceding categories apply.

F. *Language Used* – This variable describes the language the student is using. Three types of language use are operationalized as follows:

1. English – This category includes students who use English in verbal interactions or materials written in English (e.g., the student is speaking in English and/or using an English textbook).

2. Spanish – This category includes students who use Spanish in verbal interactions or materials written in Spanish (e.g., the student is speaking in Spanish and/or using a Spanish textbook).

3. Both English and Spanish – This category includes students who use both English and Spanish in verbal interactions or materials written in both English and Spanish (e.g., the student is talking partially in English and partially in Spanish and/or using materials written in English and Spanish).

ADVANTAGES AND DISADVANTAGES OF THE COS

Advantages of the COS

The COS provides a number of advantages over other systematic classroom observation measures. As indicated earlier, the COS has been found to be reliable and valid. The reliability of data, in particular, has been found to be quite high and consistent across all studies. Interrater reliability for the COS has been found to be very high ($r > .95$) in most studies (Padrón & Waxman, 1999; Padrón et al., 1999; Waxman & Huang, 1996, 1997; Waxman, Huang, Anderson, & Weinstein, 1997; Waxman et al., 1995). A second advantage of the COS is that it does not require extensive training in order to use the instrument. Several other observation instruments require extensive and expensive training that can last 2 or 3 days. On the other hand, an observer can be trained to use the COS in a few hours at most.

A third important advantage of the COS is that it allows examination of subgroup differences. For example, results can be reported by various categories, such as gender, grade, bilingual/English-monolingual, and resilient/nonresilient. Similarly, because the COS focuses on individual students and generally uses the student as the unit of measurement, a smaller sample of classrooms is required for some statistical analyses than for instruments focusing on the teacher as the unit of measurement.

For example, a COS study of 10 classrooms will yield a sample of about 60 students, which would allow the use of inferential statistics to make comparisons across student subgroups.

A fourth major advantage is that the COS can be easily modified and adapted for particular research studies. The original instrument, for example, did not include a category for the language(s) used by the student. The Language Used category was specifically developed for a study involving English language learners (ELLs). That category has now become critical when examining language-diverse classrooms because it provides information about the language (e.g., English vs. Spanish) that students use and the context in which the first or second language is used. In another study, the technology component was added to the instrument to examine the extent to which students are using technology (e.g., computer, calculator) in the classroom.

Because the focus of the COS is on the student, another benefit is that teachers do not feel threatened by the observations. Very few teachers, for example, have ever voiced concerns about having researchers come to their classroom to observe students. In several cases, teachers have welcomed the opportunity for observers to focus on a particular student or set of students. Consequently, the final advantage of the COS is its ability to provide teachers and other school personnel with systematic feedback about their students or individual students. This will be discussed more thoroughly in the summary section.

Disadvantages of the COS

Some of the disadvantages of the COS are those that are also typical of other observational instruments. First, a limited number of variables and activities are included. Second, the observer needs to be very focused during the observation period so that accurate information can be provided. Third, whenever an observer enters the classroom, the observation can be considered obtrusive; therefore, the researcher must be careful to have all the preparation materials needed (e.g., class seating chart) before the time of the observation. Some of the materials that are needed for conducting the observation require the cooperation of others, such as teachers, parents, and principals. The classroom teacher, for example, needs to provide a class roster or seating chart that identifies the students who will be observed. In addition, because the focus is on the individual student, permission forms signed by students' parents are sometimes needed before any observations can be conducted. Another

disadvantage of the COS is that it is time-based. Because the observations are conducted in 30-second intervals, the observer needs to have
a watch or timer with a second hand. This process of continuously observing with a timer can be cumbersome for observers and sometimes
increases the obtrusiveness of the observation. There are other general
problems associated with most systematic classroom observation instruments, such as (a) misinterpreting classroom behavior, (b) personal
biases, (c) primacy or recency effects, and (d) leniency or generosity errors (Evertson & Green, 1986; Good & Brophy, 2000) that also could affect
the use of the COS. Finally, there is the possibility that the COS could be
misused to examine the behaviors of particular students. Although the
COS yields very reliable and valid data about groups of students, it is
not designed to provide representative data about individual students.
A larger number of observations across time (e.g., days and weeks) is
required to obtain reliable and valid data about individual students.

STUDIES USING THE COS

The COS has recently been used in a variety of research studies – for
example, in several descriptive studies that focus on classroom instruction and student behaviors in various settings. The COS has also been
used to investigate differences between (a) resilient and nonresilient
students, (b) types of teachers using various instructional methods,
(c) effective and ineffective schools, and (d) differences in classroom
behaviors by technology use. This section will describe four different
types of studies in which the COS was used.

Differences Between Resilient and Nonresilient Students

Padrón et al. (1999) compared the classroom instruction and learning environment of resilient and nonresilient students in elementary schools
serving predominantly minority students. The participants were fourth-
and fifth-grade students from three elementary schools located in a major metropolitan area in the south central region of the United States.
Trained observers systematically observed 57 resilient and 56 nonresilient students identified by teachers during their regular reading and
language classes. Table 4.1 reports the findings, which revealed that resilient students spent significantly more time interacting with teachers
for instructional purposes, whereas nonresilient students spent more
time interacting with other students for social or personal purposes.

TABLE 4.1. *Comparison of Resilient and Nonresilient Students' Classroom Behaviors*

	Resilient (n = 57)		Nonresilient (n = 56)		
	M	*SD*	*M*	*SD*	*t*-Value
Interactions					
No interaction/independence	68.84	30.78	67.25	30.43	0.28
Interactions with teacher – Instructional	10.39	13.42	5.94	10.37	1.97*
Interactions with teacher – Social, Personal	3.57	12.93	5.28	10.15	−0.78
Interactions with other students – Instructional	14.69	24.02	13.70	26.16	0.21
Interactions with other students – Social	2.50	6.65	7.82	16.80	−2.22*
Selection of Activity					
Teacher-assigned activity	96.73	15.38	95.61	17.96	0.35
Student-selected activity	3.27	15.38	4.39	17.96	−0.35
Activity Types					
Working on written assignments	30.04	28.32	20.90	26.11	1.78
Interacting – Instructional	20.10	25.01	17.12	28.39	0.59
Interacting – Social (e.g., talking)	11.05	21.27	10.51	17.27	0.15
Watching or listening	28.61	26.89	19.17	22.78	2.01*
Reading	15.27	25.28	16.56	27.55	−0.26
Painting, drawing, creating graphics, etc.	6.47	20.69	7.94	20.84	−0.38
Not attending to task	8.40	16.64	28.08	30.50	−4.25**
Other	9.98	17.27	10.92	17.46	−0.29
Setting					
Whole class	77.60	36.97	75.21	38.11	0.34
Small group	15.55	35.09	7.19	24.33	1.48
Pairs	2.95	10.24	13.55	30.73	−2.47*
Individual	3.90	10.77	4.03	10.65	−0.07
Manner					
On task	85.30	18.86	60.63	33.63	4.82**
Off task	14.70	18.86	39.37	33.63	−4.82**
Language Used					
English	89.86	27.86	88.60	28.98	0.24
Spanish	6.05	22.25	7.56	23.78	−0.35
Both English and Spanish	4.09	13.58	3.84	11.43	0.10

*$p < .05$. **$p < .001$.

Source: Padrón, Y. N., Waxman, H. C., & Huang, S. L. (1999). Classroom and instructional learning environment differences between resilient and non-resilient elementary school students. *Journal of Education for Students Placed at Risk of Failure, 4*(1), 63–81.

Resilient students were also observed watching or listening significantly more often than nonresilient students, whereas nonresilient students were observed more often not attending to the task. The percentage of time that resilient students were on task was much higher than that of nonresilient students.

Differences in Student Behavior by Teacher Use of the Standards for Effective Pedagogy

Padrón and Waxman (1999) examined the degree to which teachers used the Five Standards for Effective Pedagogy (Tharp, 1997) and then categorized teachers into three levels of use: (a) No Use of Standards, (b) Slight Use of Standards, and (c) Moderate Use of Standards. Classroom teachers were first observed to examine the extent to which they exhibited the standards. Then the COS was used to examine how student behaviors differed in the three types of classrooms. Table 4.2 reports the results, which revealed that students in the Moderate Use of Standards group were observed less frequently working on written assignments than students in the Slight Use of Standards and No Use of Standards groups, whereas students in the Moderate Use of Standards and Slight Use of Standards group were observed more frequently watching or listening to teachers than students in the No Use of Standards group. Students in the Moderate Use of Standards group spent significantly more time reading than students in the Slight Use of Standards and No Use of Standards groups. Furthermore, students in the No Use of Standards group were observed more frequently doing no activity or transition than students in the Moderate Use of Standards and Slight Use of Standards groups.

Students in the Slight Use of Standards group were more frequently observed in whole-class settings than students in the Moderate Use of Standards or No Use of Standards group. Students in the Moderate Use of Standards group were observed more frequently in whole-class settings than students in the No Use of Standards group. Students in the Moderate Use of Standards group were observed more frequently in small group or in pairs than students in the Slight Use of Standards and No Use of Standards groups, whereas students in the No Use of Standards group were observed more frequently in individual settings than students in the Moderate Use of Standards and Slight Use of Standards groups.

ABLE 4.2. *Comparison of Students' Classroom Behaviors by Teacher Group*

	No Use of Standards (n = 42)		Slight Use of Standards (n = 40)		Moderate Use of Standards (n = 35)		
	M	SD	M	SD	M	SD	F
nteractions							
No interaction/ independence	96.27	8.19	91.57	18.64	92.61	16.41	1.22
With teacher – Instructional	2.13	5.99	7.09	17.60	3.16	7.34	2.11
With other students – Instructional	0.79	5.14	0.42	2.64	3.87	11.36	2.19
Other	0.79	3.59	0.92	4.06	0.36	2.11	0.15
Activity Types							
Working on written assignments	26.37a	30.36	17.44a	23.69	1.22b	5.34	11.22***
Interacting – Instructional	4.71	13.50	5.73	9.97	7.19	17.23	0.38
Watching or listening	24.13b	31.25	59.21a	31.59	54.39a	30.36	14.87***
Reading	9.52b	17.70	19.72b	21.28	39.84a	30.99	15.72***
Not attending to task	20.41	30.31	10.69	19.85	12.27	24.71	1.58
No activity/transition	17.16a	26.62	2.92b	7.99	1.63b	7.57	10.81***
Other	5.56	20.38	0.00	0.00	2.85	10.84	1.86
Setting							
Whole class	53.14c	39.04	100.00a	0.00	83.87b	21.85	33.05***
Small group/pairs	1.78b	6.51	0.00b	0.00	12.85a	18.29	14.65***
Individual	45.07a	40.58	0.00b	0.00	3.26b	11.54	40.36***
Manner							
On-task	61.62b	34.38	86.38a	20.85	85.68a	24.92	10.58***
Waiting for teacher	10.56a	18.61	2.64b	8.12	0.00b	0.00	7.35**
Distracted/Disruptive	27.82a	32.60	10.97b	19.68	14.31b	24.92	4.92**

Note: Means with the same letter are not significantly different.
*p < .05. **p < .01. ***p < .001.
Source: Padrón, Y. N., & Waxman, H. C. (1999). Classroom observations of the Five Standards of Effective Teaching in urban classrooms with ELLs. *Teaching and Change, 7*(1), 79–100.

Differences Between Effective and Ineffective Schools for African American Students

Waxman and Huang (1997) investigated differences between four effective and four ineffective urban elementary schools that served predominantly African American students. About 250 fourth- and fifth-grade students from the effective schools and about 450 fourth- and fifth-grade students from the ineffective schools were systematically observed using the COS near the end of the school year. Table 4.3 summarizes the multivariate analysis of variance results, which revealed a significant multivariate effect for type of school (i.e., effective vs. ineffective) on the Setting, Interactions, and Selection of Activity sections of the COS. Follow-up univariate tests revealed that there were significant differences between the effective and ineffective schools on Whole Class Setting, Individual Setting, No Interaction, Interaction with Teacher, Interaction with Others, Working on Written Assignments, Reading, Working with Manipulative Material, and Other Activities. Students from the effective schools were observed significantly more (a) Working in an Individualized Setting, (b) Interacting with Teacher, and (c) Working on Written Assignments. On the other hand, students from the ineffective schools were observed in (a) Whole Class Settings, (b) Not Interacting, (c) Interacting with Others, (d) Reading, and (e) Working with Manipulative Materials significantly more than students from the effective schools.

Classroom Instruction Differences by Level of Technology Use in Middle School Mathematics

Waxman and Huang (1996) examined whether (a) classroom interaction, (b) selection of activities, (c) instructional activities, (d) organizational setting of the classroom, and (e) student on-task and off-task behaviors in the classroom differ significantly according to the degree of implementation of technology in middle school mathematics classrooms. The participants were 2,189 middle school students who were randomly chosen from a multiethnic school district located in a major metropolitan city in the south central region of the United States. The COS was modified to include four items to assess the extent to which students used instructional technology (e.g., calculator or computer) in mathematics.

After all COS observation data were aggregated by class to determine how often students in each class were observed using technology in their classes, three levels or categories of technology use were determined: (a) Moderate Use of Technology (MTU) – classes where students used technology more than 20% of the time, (b) Slight Use of Technology (STU) – classes where students used technology between 11% and 19% of the time, and (c) Infrequent Use of Technology (ITU) – classes where students used technology less than 10% of the time. Students in the MTU

TABLE 4.3. *Comparison of MANOVA and ANOVA Results Between Effective and Ineffective Schools on Observed Student Behaviors*

	MANOVA		Effective (*n* = 259)		Ineffective (*n* = 454)		ANOVA
Behavior Categories	*df*	*F*	*M*	*SD*	*M*	*SD*	*F*
Interaction	2,710	37.06***					
No interaction/ Independence			37.30	38.05	61.44	41.45	59.34***
Interaction with teacher			59.81	39.01	33.19	41.43	70.91***
Interaction with others (e.g., students)			2.89	6.94	5.37	11.58	9.84**
Selection of Activities	1,711	.01					
Teacher-assigned activity			99.10	4.74	99.07	6.47	
Student-selected activity			0.90	4.74	0.93	6.47	
Activity Types	11,701	4.35***					
Working on written assignments			20.85	26.49	16.21	21.08	6.60*
Interacting			5.17	9.20	5.53	9.61	0.23
Watching or listening			54.44	30.85	53.52	29.59	0.15
Reading			4.29	13.69	6.92	17.34	4.39*
Getting/returning materials			2.32	5.06	3.00	5.78	2.49
Coloring, drawing, painting, etc.			1.00	7.46	1.43	7.45	0.54
Working with manipulative materials/equipment			0.39	2.61	4.12	15.20	15.36***
Presenting/acting			0.46	2.11	1.15	4.36	5.60*
Tutoring peers			0.31	3.62	0.04	0.66	2.30
Not attending to task			4.05	10.50	3.17	8.94	1.41
Other			5.10	15.23	3.03	7.61	5.76*
Setting	2,710	3.74*					
Whole class			79.85	32.74	85.72	24.98	7.21**
Small group			6.45	19.01	4.89	16.81	1.28
Individual			13.70	27.69	9.39	19.53	5.88*
Manner	2,710	1.27					
On task			93.43	13.42	91.68	16.49	
Off task			6.57	13.42	7.88	15.33	

*p < .05. **p < .01. ***p < .001.

Source: Waxman, H. C., & Huang, S. L. (1997). Classroom instruction and learning environment differences between effective and ineffective urban elementary schools for African American students. *Urban Education, 32*(1), 7–44.

TABLE 4.4. *Classroom Observation Schedule Results by Level of Technology Use*

	Infrequent Use (n = 720)		Slight Use (n = 749)		Moderate Use (n = 720)		
	M	SD	M	SD	M	SD	F
Classroom Interaction							
(*Wilks's lambda* = .934, F = 12.52, p = .0001, df = 12,4362)							
No interaction/Independence	21.97c	27.73	33.72b	28.84	38.08a	30.89	58.84**
Instructional interaction with teacher	60.27a	31.57	50.79b	30.79	44.93c	30.65	44.88**
Managerial interaction with teacher	7.63	10.65	8.64	11.70	7.58	10.42	2.20
Instructional interaction with students	3.98a	13.10	2.56b	7.59	4.46a	10.32	6.47*
Managerial interaction with students	4.04	10.90	3.51	9.67	3.23	8.88	1.27
Other interactions (e.g., support staff)	2.11	11.63	0.65	4.66	1.72	12.28	4.14
Selection of Activity							
(*Wilks's lambda* = .997, F = 1.69, p = .1487, df = 4,4370)							
Teacher-assigned activity	98.53	10.71	98.80	9.29	99.56	4.57	
Student-selected activity	1.33	10.06	1.07	8.56	0.30	2.66	
Instructional Activities							
(*Wilks's lambda* = .940, F = 7.54, p = .0001, df = 18,4356)							
Working on written assignment	27.82b	26.95	36.01a	27.34	36.51a	28.08	22.88**
Taking quizzes/tests	6.26b	20.54	8.29b	21.50	11.85a	27.10	10.72**

Interacting	15.35	19.43	14.00	18.08	15.91	19.20	1.99
Watching or listening	61.97a	32.82	53.02b	30.76	49.71c	32.37	28.41**
Getting/returning materials	5.54	9.80	6.14	9.52	5.21	9.53	1.77
Doing activities/learning games	2.57	11.22	2.02	9.54	2.06	9.27	0.68
Working on manipulatives	1.23	6.82	1.77	8.06	1.39	8.41	0.92
No activity	5.10	12.54	3.53	9.17	4.45	14.17	3.13
Other (e.g., reading, drawing)	7.28	16.23	6.44	14.84	8.11	19.68	1.76

Classroom Setting

(Wilks's lambda = .932, F = 19.42, p = .0001, df = 8,4366)

Whole class	71.96a	32.22	60.53b	32.23	52.97c	32.81	62.58**
Small group	2.45a	13.36	0.73b	5.04	2.05a	9.79	6.04*
Independent	22.98b	30.24	36.20a	31.67	39.25a	33.40	53.44**
Other (e.g., paired or medium group)	2.19b	8.89	2.27b	10.45	4.75a	16.63	9.94**

Student Behaviors

(Wilks's lambda = .986, F = 5.28, p = .0001, df = 6,4368)

On task	80.29b	24.51	81.60b	21.82	83.97a	20.45	5.02*
Off task (e.g., distracted or uninvolved)	14.99a	22.39	11.80b	19.08	10.96b	18.36	8.16**
Waiting	4.30b	8.52	6.07a	10.45	4.66b	7.88	7.86**

Note: Means with the same letter are not significantly different.

$*p < .01$; $**p < .001$.

Source: Waxman, H. C., & Huang, S. L. (1996). Classroom instruction differences by level of technology use in middle school mathematics. *Journal of Educational Computing Research, 14*(2), 157–169.

group used technology about 28% of the time, significantly more than students from the other two groups. Students in the STU group used technology about 15% of the time, significantly more than students in the ITU group, who used technology only 6% of the time. Calculators were the most prevalent type of technology used, whereas computers were used only about 1% of the time.

Table 4.4. reports the overall results from the study, which indicated that there were significant differences in classroom instruction by the amount of technology used. Instruction in ITU classrooms tended to be whole-class approaches where students generally listened or watched the teacher. Instruction in MTU classrooms had much less whole-class instruction and much more independent work. Students from the MTU group were also observed working in pairs or medium-sized groups (~6–10 students) significantly more often than students in the ITU and STU groups. The overall results, however, for both the STU and ITU groups reveal that very little small-group work occurs in most of these classrooms. These findings lend support to other research that also found that technology use may change teaching from the traditional teacher-centered model to a more student-centered approach. Another important finding from the study was that students in MTU classrooms were on task significantly more often than students from the other two groups. These findings are similar to prior research that found that computer-based instruction increases students' time on task.

USING FEEDBACK FROM THE COS TO INFORM PRACTICES

One of the traditional problems hindering teachers' classroom instruction has been the lack of valid and accurate information that teachers could use to facilitate their professional growth (Johnson, 1974). Many teachers, even experienced ones, are not always aware of the nature of their interactions with individual students (Doyle, 1979). Good and Brophy (2000), for example, point out several classroom problems such as teacher domination of classroom communication, lack of emphasis on meaning, and few attempts to motivate students that are often caused by lack of teacher awareness and information. Consequently, one of the most important purposes of systematic classroom observation is to improve teachers' classroom instruction (Waxman, 1995; Waxman & Huang, 1999). Feedback from individual classroom profiles derived from systematic observations has been found to help teachers understand their own strengths and weaknesses and has consequently enabled them to improve their instruction significantly. Through feedback, teachers can become aware of how their classroom functions and thus bring about the changes they desire (Brophy, 1979; Stallings, Needels, & Sparks, 1987). This process typically involves having trained observers systematically observe teachers and their students in their classrooms and later providing teachers with information about their instruction in clinical sessions. This approach is based on the assumption that teachers value accurate information that they can use to improve their instruction.

Similar to other observation instruments, feedback from the COS has been found to help teachers understand their current instructional strengths and weaknesses (Padrón et al., 1999; Waxman, 1995; Waxman & Huang, 1999; Waxman et al., 1995). In several studies in which the COS was used, the researchers provided teachers with an individual classroom profile. These profiles contained the classes' individual data and a summary of the aggregated data across all the schools in the sample (e.g., a school district). For example, the class means for each of the indicators on the COS were presented along with the overall school district mean value. This allowed each teacher to compare his or her class means to the district's average. In some cases, school meetings were held in which all the teachers and administrators received the profiles and discussed the implications. Feedback from these profiles was used to stimulate dialogue and discussion about instructional strengths and weaknesses in the school. The profiles also helped initiate discussion about specific instructional areas in the school that needed to be improved.

It should be pointed out again that these profiles provide some guidelines for practice; they were not attempts to tell teachers what to do. These profiles provide teachers with concepts and criteria that they can use to think about their own teaching (Nuthall & Alton-Lee, 1990). Feedback sessions are not designed to have teachers specifically follow or apply our research findings to rules or guidelines to follow. Rather, they are intended to be used as a guide for teachers so that they and their colleagues can reflect on their own practices and decide what action to take. Additional professional development sessions would be appropriate if teachers want to build upon the strengths and correct the weaknesses of their profiles in order to improve their instruction learning environment. Quality professional development is one of the keys to successful school reform, and feedback from the COS can be the catalyst for this process.

SUMMARY

Although research on classroom observation has made significant progress over the past several decades, there are still several areas that need further investigation. In order to capture all the processes and nuances that occur in classrooms, triangulation procedures are needed to collect data from multiple perspectives (Evertson & Green, 1986). Collecting multiple measures or indicators of classroom processes may help alleviate some of the concerns and criticisms of observational research and provide us with a more comprehensive picture of what occurs in classrooms. All of the COS studies reported earlier, for example, collected either additional classroom learning environment data or teacher observation data. The Teacher Roles Observation Schedule (Waxman et al., 1990a, 1990b), for example, is a low-inference, time-based instrument that measures teachers' classroom behaviors and is often used in conjunction with the COS. The My Class Inventory (Fraser, Anderson, & Walberg, 1982) is a student self-report instrument that is also used with the COS to assess students' perceptions of their classroom learning environments. These additional types of data provide valuable information and often support the findings obtained through the COS. Furthermore, teacher self-report data, teacher, administrator, and student interview data, and qualitative ethnographic data (e.g., participant observation) could all be used to help supplement the COS data.

Overall, findings from the COS have provided researchers, administrators, and teachers with important information about a number of classroom processes. More importantly, this information has been useful in providing information on how to improve classroom instruction. Future studies using the COS may want to explore adapting the instrument to include more learning activities, as well as developing new categories for technology use in order to investigate the increased use of new technology currently being used in classrooms. New categories that examine the inclusion of culturally responsive activities may be another new direction for the COS. In addition, future studies may want to explore the development of norms for some of the student behaviors so that educators can see how the behaviors in their classrooms and schools compare to those found in other similar settings.

Note

This research was supported in part by a Department of Education, Office of Educational Research and Improvement grant from the National Center for

Research on Education, Diversity & Excellence. The opinions expressed in this chapter do not necessarily reflect the position, policy, or endorsement of the granting agency.

A previous version of this chapter was presented at the annual meeting of the American Educational Research Association, New Orleans, April 2000.

References

Anderson, L. W. (1987). The classroom environment study: Teaching for learning. *Comparative Education Review, 31*(1), 69–87.

Brophy, J. E. (1979). *Using observation to improve your teaching* (Occasional Paper No. 21). East Lansing: Institute for Research on Teaching, Michigan State University.

Brophy, J. E., & Good, T. L. (1986). Teacher behavior and student achievement. In M. C. Wittrock (Ed.), *Handbook of research on teaching* (3rd ed., pp. 328–375). New York: Macmillan.

Doyle, W. (1977). Paradigms for research on teacher effectiveness. In L. S. Shulman (Ed.), *Review of research in education* (Vol. 5, pp. 163–198). Itasca, IL: Peacock.

Doyle, W. (1979). Making managerial decisions in classrooms. In D. L. Duke (Ed.), *Classroom management* (pp. 42–74). Chicago: National Society for the Study of Education.

Evertson, C., & Green, J. L. (1986). Observation as inquiry and method. In M. C. Wittrock (Ed.), *Handbook of research on teaching* (3rd ed., pp. 162–207). New York: Macmillan.

Fraser, B. J., Anderson, G. J., & Walberg, H. J. (1982). *Assessment of learning environments: Manual for Learning Environment Inventory (LEI) and My Class Inventory (MCI)* (3rd ed.). Perth: Western Australian Institute of Technology.

Good, T. L., & Brophy, J. E. (2000). *Looking in classrooms* (8th ed.). New York: Longman.

Johnson, D. W. (1974). Affective outcomes. In H. J. Walberg (Ed.), *Evaluating educational performance* (pp. 99–112). Berkeley, CA: McCutchan.

Nuthall, G., & Alton-Lee, A. (1990). Research on teaching and learning: Thirty years of change. *The Elementary School Journal, 90,* 546–570.

Padrón, Y. N., & Waxman, H. C. (1999). Classroom observations of the Five Standards of Effective Teaching in urban classrooms with English language learners. *Teaching and Change, 7*(1), 79–100.

Padrón, Y. N., Waxman, H. C., & Huang, S. L. (1999). Classroom and instructional learning environment differences between resilient and non-resilient elementary school students. *Journal of Education for Students Placed at Risk of Failure, 4*(1), 63–81.

Schunk, D. H. (1992). Theory and research on student perceptions in the classroom. In D. H. Schunk & J. L. Meece (Eds.), *Student perceptions in the classroom* (pp. 3–23). Hillsdale, NJ: Erlbaum.

Stallings, J. A., & Mohlman, G. G. (1988). Classroom observation techniques. In J. P. Keeves (Ed.), *Educational research, methodology, and measurement: An international handbook* (pp. 469–474). Oxford: Pergamon Press.

Stallings, J. A., Needles, M. C., & Sparks. (1987). Observation for the improvement of student learning. In D. C. Berliner & B. V. Rosenshine (Eds.), *Talks to teachers* (pp. 129–158). New York: Random House.

Tharp, R. G. (1997). *From at-risk to excellence: Research, theory, and principles for practice* (Research Report No. 1). Santa Cruz: Center for Research on Education, Diversity & Excellence, University of California.

Walberg, H. J. (1986). Synthesis of research on teaching. In M. C. Wittrock (Ed.), *Handbook of research on teaching* (3rd ed., pp. 214–229). New York: Macmillan.

Waxman, H. C. (1995). Classroom observations of effective teaching. In A. C. Ornstein (Ed.), *Teaching: Theory into practice* (pp. 76–93). Needham Heights, MA: Allyn & Bacon.

Waxman, H. C., & Huang, S. L. (1996). Classroom instruction differences by level of technology use in middle school mathematics. *Journal of Educational Computing Research, 14,* 147–159.

Waxman, H. C., & Huang, S. L. (1997). Classroom instruction and learning environment differences between effective and ineffective urban elementary schools for African American students. *Urban Education, 32,* 7–44.

Waxman, H. C., & Huang, S. L. (1999). Classroom observation research and the improvement of teaching. In H. C. Waxman & H. J. Walberg (Eds.), *New directions for teaching practice and research* (pp. 107–129). Berkeley, CA: McCutchan.

Waxman, H. C., Huang, S. L., Anderson, L. W., & Weinstein, T. (1997). Classroom process differences in inner-city elementary schools. *Journal of Educational Research, 91,* 49–59.

Waxman, H. C., Huang, S. L., & Padrón, Y. N. (1995). Investigating the pedagogy of poverty in inner-city middle level schools. *Research in Middle Level Education, 18*(2), 1–22.

Waxman, H. C., Wang, M. C., Lindvall, C. M., & Anderson, K. A. (1990a). *Classroom Observation Schedule technical manual* (rev. ed.). Philadelphia: Center for Research in Human Development and Education, Temple University.

Waxman, H. C., Wang, M. C., Lindvall, C. M., & Anderson, K. A. (1990b). *Teacher Roles Observational Schedule technical manual* (rev. ed.). Philadelphia: Temple University, Center for Research in Human Development and Education.

Weinstein, R. S. (1989). Perceptions of classroom processes and student motivation: Children's views of self-fulfilling prophecies. In C. Ames & R. Ames (Eds.), *Research on motivation in education: Goals and cognitions* (Vol. 3, pp. 187–221). San Diego, CA: Academic Press.

Winne, P. H. (1985). Steps toward promoting cognitive achievements. *The Elementary School Journal, 85,* 673–693.

APPENDIX: Classroom Observation Schedule

School Name _____ ID# ___

Teacher Name _____ ID# ___

Data Control No._____ Grade___   Student Name _____ ID#___

Subject: Reading Lang. Arts Math Obs# ___   Ethnicity: W B H A O   Sex: M F

		1 2 3 4 5	6 7 8 9 10	Total
A.	INTERACTIONS (check one)			
	1. No interaction/independence	O O O O O	O O O O O	----
	2. With teacher – Instructional	O O O O O	O O O O O	----
	3. With teacher – Managerial	O O O O O	O O O O O	----
	4. With teacher – Social, Personal	O O O O O	O O O O O	----
	5. With support staff	O O O O O	O O O O O	----
	6. With other students – Instructional	O O O O O	O O O O O	----
	7. With other students – Social, personal	O O O O O	O O O O O	----
	10. Other _____	O O O O O	O O O O O	----
B.	SELECTION OF ACTIVITY (check one)			
	1. Teacher assigned activity	O O O O O	O O O O O	----
	2. Student selected activity	O O O O O	O O O O O	----
C.	ACTIVITY TYPES (check as appropriate)			
	1. Working on written assignments	O O O O O	O O O O O	----
	2. Interacting – Instructional (e.g., discussing)	O O O O O	O O O O O	----
	3. Interacting – Social (e.g., talking)	O O O O O	O O O O O	----
	4. Watching or listening	O O O O O	O O O O O	----
	5. Reading	O O O O O	O O O O O	----
	6. Getting/Returning materials	O O O O O	O O O O O	----
	7. Painting, drawing, creating graphics, etc.	O O O O O	O O O O O	----
	8. Working with technology	O O O O O	O O O O O	----
	9. Working with manipulative material/equipt.	O O O O O	O O O O O	----
	10. Viewing video/slides	O O O O O	O O O O O	----
	11. Playing games	O O O O O	O O O O O	----
	12. Presenting/acting	O O O O O	O O O O O	----
	13. Tutoring peers	O O O O O	O O O O O	----
	14. Not attending to task	O O O O O	O O O O O	----
	15. No activity/transition	O O O O O	O O O O O	----
	16. Other _____	O O O O O	O O O O O	----
D.	SETTING (check one)			
	1. Whole class	O O O O O	O O O O O	----
	2. Small group	O O O O O	O O O O O	----
	3. Pairs	O O O O O	O O O O O	----
	4. Individual	O O O O O	O O O O O	----

E. MANNER (check one)
    1. On task   O O O O O   O O O O O   ----
    2. Waiting for teacher   O O O O O   O O O O O   ----
    3. Distracted   O O O O O   O O O O O   ----
    4. Disruptive   O O O O O   O O O O O   ----
    5. Other _____   O O O O O   O O O O O   ----

F. LANGUAGE USED (check one)
    1. English   O O O O O   O O O O O   ----
    2. Spanish   O O O O O   O O O O O   ----
    3. Both English and Spanish   O O O O O   O O O O O   ----

5

Development and Use of a Classroom Observation Instrument to Investigate Teaching for Meaning in Diverse Classrooms

Stephanie L. Knight and Robert G. Smith

As the number of states and local school districts requiring high-stakes testing grows, controversy intensifies around the issue of the impact of such testing on the quality of instruction and on the education of the students who ostensibly are its intended beneficiaries (National Research Council, 1999; Sadowski, 2000). Many parents, students, and educators express concerns about the emphasis on improving the passing rates on high-stakes tests (Rose & Gallup, 2000; Schrag, 2000). They fear that such a focus militates against good instruction and tends to reduce the scope of the curriculum to that which is tested. Implicit in these concerns is the assumption that getting good results on the tests requires repetitive drill and practice on isolated skills and content to the exclusion of what might be termed *teaching for meaning*. These concerns also assume that teaching for meaning will result in poorer performance on the tests.

Particularly troubling is the effect on those students who experience difficulty with learning, live in high-poverty conditions, and represent a diversity of cultural and linguistic backgrounds. Educators use various terms to describe these students (*at risk, educationally disadvantaged, marginal,* etc.) to capture the disconnection between students and the conditions designed for their learning. Typically, although attention may be directed to their needs, little effort has been expended to identify and build on the assets that they bring with them from their diverse backgrounds (Levin, 1987). Although a disproportionate number of these students come from low-income, minority homes (Pianta & Walsh, 1996), students at risk of failure can include exceptional learners of both genders and of any race, family structure, or economic background.

97

Emphasizing remediation through drill and practice appears to be the typical response to students who fail high-stakes criterion-referenced tests. This response, of course, ensures that the students fall further behind in their education, and although it may help some of them to pass a test, it is not clear that it is as effective in increasing test performance as other approaches or that it helps to improve their learning. To address the learning problems of students from diverse circumstances and to alleviate the mismatch between the individual and the learning environment, educators have sought ways to create conditions for success. Numerous programs have been implemented in schools to counter these problems (see, e.g., Madden, Slavin, Karweit, Dolen, & Wasik 1993; Slavin, Karweit, & Madden, 1989). Although some instructional interventions have shown promise in reducing the achievement gap between students at risk and their peers (Ferguson, 1998a, 1998b; Slavin, Karweit, & Madden, 1989), previous traditional programs have had little or no impact (Forsyth, 1998), and current barriers to reform place many new programs in jeopardy (Schaffer, Nesselrodt, & Stringfield, 1997).

The failure of many of these reform efforts may be traced to faulty assumptions underlying their basic approaches. Some of these problematic approaches include deficit models focused on remediation (Sinclair, 1993), lack of an integrated conceptualization of the problem (Levin, 1987), and overreliance on instruction in basic skills directed to passive learners at the expense of more personally and conceptually meaningful content (Haberman, 1991; Knapp & Shields, 1990). Of particular concern, many schools fail to provide a challenging environment for their culturally diverse and language minority student populations (Cawelti, 1994). Some evidence exists that these student populations do better with teachers who engage students actively in critical thinking activities, provide cooperative and supportive classroom environments, and link classroom content to students' experiences and interests (Foster & Peele, 1999; Murrell, 1999; Waxman & Padrón, 1995). Nevertheless, children at risk are more and more likely to attend schools much like those of a previous generation, but that are more rigid and more likely to have teachers who have a management orientation to instruction (Pianta & Walsh, 1996).

To counter this problem, some researchers have suggested that educators provide students considered at risk with more meaningful instruction that embeds skill learning in activities that feature conceptually challenging content and draw on the prior experiences and cultures of students to provide relevance (Knapp, 1992; Knapp & Adelman, 1995).

Using norm-referenced standardized tests as the outcome measures, Knapp and his associates conducted a study of teaching for meaning in high-poverty locations in selected areas of the country. They concluded that the students of teachers who taught for meaning and the students of teachers who taught discrete, isolated basic skills scored about the same on basic skills. However, on more advanced thinking, the students of teachers who taught for meaning performed better than the students of teachers who taught discrete, isolated basic skills (Knapp & Adelman, 1995).

Unclear is whether Knapp et al.'s findings would extend to performance on the high-stakes criterion-referenced measures used by most states. It also appears that although several programs provide meaningful instruction, a particular challenge lies in identifying and evaluating the classroom processes associated with this approach. Systematic observation traditionally has been used for more direct approaches that feature observable, quantifiable behaviors typically associated with basic skills instruction (see, e.g., Good & Brophy, 2000). Typically, qualitative methodology has been used extensively to examine multicultural classroom settings (see, e.g., Mehan, Lintz, Okamoto, & Wills, 1995) and to capture higher-order processes in classrooms. Few systematic observation instruments exist for instruction focused on higher-order processes. This chapter describes an instrument that focuses on teaching for meaning developed for the purpose of observing in classrooms populated by many at-risk students. Specifically, the chapter summarizes the use of the instrument in two studies conducted to determine the implementation and quality of teaching for meaning behaviors and their relationship to performance on a high-stakes state test and other measures. The instrument differs from other classroom observation instruments in its (a) focus on teaching behaviors related to teaching for higher-order learning and (b) use of quantitative measures of teaching for meaning. This is an advantage of the instrument because it allows for quantification of variables often captured only by qualitative data. This quantification is particularly useful for comparison with test scores. However, a disadvantage is that reducing the complex behaviors involved in teaching for higher-order outcomes may also reduce the richness of the description.

TEACHING FOR MEANING OBSERVATION INSTRUMENT

Both studies described in this chapter were conducted in conjunction with a multiyear project in a single district. The Connections project,

Teaching for Meaning (TFM), was a districtwide effort that focused on enabling elementary teachers to design and implement instruction that is meaningful to the diverse group of students they teach. Drawing on work by Knapp and his colleagues described previously (Knapp, 1992; Knapp and Adelman, 1995), as well as on recent research on effective strategies for culturally and linguistically diverse classrooms (see, e.g., Polite & Davis, 1999; Tharp, Estrada, Dalton, & Yamauchi, 2000), teachers participated in a series of workshops to help them acquire the following skills and knowledge:

1. management of classrooms in ways that increase engaged, academic learning time while decreasing time spent on provision of external rewards and punishments;
2. diagnosis of prior knowledge of students, determination of the appropriate level of instruction, and connection of new learning to prior knowledge;
3. analysis and implementation of instructional activities that emphasize perceiving relationships among parts rather than isolating discrete skills;
4. academic content characterized by complex concepts and generalizations; and
5. responding to cultural and social diversity by integrating the backgrounds of students with meaningful instruction.

In addition to workshops to provide them with skills and knowledge related to TFM, teachers participated in ongoing activities to promote inquiry and reflection. They formed study teams to identify and address individual student problems of learning, designed teacher research projects around TFM, and used peer coaching to assist each other in implementation of TFM. The combination of these three types of collaborative inquiry provided a framework for joint reflection that supports and enhances teacher professional development (Knight & Smith, 1995; Smith & Knight, 1997).

Components of the TFM Instrument

The Teaching for Meaning (TFM) Classroom Observation Form (Knight & Ackerman, 1997; see the appendix) was developed to assess behaviors associated with teaching for meaning in the project just described. To assess implementation of project objectives, the TFM instrument included three components: (a) determination of student engagement rates, (b) a log to record qualitatively classroom processes and events related to the TFM behaviors, and (c) indicators of seven target behaviors representing teaching for meaning that were rated using a Likert-type scale. Engagement rates were obtained using scans of the classroom at 5-minute intervals to record the number of students in the class and the number engaged in off-task behaviors at that time. The log was divided into segments representing the period of time between the engagement scans. Directions associated with the log prompted observers to record specific instances of TFM behaviors and the context in which they occurred. Content validity of the instrument was established through discussion of the indicators with project developers and coordinators and through examination of research cited previously related to effective teaching for culturally, linguistically, and socioeconomically diverse populations.

TFM Observation Procedures

At 5-minute intervals, observers conducted a total of ten 1-minute scans of the classroom and recorded the number of students present and the number of students engaged in off-task behavior during the scan. During the 5-minute intervals between scans, they recorded classroom processes and interactions in a log, noting, in particular, behaviors associated with the TFM objectives described previously. At the end of the class period, the Likert-type scale described previously was completed for each indicator based on notes from the log. In this way, observers were able to determine to what extent these behaviors occurred during the period observed.

Interobserver reliability was obtained through (a) training using videos, (b) comparisons with expert ratings, and (c) paired observations in the field. Cohen's kappa was used to calculate reliability estimates. All nine observers met the .85 reliability criterion for a video coded by the trainer prior to conducting observations and during paired observations with another observer in the field.

Degree of Implementation Score. Using the average of engagement rate and the seven TFM research-based indicators for the two observations during each time period, a TFM degree of implementation was calculated for each teacher in the sample. Degree of implementation for TFM was defined as a numerical value derived from the following evidence: (a) management of classrooms in ways that increase engaged academic learning time while decreasing time spent on provision of external rewards and punishments, (b) use of discussion in small or large groups, (c) emphasis on complex concepts and generalizations, (d) teaching of skills in context, (e) linkage of content to other content, (f) linkage of content to the prior knowledge and experiences of students, and (g) evidence of appropriate reference to the culture of students in the class. Two of the preceding variables, *Emphasis on complex concepts and generalizations* and *Teaching of skills in context* were weighted more heavily in the determination of the value. When polled, project developers ranked these two indicators as higher in importance than the other five indicators on the observation instrument. They explained that in the absence of emphasis on complex concepts and generalizations and teaching of skills in context, they would not consider TFM to be adequately implemented.

In addition to weighting some behaviors more heavily than others, the TFM degree of implementation score contains an index for observed student intrinsic motivation based on the relationship between student engagement and teacher use of extrinsic controls and rewards. The assumption is that high student engagement, in the absence of externally imposed controls and rewards, indicates high student interest in class tasks and activities. The index was computed by dividing the percentage of student time on task by the extent of extrinsic motivators observed being used by the teacher in the class and dividing the result by 10. The index was added to the other six weighted and unweighted scores to determine the degree of implementation of TFM.

STUDY 1

The purpose of the first study that employed the TFM instrument was to determine the effectiveness of a program that targeted meaningful teaching of language arts to elementary students in six schools with large at-risk populations. Specifically, the objectives of the study included analysis of (a) data collected during observations of participating teachers to determine the implementation and quality of target behaviors and (b) state criterion-referenced test passing rates for participating schools.

Participants

A sample ($N = 28$) of approximately one-third of all teachers participating in the project was selected for observation based on the school, grade level, and subject area of emphasis. The teachers observed represented the six participating schools and had all chosen language arts/reading as their area of emphasis for the project. Three kindergarten teachers, three first-grade teachers, six second-grade teachers, seven third-grade teachers, six fourth-grade teachers, and three fifth-grade teachers comprised the sample.

Procedures

Classroom observations of the sample of teachers were conducted prior to implementation of project activities in the fall and at the completion of the first year of implementation in the spring. Two observations during each time period were conducted for each teacher, and means were calculated to yield initial and final observation scores. Teachers were observed during both time periods teaching the same subject area, language arts, at the same time of day. Prior to observations, teachers were informed that they would be observed using an observation instrument designed to record TFM student and teacher behaviors. They were informed of the intent of the observation to increase the probability that they would include TFM in their planned lesson. Scores on the instrument therefore represented what teachers could do in relation to TFM and not necessarily what they typically do.

Results and Discussion

Mean scores for TFM engagement rates and the seven weighted and unweighted behavioral indicators were calculated separately for the fall and spring observations to determine baseline behaviors and subsequent acquisition and implementation of TFM objectives. Engagement rates were represented by mean percentages of on-task behavior noted during scans. A higher mean percentage represents higher student engagement. Prior to computation of the degree of implementation, mean percentages for on-task rates were divided by 10 to yield a value ranging from 0 to 10, consistent with the value of the two weighted indicators. TFM behaviors were represented by means that ranged from 1 to 5 for unweighted items or 5 to 10 for weighted items. The value for *Extrinsic controls* was reversed so that the direction of the mean would be consistent with the other indicators; that is, low use of extrinsic motivators and controls is a characteristic of TFM and was represented as such in the implementation score. Degree of implementation was calculated from

TABLE 5.1. *On-Task Behavior Before and After Implementation of TFM Objectives by School*

School	Preobservation			Postobservation		
	X	SD	n	X	SD	n
A	85.6%	13.6	14	86.2%	7.5	14
B	92.5	3.3	10	88.9	7.2	10
C	91.7	5.2	8	87.1	9.8	8
D	90.2	2.8	8	86.6	9.8	8
E	77.2	17.8	4	94.4	2.7	4
F	87.2	15.9	12	92.3	7.5	12
TOTAL	88.1	11.6	56	88.8	8.1	56

these values, with higher scores representing greater implementation of TFM behaviors. *T*-tests for correlated means were conducted to determine whether differences in behaviors noted between initial and final observations were statistically significant.

Degree of Implementation. On-task behavior was high prior to implementation of TFM (88%) and remained high after implementation (89%) (see Table 5.1). Although the difference was not statistically significant and was very small, it represents a slight increase in on-task behavior and therefore an increase in student engagement rates. This is particularly interesting because some researchers (e.g., Doyle, 1986) have noted that the kinds of higher-order teaching and learning activities represented by TFM may likely result in classroom management difficulties for teachers. In this case, implementation of TFM resulted in no significant reduction in student engagement, and the direction of the means indicated a slight improvement. However, some variability by school existed because the range of on-task behavior varied from 77% to 93% for the preobservations and from 86% to 94% for the postobservations.

Mean scores for the seven indicators prior to implementation of TFM range from lows of 1.84 for *Extrinsic controls* and 1.86 for *Linkage of new content to other content* to a high of 2.89 for *Skills taught in context* (see Table 5.2). All means initially were less than 3.0 and only three were higher than 2.5, indicating low use of TFM behaviors prior to participation in the Connections project. Conversely, the pattern for the postobservations reveals four of the seven means to be higher than 3.0. For the postobservations, *Extrinsic controls* was lowest (2.26) and *Linkage of new content to other content* was highest (2.96).

TABLE 5.2. *Means, Standard Deviations, and Statistical Significance Tests for TFM Indicators*

Indicator	Preobservation		Postobservation			
	TFM Indicators	SD	TFM Indicators	SD	t	ES
Discussion	2.72	.99	3.26	1.35	2.17*	.55
Complexity	2.41	.81	3.24	1.22	2.44*	1.02
Context	2.89	1.07	3.56	.83	2.66*	.63
Extrinsic	1.84	.82	2.26	1.11	1.33	.51
Culture	2.04	.63	2.76	1.05	3.33**	1.14
Prior knowledge	2.54	.81	3.34	.98	3.55**	.99
Content linkage	1.85	.74	2.96	1.01	3.88**	1.5

$*p < .05; **p < .01.$

TABLE 5.3. *Degree of Implementation of TFM Objectives by School*

School	Preimplementation			Postimplementation		
	X	SD	n	X	SD	n
A	32.2	7.4	14	37.8	5.6	14
B	35.9	8.9	10	35.5	6.6	10
C	34.5	4.3	8	40	8.1	8
D	31.6	3.4	8	37.1	4.3	8
E	33.6	5.3	4	40.2	4.5	4
F	29.5	5.9	12	40.7	7.4	12
TOTAL	32.6	6.5	56	38.4	6.4	56

Differences between TFM indicators prior to implementation and at the end of the first year for six of the seven indicators are statistically significant (see Table 5.2). The only difference that was not statistically significant was for *Extrinsic controls*. Teachers used few extrinsic motivators prior to the project's implementation and continued to use few after implementation despite the slight increase in the mean value. Although the means for the initial observations indicated low to average implementation of TFM behaviors, the final observations revealed average to high implementation of target behaviors. With the exception of the direction of the means from initial to final for *Extrinsic controls*, which was not statistically significant, differences were in favor of TFM objectives.

After training, the degree of implementation for all teachers increased from 32.6 to 38.4 out of a possible 56 (see Table 5.3). This difference was statistically significant at the .01 level of probability. Individual schools exhibited degrees of implementation that ranged from 29.5 to 35.9 for the first observation and from 35.5 to 40.7 for the final observation. Five of the six included schools increased their degrees of implementation after training. One of the six schools, initially with the highest score, decreased slightly after participation and emerged as the school with the lowest degree of implementation at the end of the study. This finding indicates that although training was effective overall, implementation varied by school.

Effect sizes were also computed that allow us to express observed sample means in standard deviation units. The larger the effect size, the larger the difference between the two groups. For example, the effect size of 1.02 for *Complexity of concepts* indicates that the mean values of the final observation group were slightly more than one standard deviation higher after implementation of the TFM objectives. The effect size of .55 for *Discussion* indicates that the mean values of the postobservations were slightly more than half a standard deviation higher after implementation of the TFM objectives. In general, effect sizes were moderate to large and ranged from .51 for *Extrinsic motivators* to 1.5 for *Content linkage*. The effect size for degree of implementation of TFM indicated that the mean value for teachers was .89 standard deviation higher after participation in the project.

Power was also calculated to show the ability to detect a true difference when it actually exists in the population (in other words, the probability of correctly rejecting a false null hypothesis). The statistical power of .995 for complexity of concepts implies that the research design has a 99.5% chance of detecting that the postobservation mean for this variable will be 1.02 standard deviation units above the preobservation mean. The power of our findings, which ranges from .84 to .995, adds confidence to our results.

Comparison of TAAS Passing Rates. Passing rates for the Texas Assessment of Academic Skills (TAAS) for All Tests and for Reading prior to implementation of TFM and after the first year of implementation were compared for five of the six participating schools (see Table 5.4). One school was new and did not have TAAS results available for the time period. For each participating school, the passing rate for All Tests was higher after implementation of TFM. For four of the five schools, the passing rate for Reading also was higher after implementation. The

TABLE 5.4. *TAAS Passing Rates Before and After Implementation in Participating Schools*

School	All Tests		Reading	
	Pre	Post	Pre	Post
A	64%	74.1%	82%	87%
B	70	76.4	82	82.6
C	60	65.5	76	80.4
D	56	69.4	72	79.7
F	71	76.1	83	81.1

Note: School E was excluded because it was new and did not have pre-TAAS scores.

school with a slightly lower passing rate in Reading after implementation still maintained a better than 80% passing rate.

Comparison of the degree of implementation scores for each school and their performance on the TAAS provides some evidence for the criterion validity of the TFM instrument. School D, which had the greatest increase in the degree of implementation score and the highest score overall after training, also exhibited the greatest gain in percentage of students mastering the reading portion of the TAAS. Nevertheless, the lack of a control group to compare the results of participation in TFM and typical classroom instruction is somewhat limiting. Although these increases cannot be attributed directly to the TFM project, the intense emphasis on objectives compatible with increases in TAAS performance may be related to the improvement. This pattern was not totally consistent across schools. More in-depth qualitative analyses of implementation processes at the school level are needed to fully understand the differences by school. However, the findings from this study indicate that the TFM observation instrument can be used to document changes in classroom processes as a result of participation in professional development.

STUDY 2

The second study was conducted during the second year of the TFM project and investigated the relationship between the structure of teachers' concept maps and the TFM observation instrument (Woods, 2000). The specific research question was "To what degree does teachers' conceptual knowledge related to TFM predict their teaching behavior?"

In order to effectively model deep and meaningful processing according to the TFM model, participating teachers had to broaden the scope of their content delivery beyond mere rote learning activities, encourage the development of intrinsic motivation for learning in students, and bridge cultural chasms effectively. Participating teachers also needed a well-established knowledge base in their content field and a well-developed cognitive model to represent the intricacies of the tenets of TFM. Thus, a concept map (i.e., Jones & Vesilind, 1996; Novak & Gowin, 1989) training component was designed to facilitate our understanding of the relationship between the formal knowledge embedded in the professional development activities, the practical knowledge developed through experience, and teachers' classroom behaviors. In addition, the concept map allowed teachers to examine their own understanding of meaningful teaching.

Participants

A sample ($N = 15$) of approximately one-third of the teachers participating in the project during the second year was selected for observation based on school and grade level. The teachers observed represented the six participating schools and had all chosen language arts/reading as their area of emphasis for the project. Included in the sample were kindergarten through fifth-grade teachers.

Procedures

Similar to Study 1, classroom observations using the TFM instrument described previously were conducted in the fall prior to implementation of project activities and in the spring at the completion of the first year of implementation. Two observations during each time period were conducted for each teacher, and means were calculated to yield initial and final observation scores. As in the first study, teachers were informed prior to both observation periods that they and their students would be observed for TFM behaviors. As for Study 1, reliability was obtained through comparison of observers' and trainers' scores on a video featuring TFM and between pairs of observers during the field observations. All observers obtained reliability coefficients of at least .85 for both video and field observations.

Creation of Concept Maps. To assess conceptual change, the teachers were asked to create concept maps that illustrated their understanding of the concepts and principles related to TFM at the two time periods to be described. In conjunction with the initial TFM workshop, teachers were given instruction and practice in creating concept maps. Teachers then constructed maps at the beginning of the year immediately after their initial training in early October and in April after participation in the Connections project activities. Maps were scored using a system adapted from Novak and Gowin (1989) that determined the extent of relationships in propositional knowledge (Woods, 2000). Concepts are defined as "a regularity in events or objects designated by some label," such as *chair* (Novak & Gowin, 1989, p. 4). Propositions are basic units of information that roughly correspond to *ideas* (Gagne, 1985). A proposition consists of a set of *arguments* that tend to be nouns or pronouns and a *relation* that constrains the arguments and typically is a verb.

The four components of propositional knowledge investigated through the concept maps include the following:

1. Propositions – the number of propositions about TFM depicted by teachers;
2. Hierarchy – the depth of their knowledge, as represented by a hierarchy of propositions ranging from overarching concepts to more specific ones;
3. Cross-links – the cross-linkages or connections that teachers perceive between propositions; and
4. Examples – the number of examples of TFM elements mentioned by teachers.

In addition to the scores allocated to the respective dimensions, the maps received a *total score* representing aggregate performance along the four dimensions and a *criterion score* based on the ratio between the individual teacher-constructed maps and a map constructed by an expert in the project. The criterion score is represented as a percentage score.

Results and Discussion

In addition to determining the classroom behaviors of teachers and students after participation in Connections activities, the change in conceptual knowledge of participating teachers was examined. Then the relationship between teachers' knowledge and behaviors at the beginning and end of the project was investigated to determine the concurrent validity of the TFM instrument.

TABLE 5.5. *Means and Standard Deviations for TFM Indicators*

Indicator	Preobservation		Postobservation	
	X	SD	X	SD
Off task	.089	.07	.089	.05
Discussion	4.17	.82	4.13	1.04
Complexity	3.60	.87	3.00	1.25
Context	3.93	1.05	3.43	1.18
Extrinsic	1.23	.46	2.10	.97
Culture	3.03	1.11	2.27	1.12
Prior knowledge	3.63	1.09	3.33	1.33

Classroom Behaviors. Mean scores for TFM engagement rates and the seven behavioral indicators were calculated for the fall and spring observations to determine baseline behaviors and subsequent acquisition and implementation of TFM objectives (see Table 5.5). Engagement rates are represented by mean percentages of off-task behavior noted during scans. A lower mean percentage represents higher student engagement. As in Study 1, TFM behaviors are represented by means that range from 1 to 5 for individual items or 5 to 35 for total scores, with higher scores representing greater implementation of TFM behaviors. *T*-tests for correlated means were conducted to determine whether differences in behaviors noted between pre- and postobservations were statistically significant.

Similar to findings from Study 1, off-task behavior was low prior to implementation of TFM (8.7%) and remained low after implementation (8.9%). The difference was not statistically significant and represents negligible change in off-task behavior and therefore in student engagement rates. As in Study 1, implementation of TFM resulted in no significant reduction in student engagement. However, some variability occurred because the range of off-task behavior varied from 2% to 27% for the initial observations and from 2% to 17% for the final observations.

Mean scores for the seven TFM indicators prior to implementation of TFM ranged from a low of 1.23 for *Use of extrinsic controls* to a high of 4.17 for *Discussion*, with all means except those for *Use of extrinsic controls* and *Linkage to other content areas* (2.70) greater than 3.0 and six of the seven higher than 2.5. As previously described, *Use of extrinsic controls* would not be consistent with TFM; therefore, a low score in this area is positive. The pattern for the postobservations reveals five of the seven means to be higher than 2.5, with only four of the seven higher than 3.0. For the postobservations, *Discussion* was also highest and *Use of extrinsic controls* was lowest.

Differences between TFM indicators prior to implementation and at the end of the year were statistically significant for three of the seven indicators: *Complex concepts* ($t = -2.17, p < .05$), *Use of extrinsic controls* ($t = -3.45, p < .01$), and *Use of students' culture* ($t = -2.55, p < .05$). However, none of the changes from pre- to posttest are in the desired direction. Teachers used few extrinsic motivators prior to the project's implementation but significantly increased their use after implementation. In addition, they significantly decreased their references to and instruction on complex concepts and linkage to the culture of the students. None of these changes are consistent with the behaviors emphasized in the training for TFM.

When comparing Study 2 data with the data from Study 1, Study 2 teachers began the school year exhibiting higher implementation of TFM behaviors than teachers involved the previous year. In fact, all of the means for the initial observations were higher than the final observation means of the previous year. Nevertheless, by the end of the second year, teachers exhibited scores that were lower on all the TFM indicators except *Discussion* than those of the Study 1 cohort at the end of the previous year. Inspection of the logs kept by observers during the observations, as well as follow-up interviews with observers, revealed that during the postobservations many teachers were engaged in preparation for the statewide test (TAAS) that was administered later that month. Therefore, notes in the logs suggested that students were often given review worksheets during the observed period and were engaged in discussion about test items related to the TAAS. Although teachers were aware that observers were recording instructional behaviors related to the TFM project, many spent a large part of the period in test preparation. The relatively narrow focus of the test review and the worksheet/discussion delivery mode may have contributed to the decline in TFM behaviors.

Conceptual Knowledge. In the study conducted by Woods (2000) in conjunction with the observational study, mean scores for four map dimensions, total scores, and criterion scores for the fall and spring collections of concept maps were calculated to compare the depth and complexity of baseline TFM knowledge and knowledge after participation in TFM. *T*-tests for correlated samples for the four dimensions and the two summative scores were calculated to determine whether changes in representations of teachers' knowledge were statistically significant. Regression analyses were used to determine the relationship between the conceptual knowledge that teachers acquired through their experiences in the Connections project and the classroom teaching behavior that they exhibited.

Results indicated that all four map dimensions exhibited increases in mean scores from initial to final maps. Among the four dimensions comprising the total score, however, only *Propositions* and *Examples* exhibited statistically significant differences from initial to final maps. In addition, the summative scores analyses revealed statistically significant increases in the pre- to postmap means of both the *Total* and *Criterion* map scores. It should be noted that although teachers varied in their conceptual knowledge base and teaching behaviors, no extreme outliers existed for either variable.

Significant changes in these indicators are encouraging, however, suggesting that teachers gained a broader declarative knowledge base related to TFM after participation in the Connections project activities. This finding suggests that not only did the overall content and organization of the concept maps grow, but they tended to grow in terms of knowledge deemed central to TFM by the constructor of the criterion map. The finding that the depth and complexity of the knowledge base did not significantly change from pre- to postmap is not surprising given that this type of knowledge might take longer to develop.

Results of the two regression analyses indicated a relationship between teachers' classroom behaviors and their conceptual knowledge of TFM. The first model tested the regression coefficient of the predictor variable of pretest concept map criterion score on the program's pretest degree of implementation score. The second model tested the regression coefficient of the predictor variable of final concept map criterion score on the program's posttest degree of implementation score. Both were statistically significant, suggesting that the criterion scores of the initial and final concept maps collected from participating teachers were generally good predictors of their final behavioral implementation scores. However, due to the decline of posttest implementation scores, the relationship was not as profound.

IMPLICATIONS OF TEACHING FOR MEANING

For several decades, educators have focused on improvement of the perceived weaknesses of our public schools through a number of reform efforts (Fullan, 1993). Despite these efforts, educators have failed to achieve two traditionally held values for public schooling, equity and excellence, on a widespread basis in public schools. Current state-level reform efforts across the country have focused on excellence by targeting the outcomes of education – in particular, the results of standardized tests. They have suggested that accountability provides the solution to perceptions of the decline of excellence in our public schools. Therefore, competency and assessment testing have increased dramatically over the past 25 years (NCEST, 1992). Accountability is currently the single most prominent issue in educational policy at the national, state, and local levels (Linn, 2000; Olson, 1999).

Criticism of the impact of increased accountability includes the concern that high-stakes testing narrows the depth and breadth of content and experiences of all students (Gallagher, 2000) and disadvantages minority students in particular (Jencks, 1998). Teachers and teacher educators argue that accountability reforms reduce classroom work to drill and practice, increase extrinsic sanctions at the expense of intrinsic rewards, focus on lower-order skills at the expense of higher-order content and processes, emphasize knowledge and skills that are easily measured, and unfairly disadvantage second-language and minority students (Gallagher, 2000).

The findings from the second study described in this chapter provide some evidence for these concerns. The TFM studies were conducted during a period of increasing focus on school accountability measures. As teachers increasingly felt pressure to improve student performance on the state test, they abandoned TFM instructional behaviors in favor of those that have been associated with gains in standardized tests (see, e.g., Brophy & Good, 1986). The conventional wisdom, when confronted with test performance concerns, suggests that teachers should address deficits by teaching discrete skills directly (Knapp & Adelman, 1995). In this case, teachers reduced their instructional behaviors related to complex concepts, reduced the strategies designed to help students link what they were learning with their own culture, and increased the use of extrinsic rewards – presumably to keep students on task during the drill and practice and seatwork related to the test. One of the two behaviors that decreased significantly during this period, emphasis on complex concepts, is considered a highly critical component of TFM.

Of particular concern in this study was the decrease in teacher behaviors encouraging the linkage of content to culture. In an era of high-stakes testing, children of color and poor children have experienced significantly lower levels of school success than their White and more economically advantaged peers, regardless of how that success has been defined and measured, such as standardized test scores, graduation rates, college admission rates, or enrollment in advanced courses (Banks, 1997; Ogbu, 1992). Interventions that address cultural mismatch have been suggested and have had some impact on the achievement gap (e.g., Ladson-Billings, 1994; Losey, 1995; Polite & Davis, 1999). Approaches from this perspective typically focus on teacher behaviors and activity structures that reflect cultural values (Tharp, 1997). The decrease of this key feature exhibited by teachers in the second study raises concern for the large numbers of minority and second-language learners in the schools participating in the study. The instruction that characterized the classrooms during the second study was consistent with the "pedagogy of poverty" described by Haberman (1991) and Waxman and Padrón (1995). Several studies have documented the problems with this approach, including passive student roles in classroom learning and few opportunities to engage in higher-order thinking activities (Knapp & Adelman, 1995; Waxman & Padrón, 1995).

Some researchers have suggested that the achievement gap may be a harbinger of problems in general with a passive educational delivery system that is inadequate for all students (Singham, 1998). Whites and Asians can justify their efforts based on perceptions that their performance will reap later rewards. Blacks and other involuntary minorities see a limited connection between effort and rewards, and the educational settings they inhabit may seem largely impersonal, irrelevant, and uninteresting. If so, instructional approaches that sacrifice active student involvement in making connections would be a step in the wrong direction.

Ironically, the schools involved in both years of the study had achieved increases in their students' test scores during the first year of the Connections project when they had successfully implemented the TFM behaviors. This finding is consistent with the large-scale study conducted by Knapp and Adelman (1995) that concluded that teachers "can increase the emphasis they place on meaning and understanding without abandoning discrete basic skills" (p. 196). However, in the face of increasing pressure for accountability, teachers may need more support to maintain instructional behaviors that emphasize teaching for meaning and embedding skills instruction within complex concepts, rather than directly focusing on basic skills instruction.

IMPLICATIONS FOR USE OF THE TFM OBSERVATION INSTRUMENT

The two studies presented in this chapter provide some evidence to support the use of the TFM instrument to record changes in behavior related to teaching for higher-order skills and knowledge. The first study recorded changes in behaviors related to teaching for meaning and subsequent increases in student performance on state standardized tests. The second study (Woods, 2000) indicated that teaching behaviors can be related to knowledge associated with teachers' professional development in teaching for meaning. Because higher-order teaching behaviors are often difficult to quantify, the combined qualitative and quantitative design of the TFM instrument provides a means of quantifying behaviors without losing the qualitative aspects of interactions that might better explain instruction in this area. Without the quantitative data, the magnitude and direction of changes in behaviors and relationships with other processes and outcomes would be difficult to determine. Without the qualitative data, understanding of anomalies such as the decrease in TFM behaviors in the second study would not have been possible. The uniqueness of the instrument resides in the combination of the two methodologies to provide (a) information about the extent of use of higher-level teaching behaviors and their relationship to other variables and (b) contextual and descriptive information that is typically absent from purely quantitative approaches.

However, these results are somewhat constrained because these studies were conducted only in settings for which the instrument was designed. In order to determine applicability of the TFM instrument for other settings or levels and types of classrooms, the instrument would need to be tested in different settings. Although the seven indicators in the TFM instrument represent teaching behaviors that might be common across instructional approaches, observations in different settings using different approaches might provide additional behavioral examples of the indicators that would be helpful during training. Furthermore, additional indicators might be added to extend applicability of the instrument.

In addition to research to examine the extended applicability and validity of the instrument, future studies need to be conducted to address the concerns related to possible links between classroom instruction and disparities in student performance between cultural, linguistic, and socioeconomic groups. As previously described, passive approaches that emphasize rote learning, acquisition of skills separate from their use, and emphasis on facts and lower-level concepts are common in educational settings that serve underserved populations (Singham, 1998). In contrast, sociocultural research in the past decade suggests that the incorporation of instruction with elements similar to the indicators measured by the TFM observation instrument, including linkage of students' knowledge and experiences to class activities and content, may provide more opportunity for success for all students (McIntyre, Roseberry, & Gonzalez, 2001; Tharp et al., 2000). Therefore, systematic investigation of the instructional behaviors included in the TFM in diverse classrooms may provide information for improvement of instruction for all students. In particular, future studies using the TFM observation instrument to document the behaviors used by teachers successful in closing achievement gaps, particularly in comparison with their less successful counterparts, may provide useful information for development of successful models for teaching. Furthermore, studies using the TFM instrument to assess program implementation or the results of teacher professional development endeavors can be designed to assess not only the impact of programs, but also the contextual elements that contribute to their success or failure.

In summary, appropriate uses of the TFM instrument include evaluation of professional development designed to increase teaching for meaning, description of classroom instruction in diverse classrooms, investigation of relationships between teachers' behaviors and teacher or student outcomes, and feedback for teachers for purposes of instructional improvement. Use of the instrument for teacher hiring or termination decisions, for evaluation of the teacher, or for other high-stakes accountability purposes involving classroom instruction would be inappropriate. In addition, although the instrument can capture some behaviors associated with direct instruction approaches (e.g., time on task), other instruments would better serve that purpose.

References

Banks, J. A. (1997). *Educating citizens in a multicultural society.* New York: Teachers College Press.

Brophy, J. E., & Good, T. L. (1986). Teacher behavior and student achievement. In M. C. Wittrock (Ed.), *Handbook of research on teaching* (3rd ed., pp. 328–375). New York: Macmillan.

Cawelti, G. (1994). *High school restructuring: A national study.* Arlington, VA: Educational Research Service.

Doyle, W. (1986). Classroom organization and management. In M. Wittrock (Ed.), *Handbook of research on teaching* (3rd ed., pp. 392–431). New York: Macmillan.

Ferguson, R. (1998a). Can schools narrow the Black–White test score gap? In C. Jencks & M. Phillips (Eds.), *The Black–White test score gap* (pp. 318–374). Washington, DC: The Brookings Institution.

Ferguson, R. (1998b). Teachers' perceptions and expectations and the Black–White test score gap. In C. Jencks & M. Phillips (Eds.), *The Black–White test score gap* (pp. 273–317). Washington, DC: The Brookings Institution.

Forsyth, J. (1998). *Comprehensive models for school improvement.* Arlington, VA: Educational Research Service.

Foster, M., & Peele, T. (1999). Teaching Black males: Lessons from the experts. In V. Polite & J. Davis (Eds.), *African American males in school and society* (pp. 8–19). New York: Teachers College Press.

Fullan, M. (1993). *Change forces.* New York: Falmer.

Gagne, E. (1985). *The cognitive psychology of school learning.* Boston: Little, Brown.

Gallagher, C. (2000). A seat at the table: Teachers reclaiming assessment through rethinking accountability. *Phi Delta Kappan, 81*(7), 502–507.

Good, T. L., & Brophy, J. E. (2000). *Looking in classrooms* (8th ed.). New York: Longman.

Haberman, M. (1991). The pedagogy of poverty versus good teaching. *Phi Delta Kappan, 73*(4), 290–294.

Jencks, C. (1998). Racial bias in testing. In C. Jencks & M. Phillips (Eds.), *The Black–White test score gap* (pp. 55–85). Washington, DC: The Brookings Institution.

Jones, M., & Vesilind, E. (1996). Putting practice into theory: Changes in the organization of preservice teachers' pedagogical knowledge. *American Educational Research Journal, 33*(1), 91–118.

Knapp, M. S. (1992). Academic challenge in high-poverty classrooms. *Phi Delta Kappan, 76*, 700–706.

Knapp, M. S., & Adelman, N. E. (1995). *Teaching for meaning in high-poverty classrooms.* New York: Teachers College Press.

Knapp, M. S., & Shields, P. (1990). *Better schooling for the children of poverty: Alternatives to conventional wisdom.* Berkeley, CA: McCutchan.

Knight, S. L., & Ackerman, C. (1997). *Teaching for Meaning (TFM) Classroom Observation Manual.* College Station: Texas A&M University.

Knight, S. L., & Smith, R. G. (1995, April). *Examining the effects of teacher inquiry on teacher perceptions and cognitions.* Paper presented at the annual meeting of the American Educational Research Association, San Francisco.

Ladson-Billings, G. (1994). *The dreamkeepers: Successful teachers of African American children.* San Francisco: Jossey-Bass.

Levin, H. (1987). Accelerated schools for disadvantaged students. *Educational Leadership, 44*(6), 19–21.

Linn, R. (2000). Assessments and accountability. *Educational Researcher, 29*(2), 4–16.

Losey, K. (1995). Mexican American students and classroom interaction: An overview and critique. *Review of Educational Research, 65*(3), 283–318.

Madden, N. A., Slavin, R. E., Karweit, N. L., Dolan, L. J., & Wasik, B. A. (1993). Success for all: Longitudinal effects of a restructuring program for inner-city elementary schools. *American Educational Research Journal, 30*(1), 123–148.

McIntyre, E., Roseberry, A., & Gonzalez, N. (2001). *Classroom diversity: Connecting curriculum to students' lives.* Portsmouth, NH: Heinemann.

Mehan, H., Lintz, A., Okamoto, D., & Wills, J. (1995). Ethnographic studies of multicultural education in schools. In J. Banks & C. Banks (Eds.), *Handbook on research of multicultural education* (pp. 129–144). New York: Macmillan.

Murrel, P. (1999). Responsive teaching for African American male adolescents. In V. Polite & J. Davis (Eds.), *African American males in schools and society* (pp. 82–96). New York: Teachers College Press.

National Council on Education Standards and Testing. (1992). *Raising standards for American education: A report to Congress.* Washington, DC: Author.

National Research Council. (1999). *High stakes: Testing for tracking, promotion, and graduation.* Washington, DC: National Academy Press.

Novak, J., & Gowin, D. (1989). *Learning how to learn.* New York: Cambridge University Press.

Ogbu, J. (1992). Understanding cultural diversity and learning. *Educational Researcher, 21*(8), 5–14.

Olson, L. (1999). Shining a spotlight on results. *Education Week, 17*(17), 8–10.

Pianta, R., & Walsh, D. (1996). *High-risk children in schools.* New York: Routledge.

Polite, V., & Davis, J. (1999). *African American males in school and society.* New York: Teachers College Press.

Rose, L., & Gallup, A. (2000). The 32nd annual Phi Delta Kappa/Gallup Poll of the public's attitudes toward the public schools. *Phi Delta Kappan, 82*(1), 41–58.

Sadowski, M. (2000). Are high-stakes tests worth the wager? *Harvard Education Letter, 16*(5), 1–5.

Schaffer, E., Nesselrodt, P., & Stringfield, S. (1997). *Impediments to reform.* Arlington, VA: Educational Research Service.

Schrag, P. (2000). High stakes are for tomatoes. *Atlantic Monthly, 286*(2), 19–21.

Sinclair, R. L. (1993, October). *The National Coalition Problem Solving Process.* Paper presented at the National Coalition for Equality in Education Facilitators and Superintendents' Meeting, Vail, CO.

Singham, M. (1998). The canary in the mine: The achievement gap between Black and White students. *Phi Delta Kappan, 80*(1), 9–15.

Slavin, R. E., Karweit, N., & Madden, N. A. (1989). *Effective programs for students at risk.* New York: Allyn & Bacon.

Smith, R. G., & Knight, S. L. (1997). Collaborative inquiry: Teacher leadership in the practice of creative intelligence. In B. Sinclair & W. Ghory (Eds.), *Reaching and teaching all children: Grassroots efforts that work* (pp. 39–60). Thousand Oaks, CA: Corwin Press.

Tharp, R. G. (1997). *From at-risk to excellence: Research, theory, and principles for practice* (Research Report No. 1). Santa Cruz: Center for Research on Education, Diversity & Excellence, University of California.

Tharp, R. G., Estrada, P., Dalton, S. S., & Yamauchi, L. (2000). *Teaching transformed: Achieving excellence, fairness, inclusion, and harmony.* Boulder, CO: Westview Press.

Waxman, H., & Padrón, Y. (1995). Improving the quality of classroom instruction for students at risk of failure in urban schools. *Peabody Journal of Education, 70*(2), 44–65.

Woods, B. (2000). *Relationship between conceptual change of teachers and classroom behaviors.* Unpublished dissertation, Texas A&M University.

APPENDIX: TFM Classroom Observation Form

Observer: _____ Date: _____ PRE-Observ: _____ POST-Obser: _____
Teacher: _____ Grade: _____ Subject: _____ School: _____

I. Student Engagement

Scan 1 -   Time:___   Total number of students_____   Total number off-task _____
Scan 2 -   Time:___   Total number of students_____   Total number off-task _____
Scan 3 -   Time:___   Total number of students_____   Total number off-task _____
Scan 4 -   Time:___   Total number of students_____   Total number off-task _____
Scan 5 -   Time:___   Total number of students_____   Total number off-task _____
Scan 6 -   Time:___   Total number of students_____   Total number off-task _____
Scan 7 -   Time:___   Total number of students_____   Total number off-task _____
Scan 8 -   Time:___   Total number of students_____   Total number off-task _____
Scan 9 -   Time:___   Total number of students_____   Total number off-task _____
Scan 10 - Time:___   Total number of students_____   Total number off-task _____

II. Teaching for Meaning Scales

Key: 1 = not observed/never (0%)
     2 = only observed occasionally (25%)
     3 = observed about half of the time (50%)
     4 = observed most of the time (75%)
     5 = observed all of the time (100%)

A. Students are engaged in discussion with the teacher   1   2   3   4   5
   or with other students in pairs, small or large groups.

B. Complex concepts/generalizations are the object of class   1   2   3   4   5
   and small group discussion and activities.

C. Skills are taught in context rather than in isolation.   1   2   3   4   5

D. Teacher uses extrinsic rewards and controls for behavior.   1   2   3   4   5

E. There is evidence of appropriate reference to culture of   1   2   3   4   5
   students in class.

F. Teacher facilitates linkage of new content to prior   1   2   3   4   5
   knowledge or to information that follows.

G. Teacher facilitates linkage of new content to other   1   2   3   4   5
   content areas.

Observer: _____ Date: _____ PRE-Observ: _____ POST-Obser: _____

Teacher: _____ Grade: _____ Subject: _____ School: _____

Focus Comments: Topics of discussion; teaching strategies; teacher and student interactions; whether skills are taught and if so how; use of rewards and discipline; evidence of culture in content, speech, materials, bulletin boards, etc.; evidence of linkage to other content or to content that comes before or after current content.

Scan 1 - Time:
Discussion:

Concepts:

Skills:

Rewards:

Culture:

Linkage:

6

Patterns of Language Arts Instructional Activity and Excellence in First- and Fourth-Grade Culturally and Linguistically Diverse Classrooms

Peggy Estrada

In this chapter, I test the utility of using a recently developed live observation tool, the Activity Setting Observation System (ASOS), to quantify and analyze patterns of instructional activity using a sociocultural lens. Specifically, I used the ASOS to examine the extent to which features of effective pedagogical and organizational practices were present in language arts instructional activity in 27 culturally and linguistically diverse first- and fourth-grade classrooms. In addition, I examined the association of the presence of these features with measures of student performance.

Efforts to identify best practices for culturally and linguistically diverse students from poverty backgrounds have grown steadily in recent years. Spurred by the well-known facts of underachievement among this group and its quickly increasing numbers, a number of researchers have begun to document the kinds of classroom instruction these students typically receive, as well as to investigate the kind of instruction that is effective (e.g., Brookhart & Rusnak, 1993; Estrada & Imhoff, 2001a; Garcia, 1990; Saunders & Goldenberg, 1999; Speidel, 1987; Tharp & Gallimore, 1988; Waxman, Huang, & Padrón, 1995).

Ironically, the teaching that these children receive is often an impoverished version of the common tradition dominated by whole-group instruction, teacher talk, assignment of tasks, and assessment. Studies looking at instructional practices in classrooms serving high proportions of low-income students have shown that teachers often operate with a hierarchical or linear perspective of student learning: Basic skills must be mastered before students can engage in higher-order thinking. For example, teachers often argue that students should master the mechanics of grammar before writing extended text. The result is a ceiling on the kinds of learning opportunities afforded students, focused primarily on the rote acquisition of mechanical skills (Knapp & Shields, 1990).

In this same vein, a number of studies have documented a "pedagogy of poverty" in classroom instruction for English language learners (Haberman, 1991; Padrón & Waxman, 1993, 1999; Waxman et al., 1995). This instructional approach is dominated by direct instruction emphasizing lecture, drill and practice, remediation, and seatwork involving worksheets (Stephen, Varble, & Taitt, 1993). Whole-group organization is characteristic, with students working on teacher-assigned activities and few opportunities for student selection of activities (Waxman et al., 1995). Dialogue is similarly impoverished. Padrón and Waxman (1999) reported no teacher–student or student–student verbal interaction about two-thirds of the time. Rather, teachers spent more time explaining instead of questioning, cueing, prompting students to respond, or encouraging extended responses. Students spent much of their time passively watching and listening. Small-group activities were rare, and typically teachers did not encourage students to assist themselves or others. The effects are predictable: student compliance, limited capacity to think critically or creatively and to solve problems (Cummins & Sayers, 1990).

More recently, the widespread focus on accountability systems that reward schools or teachers for high scores and punish them for lack of progress has exacerbated this problem. When state accountability systems punish schools for absolute low performance (Goertz & Duffey, 2000), those that serve low-income and diverse students are most likely to be the target of sanctions. Under the threat of such sanctions, these schools often focus instruction on test-taking skills and rote learning of the basic skills tested (David & Shields, 2001). Classroom instruction increasingly becomes dominated by the goal of increasing short-term test scores at the expense of longer-term efforts to develop critical thinking skills.

These trends notwithstanding, the past 20 years have yielded a substantial body of knowledge regarding effective practices for diverse students. Tharp and his colleagues have synthesized this knowledge into the Five Standards for Effective Pedagogy, using sociocultural theory to unify and distill commonalties into a coherent whole (Dalton, 1998; see Tharp, Estrada, Dalton, & Yamauchi, 2000, for a complete discussion and review of the literature). These practices emphasize teacher–student and student–student collaboration and dialogue (e.g., Brown &

Campione, 1994; Nystrand & Gamoran, 1991; Slavin, 1996), language and conceptual development (e.g., Lemke, 1990; Speidel, 1987), building on prior knowledge and experience (e.g., Lipka, 1994; Moll, Amanti, Neff, & Gonzalez, 1992), and higher-order, complex thinking (Cohen, 1994; Langer, 1995). A distinct feature of our approach is that it moves away from the polemics of teacher- versus child-centered instruction, with active roles for both teachers and students, while according the teacher primacy as instructional leader and guide in developing conceptual knowledge and literacy in the subject matter areas. We also specify the classroom organizational conditions necessary to support effective pedagogy (Tharp et al., 2000). Neither complete nor static, the Standards represent our current knowledge. Inherent in the Standards is the idea of adaptation to local contexts, so although the form may differ, the underlying principles will still be recognizable.

From a sociocultural perspective, the mind is socially constructed through the appropriation and transformation of social interactions that are mediated via linguistic and visual symbols (Rogoff, 1990; Tharp & Gallimore, 1988; Vygotsky, 1978; Wertsch, 1985). These interactions occur within culturally sanctioned activities that are situated in a sociohistorical context. Thus, the activities in which people engage, the dialogue (and other symbolic systems) and problem solving that accompany those activities, and the persons involved are critical to understanding the development of cognitions, perceptions, motives, values, and performance capacities. Activity as an organizing principle of human behavior, then, is central.

Applying this view to the complex world of classrooms suggests that different patterns of instructional activity afford different opportunities for teaching and learning. And it suggests that maximizing excellence for all students involves a pedagogical and organizational pattern distinct from the pedagogy of poverty described previously.

EFFECTIVE PEDAGOGY IN INSTRUCTIONAL ACTIVITY

Grounded in sociocultural theory and educational research, the Five Standards emphasize that teaching and learning occur best in joint productive activity involving teachers and students, that is, when experts and novices work together for a common product or goal and during the activity have opportunities to converse about it (Rogoff, 1990; Tharp & Gallimore, 1988; Tharp et al., 2000). According to this view, effective teaching and learning involve teachers and students actively engaged in *constructing knowledge together*. The first standard, *Joint Productive Activity*, involves facilitating learning through teachers and students (and peers) working collaboratively on relevant instructional products and engaging in dialogue about their work. The second standard, *Developing Language and Literacy Across the Curriculum*, involves developing competence in the language and literacy of instruction and in the academic disciplines throughout all instructional activities. The third standard, *Contextualization*, involves connecting teaching and the curriculum to students' experiences and skills from the home and community as well as to prior school knowledge. The fourth standard, *Cognitive Complexity*, involves challenging students to engage in complex thinking in all of the subject matter areas. The fifth standard, *Instructional Conversation*, involves teaching through conversation by engaging students in purposive, sustained dialogue.

EFFECTIVE ORGANIZATION OF INSTRUCTION ACTIVITY

My colleagues and I propose that effective organization of activity enables the enactment of effective pedagogy. According to this view, three conditions are necessary: simultaneity, diversification, and values consistency (Estrada, 1997; Estrada & Imhoff, 2001b; Tharp et al., 2000). Due to space limitations, only the first two are discussed here. Effective organization promotes effective pedagogy in at least three ways. First, teachers can work with groups that are small enough for responsive teacher assessment and assistance and inclusive student participation. Second, it promotes the development of a wide repertoire of competencies in all students. Third, it promotes the development of harmony within the classroom community.

Simultaneous, Diversified Activity Settings

When instruction is organized into multiple, *simultaneous, diversified activity settings*, teachers and students work toward a variety of integrated goals and tasks within the same instructional time unit (e.g., in literacy classes, toward the goals of vocabulary development, literary analysis, reference skill development, and creative writing, sometimes working individually and sometimes collaboratively) under a variety of simultaneous configurations (teacher-led small group, cooperative small group, pairings, individual). Teachers can work with small groups of students while the remainder of students are productively engaged.

Diversification of Activity and Persons

The rationale for diversification of activities and persons within activities is that it provides a condition basic to education: more inclusive participation and more new learning for all. Although the many natal cultures and performance levels represented in most classrooms can present knotty issues, the answer to diversity is diversity (Estrada, 1997; Estrada & Imhoff, 2001b; see Tharp et al., 2000, for a detailed description of the relevant dimensions for diversification of activities and persons). A fundamental idea from this perspective is that all students should engage in familiar and unfamiliar activities with familiar and unfamiliar peers. Doing so provides opportunities for students to demonstrate current capacities and learn new ones, as well as to develop new relationships (cf. Cohen & Lotan, 1997; Hallinan, 1976).

RESEARCH FOCUS

Unfortunately, until recently, few observation instruments using a sociocultural lens have been available for analyzing and quantifying key features of effective pedagogy and organization. Historically, quantitative observational measures (e.g., Stallings and Flanders's observation instrument) were based primarily on process-product research focusing on correlates of teaching behaviors related to learning low-level skills.

By contrast, the ASOS, anchored in sociocultural theory and current research on best practices for culturally and linguistically diverse students, focuses on features of effective pedagogy connected to higher-order learning. It also provides for quantification of critical organizational features. The ASOS is a live observation tool that allows analysis, quantification, and *thin* description of activity settings as they unfold in classrooms (Rivera et al., 1999). Compared to the thicker, in-depth descriptions provided by qualitative approaches such as ethnography or sociolinguistic microanalysis of discourse, the ASOS yields a comprehensive quantitative overview of the presence of numerous relevant features of activity settings, allowing a charting of the overall pattern of pedagogy and organization simultaneously. Thus, it provides an overall thumbnail sketch of the presence (or absence) of key effective pedagogical and organizational features in instruction.

The study addressed the following questions: Is the ASOS useful for assessing the presence or absence of key effective pedagogical and organizational features in language arts instruction in culturally and

linguistically diverse classrooms? Are effective pedagogical and organizational features associated positively with one another? Is the presence of these features associated positively with measures of student
performance?

METHOD

Participants

Classrooms. The 27 participating first- and fourth-grade classrooms
represented the major variants of demographics, language programs,
and patterns of language arts instructional activity in culturally and
linguistically diverse schools. Selected to sample primary and upper elementary grades, the classes were located in eight mid-sized elementary
schools in urban, suburban, and rural areas.

Teachers. Sixteen first-grade and 11 fourth-grade teachers participated.
In both grades, just over half of the teachers were Euroamerican (56%),
with Latino teachers making up a substantial proportion (34%). One
teacher (3%) was African American, and the remainder were Other. In
both grades, the average number of years teaching was almost identical
(5 years for first-grade teachers and 5.5 for fourth-grade teachers). The
majority of first-grade (76%) and fourth-grade (63%) teachers held full
or partial bilingual credentials. Intern or emergency teachers made up
12% of the sample, all in first grade.

Students. A total of 306 first graders and 335 fourth graders participated. Latinos (60%) and Euroamericans (26%) made up the majority of
students. African Americans, Asians, Pacific Islanders, Filipinos, Native
Americans, and the Other group together made up 14% of the sample.

The vast majority of students spoke either Spanish (52%) or English
(46%), with the remaining 2% speaking Vietnamese, Chinese, Tagalog,
Cambodian, or Arabic. In first grade, nearly 60% were English language
learners (ELLs), whereas in fourth grade 41% were ELLs.

Language Programs in the Classrooms. Of the 27 classrooms, 22 were
Spanish bilingual classrooms (13 transitional or developmental bilingual and 9 two-way Spanish bilingual immersion classrooms). Three
of the classrooms were English language development classrooms. To
regroup students for instruction in their primary language, two of
these were partnered with bilingual classrooms. The other language

development classroom functioned in English only and had a multicultural student population. Two classrooms had an African American cultural focus and had primarily African American students.

Measures

For all measures, the unit of analysis was activity settings, containing both objective and subjective elements, consisting of individual(s) engaged in goal-directed behavior in which actions and operations are carried out within an ecocultural niche of a larger social system (e.g., Leont'ev, 1981; Tharp & Gallimore, 1988; Weisner, 1984; Wells, 1999; Wertsch, 1981). One activity setting is distinguished from another by its purpose. Typical classroom activity settings include teaching the elements of a story in a small reading group or demonstrating two-digit multiplication in whole group.

For measures of pedagogy and organization, the ASOS was the primary instrument (Spearman-Brown effective reliability = .99 for distinguishing the beginning and the end of an activity setting; Cohen's kappa = .65 to .82 for observer reliability of the pedagogy features; see Rivera, 1998. For this study, three observers established interobserver reliability of the pedagogy features, $r = .99$, using videotapes of language arts instruction).

For 2 full days in each classroom, single observers coded each language arts activity setting using the ASOS. To ensure that observations captured typical instruction, they occurred in late fall after school was well underway and in early spring in advance of testing and end-of-year activities. During observation, coders distinguished the boundary of an activity setting by its product, purpose, or objective (Rivera, 1998; Rivera et al., 1999). These could be tangible (e.g., completion of worksheets) or intangible (e.g., story time). Next, observers used the coding categories to identify a variety of characteristics of each activity setting.

For each activity setting, observers coded (a) the start and finish times, (b) the subject matter, (c) the general type (e.g., lecture, small-group instruction), (d) the product or purpose, (e) the location, (f) the personnel involved (i.e., teacher, aide, or other personnel; number, gender, and ethnicity of students), (g) the language of instruction, (h) the type of grouping employed (i.e., whole group, small group, pairs, or individual), and (i) a brief description. Categories added to the ASOS included the gender and ethnicity of students, the language of instruction, and the type of grouping employed during the activity settings. In addition, observers recorded narrative descriptions that were brief or longer, depending on the instructional context.

The ASOS was supplemented with a teacher interview that provided demographic information on teachers and students, daily subject matter teaching schedules, use of primary language instruction, grouping practices, and criteria used for grouping students in reading and writing.

Time Spent on Language Arts. Time devoted to language arts provided an important context for understanding patterns of language arts instructional activity in part because elementary schools do not usually allocate specific amounts of time to subjects. Calculation of the mean daily number of hours devoted to language arts was based on the start and end times of all observed language arts activity settings such as reading and writing instruction, story time, and poetry reading. Other activities involving literacy were included only if teachers specifically construed them as part of their language arts program, such as reading a historical novel in the content area of social studies.

Pedagogy. At the time of this study, an instrument was unavailable for assessment of all Five Standards for Effective Pedagogy. Therefore, using the ASOS, observers coded the simple presence or absence of six effective pedagogy *features* rather than the complete set of Standards. Two of these are among the Five Standards for Effective Pedagogy: *Joint Productive Activity* and *Contextualization*. Two of these are among the building blocks of *Instructional Conversation: teacher–student dialogue* and *responsive assistance*. The remaining two, *modeling and demonstration* and *student initiative and choice*, have been found effective in education programs for Native American communities (Rivera et al., 1999).

The threshold for identification of the pedagogy features was relatively low. To receive a "present" marking, teachers had to use a pedagogy feature only once within an activity setting. In addition, bare-bones criteria were purposefully set for identifying the pedagogical features of each activity setting within the real-time, fast-paced, complex context of classrooms. Joint Productive Activity required some collaborative interaction over task(s) leading to completion of a product. Collaboration could involve shared ownership, authorship, use, or the sharing of ideas or advice, or responsibility for a product. When Joint Productive Activity occurred, observers coded whether it involved teachers, peers, or both. Teacher–student dialogue required the discourse to extend to at least two speech turns each and to involve more than answering a student's question or providing a fact. The conversation between the teacher and student(s) had to be a continuous strand of dialogue and build upon previous statements of the participants involved. Responsive assistance required teachers or students to (a) monitor, observe, or test a student's current level of performance and then to (b) respond by adjusting, selecting, or modulating the assistance to enable the student to advance toward the learning goal. Modeling and demonstration required teachers or students to engage in actions for "showing how." It usually enabled or prepared students to engage in some form of productive activity. Contextualization required teachers to incorporate students' individual or community experience and knowledge from outside the classroom or school into the activity setting. Student initiative or choice required teachers to provide students with the opportunity to make decisions or choose between instructional activities. Students or a group of students had to initiate, generate, or choose the activity setting.

ITEM-LEVEL PEDAGOGICAL FEATURES. For each teacher, the average number of activity settings per hour in which each pedagogical feature was present was calculated by summing the number of language arts activity settings in which the feature was present over the 2-day period and then dividing by the total number of hours spent on language arts. Initial inspection of these data resulted in dropping from further analysis 6 of the 10 items that occurred very infrequently and had little variance (i.e., student choice, Contextualization of instruction in students' individual experiences, Contextualization in community experiences, Joint Productive Activity with peers, responsive assistance by peers, and modeling and demonstration by peers [see Table 6.1]).

TABLE 6.1. *Mean Number of Activity Settings Per Hour in Which Pedagogy Features Were Present in First- and Fourth-Grade Language Arts Instruction*

Pedagogy Feature	Teacher		Student	
	M	SD	M	SD
Joint productive activity	1.02	.73	.29[a]	.39
Teacher–student dialogue	1.28	.69		
Responsive assistance	1.26	.64	.14[a]	.14
Modeling and demonstration	1.18	.70	.47[a]	.34
Contextualization individual	.56[a]	.48		
Contextualization community	.03[a]	.08		
Student choice	.05[a]	.15		

[a] Pedagogy feature was excluded from the language arts pedagogy composite variable due to low frequency and variance; $N = 27$.

PEDAGOGY COMPOSITE. A principal components analysis of the four remaining items revealed that one underlying factor represented the data (factor loadings ranged from .78 to .92). Subsequently, a linear composite of the four features was created, using the time-standardized values. A median split of this variable resulted in stronger versus weaker pedagogy categories.

DIALOGICAL TEACHING COMPOSITE. Because the ASOS coding protocol identifies only the presence or absence of the pedagogical features during an activity setting, it does not distinguish between teachers who enacted the features at different rates. Therefore a scale of 1 (never occurs) to 4 (frequently occurs) was used to record the relative frequency of teacher–student dialogue and responsive assistance within an activity setting. The rationale for targeting these two features is that they most closely represent dialogical teaching, and they are key to assessment and assisted performance of students. A linear composite of these two items was created after confirming that they were highly correlated ($r = .93$, $p < .001$). A median split of this variable resulted in strong versus weaker dialogical teaching categories.

Organization

NUMBER OF ACTIVITY SETTINGS PER HOUR. For each teacher, the number of language arts activity settings over the 2-day period were summed, then divided by the total number of hours spent on language arts to produce the average number of activity settings per hour.

SIMULTANEOUS, DIVERSIFIED ACTIVITY SETTINGS. Teachers who conducted three or more activity settings simultaneously for any instructional period during language arts received a "present" code. Those who did not received an "absent" code. There was no time requirement; the shortest period was approximately 30 minutes and the longest was approximately 90 minutes.

DIVERSIFICATION OF PERSONS. This assessment was based on observations of activity settings involving ELLs and English speakers, as well as teacher interview data regarding grouping practices and whether these students worked and talked together in language arts activities. Teachers whose students always worked and talked together in language-heterogeneous groups and had some opportunities to function within the other's language code received a code of "always." When such activity was absent, they received a code of "never." When it occurred sometimes, they received a code of "sometimes." This report includes data on diversification of persons on the dimension of primary language only.

Student Performance

NORM-REFERENCED READING AND LANGUAGE TEST SCORES. Stanford 9 reading and language scale scores were available for 91% of all fourth graders. Spanish Assessment of Basic Education (SABE) reading scale scores and language reference percentile scores were available for a subsample of 59 first graders because California state testing requirements do not apply to first graders.

TEACHER RATINGS OF LANGUAGE ARTS AND OVERALL STUDENT PERFORMANCE. These ratings were based on a modified version of the Teacher Rating Scale (Goldenberg, Gallimore, Reese, & Garnier, 1998). Teachers rated students on a 1 (very poor) to 6 (excellent) scale on overall academic performance, reading performance, writing performance, math performance, quickness to learn, and motivation. Principal components analysis indicated that the six items represented one underlying component, so these items were combined to form a linear composite (factor loadings ranged from .78 to .92).

FINDINGS

Patterns of Language Arts Instructional Activity

The ASOS proved useful for assessing the presence or absence of key effective pedagogical and organizational features in language arts. The landscape that emerged indicated that, overall, teachers and students participated in relatively few settings with effective pedagogy features present, though first-grade participants did so decidedly more often than fourth-grade participants. Effective pedagogical and organizational features tended to co-occur. In about 50% of the classrooms, teachers and their students participated some of the time in activity settings with effective organizational features; the vast majority of these were in the first grade. For the most part, first- and fourth-grade teachers and their students participated in different patterns of language arts instructional activity.

Time Spent on Language Arts Instruction. First-grade teachers tended to spend more time on language arts than fourth-grade teachers (2.73 vs. 2.19 hours per day, $t(14.95) = 2.22$, $p < .05$). One interpretation might be that fourth-grade teachers feel pressure to teach more subjects such as social studies and science. To some degree, this was true. During observations, some fourth-grade teachers taught social studies, though they infrequently taught science. This fact did not entirely account for the discrepancy, however.

Some fourth-grade teachers included social studies without sacrificing language arts time. The four fourth-grade teachers who maximized time on language arts spent twice as much time on language arts as their fourth-grade counterparts – and similar amounts of time as the five first-grade teachers who also maximized language arts time (approximately 3 hours per day). All but one of these teachers participated in two-way bilingual immersion programs that required reading instruction in both languages. Two of these teachers maximized language arts and social studies instruction time by construing social studies as reading in the content areas.

Pedagogy. Across both grades, the number of activity settings in which the critical pedagogy features were present was low, ranging from 0 to 1.28 per hour (see Table 6.1). On average, teachers and students participated in approximately one activity setting per hour in which Joint Productive Activity, teacher–student dialogue, responsive assistance, and modeling and demonstration were present. Participation in activity settings with the remaining effective pedagogy features, however, was rare to nonexistent (see Table 6.1). Teachers and students participated in activity settings with Contextualization of instruction in students' individual experiences approximately once every 2 hours. They participated in almost no activity settings with Contextualization in community experiences and student choice. Students rarely participated in activity settings involving Joint Productive Activity with peers, responsive assistance by peers, and modeling and demonstration by peers (see Table 6.1).

Using the pedagogy composite to examine first- and fourth-grade teachers' practices revealed that first-grade teachers and students participated on average in nearly twice as many activity settings with Joint Productive Activity, teacher–student dialogue, responsive assistance, and modeling and demonstration present (1.45 vs. .80 per hour, $t(25) = 3.97$ $p < .001$). Even for first-grade participants, however, this rate was relatively low compared to the average number of activity settings per hour (4.16).

First- and fourth-grade teachers' use of teacher–student dialogue and responsive assistance with their students was similar, as measured by the dialogical teaching composite (1.75 vs. 1.65 per hour, respectively, *ns*). Both engaged in low levels of dialogical teaching on average, neither achieving the rating of "sometimes" on the 1 to 4 scale.

Organizational Features. Across the two grades, in about 50% of the classrooms, teachers and their students participated some of the time in activity settings with effective organizational features. Here again, however, first- and fourth-grade teachers differed in the ways they organized their language arts activity settings; effective organizational features occurred more often in first grade.

NUMBER OF LANGUAGE ARTS ACTIVITY SETTINGS. On average, first-grade teachers and their students engaged in a greater number of language arts activities settings per hour than their fourth-grade counterparts (4.19 vs. 2.90 per hour, $t(25) = 4.15, p < .001$).

SIMULTANEOUS, DIVERSIFIED ACTIVITY SETTINGS. Almost twice as many first-grade as fourth-grade teachers created simultaneous, multiple, diverse activity settings (75% vs. 36%). This form of organization occurred almost exclusively during reading instruction. During the remainder of language arts instruction, first-grade teachers and their students tended to be in single, undifferentiated activity settings. Fourth-grade teachers much more typically created single, undifferentiated activity settings such as whole-group instruction or seatwork throughout language arts instruction.

DIVERSIFICATION OF PERSONS. In both first and fourth grade two-way bilingual Spanish immersion classrooms, language-diverse students always worked together. In these programs, strict guidelines prescribed the language codes used for instructing all students, regardless of primary language, so that regrouping students on the basis of language was irrelevant.

In the remaining classrooms, language-diverse students rarely worked together. Working together occurred sometimes in 19% of these first-grade classrooms and in none of these fourth-grade classrooms. In classrooms where language-diverse students never had opportunities to work together during language arts, they were segregated in some fashion for primary language instruction – either within or across classrooms. In one fourth-grade transitional classroom, Spanish speakers occasionally joined English speakers for some reading instruction, but no activities occurred during which English speakers functioned in a Spanish-language context.

Pedagogy and Organization. Consistent with the idea that effective organization affords the enactment of effective pedagogy, teachers who

TABLE 6.2. *Distribution of Teachers by Pedagogical and Organizational Features*

	Pedagogy Composite[a]	
Organization	Stronger	Weaker
Simultaneous, diversified activity settings	41%	18%
Single, undifferentiated activity settings	11%	30%

Note: $n = 27$. Values represent the percentage of classrooms in each cell.
[a] Pedagogy composite represents the mean number of activity settings per hour in which each of the five pedagogy features was present.
* $\chi^2(26) = 4.49, p < .03$.

created activity settings with more effective pedagogical features tended to use multiple, simultaneous, diversified activity settings. The distribution of pedagogical by organizational features was significantly different than would be expected by chance ($\chi^2(26) = 4.49$, $p < .03$; see Table 6.2). Teachers with stronger pedagogy were four times as likely to use simultaneous, diverse activities versus single, undifferentiated activities. Teachers with weaker pedagogy tended to use single, undifferentiated activities.

An Overview of the Patterns. The usefulness of the ASOS in describing the whole of the characteristic patterns of language arts activity in first and fourth grades is illustrated well by a graphic representation of both pedagogical and organizational features (see Figure 6.1). Based on a median split of the pedagogy composite, the teachers were categorized as stronger or weaker implementers of the effective pedagogy features. The range of the number of activity settings per hour in first and fourth grade serves as the background context. Superimposed are the number of activity settings per hour in which each of the pedagogy features was present for first- and fourth-grade teachers with stronger and weaker pedagogy. This representation reveals that not only is the mean of the number of activity settings per hour different in the two grades, the range is quite different. Perhaps most striking is that first-grade teachers with stronger pedagogy stand out among their peers in terms of Joint Productive Activity, teacher–student dialogue, responsive assistance, and modeling and demonstration. In addition, all of these teachers used simultaneous, diversified activity settings. Fourth-grade teachers with stronger pedagogy look similar to first-grade teachers with weaker pedagogy. Fourth-grade teachers with weaker pedagogy

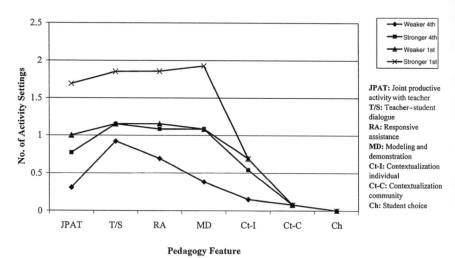

FIGURE 6.1. Average number of activity settings per hour in which effective pedagogy features are present.

created the fewest activity settings in which these pedagogy features are present. Because the remaining effective pedagogy features were infrequent to nonexistent among all teachers, the distinctions here wane.

Patterns of Language Arts Instructional Activity and Measures of Student Performance

Overall, the findings indicated that patterns of language arts activity with features of effective pedagogy and organization present were positively related to measures of student performance. To analyze covariation of implementation of effective features with measures of student performance, teachers were categorized as stronger versus weaker implementers of effective pedagogy and of dialogical teaching, and as using or not using multiple, simultaneous, diversified activity settings. Planned comparisons were conducted of student performance as measured by norm-referenced test scores and teacher ratings of performance across these categories. Comparisons of test scores were based on the pedagogy composite because this was the categorical variable with the most even distribution across the classrooms with test data. Scale test scores were used for three of four comparisons because they preserve best the distance between scores across the entire distribution. For first grade, only reference percentile scores were available in language. Because norm-referenced test percentile scores are ordinal in nature,

TABLE 6.3. *Mean Student Performance by Pedagogy and Organization*

| | Pedagogy Composite | | | | |
| | Weaker | | Stronger | | Planned Comparisons |
Norm-Referenced Tests	M	SD	M	SD	of Means
First-grade SABE reading scale scores	487.00	63.68	579.75	49.89	$t(57) = -6.09$***
First-grade SABE language reference percentile scores	50.37	22.44	75.28	19.69	$U = 148$***
Fourth-grade Stanford 9 reading scale scores	619.50	43.61	630.73	43.84	$t(279) = -2.14$*
Fourth-grade Stanford 9 language scale scores	609.04	36.97	619.19	36.19	$t(279) = -2.31$**

Teacher Ratings

Overall performance	3.80	1.48	4.06	1.33	$t(601) = -2.24$**

| | Dialogical Teaching Composite | | | | |
	Weaker		Stronger		
Overall performance	3.76	1.39	4.10	1.36	$t(601) = -2.93$**

| | Simult., Div. Activity Settings | | | | |
	Yes		No		
Overall performance	4.04	1.47	3.79	1.36	$t(601) = -2.13$*

Note: Range of teacher ratings = 1 to 6. One-tailed *t*-tests were used to compare all means except first-grade language reference percentile scores. The Mann–Whitney U test was used for this comparison.
*$p < .05$. **$p < .01$. ***$p < .001$.

the Mann–Whitney U Test, a nonparametric alternative designed to test whether two independent groups are drawn from the same population (Siegel, 1956), was used for this comparison.

Pedagogy and Norm-Referenced Tests of Student Performance. In both first and fourth grades, teacher pedagogy covaried positively with student performance on norm-referenced tests (see Table 6.3). On SABE reading scores, first graders whose teachers were stronger implementers of effective pedagogy outperformed by a wide margin their counterparts whose teachers were weaker implementers. Similarly, first graders' average SABE reference percentile score in language was 75% in stronger implementers' classrooms, whereas it was 50% in weaker implementers' classrooms.

The results were similar for fourth grade. Fourth graders whose teachers were stronger implementers of effective pedagogy scored higher on Stanford 9 reading and language tests than students whose teachers were weaker implementers (see Table 6.3).

Pedagogy, Organization, and Teacher Ratings of Student Performance. Both pedagogy and simultaneity/diversification of activity settings covaried positively with teacher ratings of student performance (see Table 6.3). Students in classrooms of teachers who were stronger implementers of features of effective pedagogy were rated as performing better by their teachers. The findings were similar for students in classrooms of teachers who were stronger in dialogical teaching and for students whose teachers used simultaneous diversified activities in language arts (see Table 6.3).

DISCUSSION

The results of the study show that the ASOS yields a useful comprehensive, quantitative overview of the patterns of language arts instruction in culturally and linguistically diverse classrooms. In a number of ways, the results are an encouraging first step in developing quantitative observational methods using a socioocultural lens. First, documenting the presence of effective pedagogical and organizational features demonstrated that teachers *can* create patterns of language arts activity that include these features, regardless of the mix of students' backgrounds. Second, teachers are able to create these kinds of teaching and learning environments across a variety of language programs. This is good news as educators come to recognize that a one-size-fits-all approach to language programs is neither desirable nor feasible (Genesee, 1999).

Third, effective features in language arts instruction in diverse classrooms are relatively rare, consistent with the work of Waxman, Padrón, and others. Across grades, activity settings characterized by the presence of effective pedagogy features were infrequent – although they were more common in first-grade classrooms. The modal experience during language arts for first-grade teachers and students was one of multiple, simultaneous, diversified activity settings during reading instruction and mostly single, undifferentiated activity settings the remainder of the time. The modal experience for fourth-grade teachers and students was one of single, undifferentiated activity settings during all of language arts instruction. Moreover, with the exception of two-way bilingual immersion programs, language-diverse students were typically segregated for language arts instruction.

Fourth, the findings were consistent with the idea that effective organization promotes effective pedagogy, with stronger pedagogy teachers tending to use multiple, simultaneous, diverse activities and weaker pedagogy teachers tending to use single, undifferentiated activities. The former trend was pronounced, whereas the latter was less so, suggesting that although effective organization enables effective pedagogy, it does not guarantee it.

Finally, the ASOS yielded preliminary evidence pointing to the benefits of effective pedagogy and organization on student performance. Overall, students whose teachers were categorized as stronger implementers tended to outperform their counterparts on norm-referenced tests, and their teachers rated them higher on overall performance. The similarity of results for the two measures of student performance is noteworthy. As indirect measures, teacher ratings of student performance must be interpreted with caution. If the positive association means simply, however, that these teachers developed more positive relationships with their students, the finding is important given the body of research indicating a positive relation between the quality of teacher–student relationships and achievement-related performance, behaviors, attitudes, and motivations (see Tharp et al., 2000, for a review of this literature). While recognizing the limitations of teacher ratings of performance, one can view them as similar though perhaps slightly better than grades because, across schools, teachers responded to a standard set of items regarding students' performances.

Taken as a whole, the findings are significant methodologically because they underscore that a quantitative approach grounded in sociocultural theory can be usefully employed to provide a thin but comprehensive description of effective features of instructional activity. Substantively, the findings are significant because they provide preliminary evidence that by implementing effective pedagogy and the necessary organizational conditions to support it, teachers can create patterns of instructional activity that promote student success under a variety of conditions.

The findings demonstrate the usefulness of the ASOS in capturing overall patterns of instruction that set the stage for further questions and areas for in-depth study. The ASOS is well suited to describing broad trends of markers of effective practices across classrooms and grade levels. It can also be used by researchers or professional developers for initial sampling of teachers across a range of practices. The ASOS should not be used to assess the quality of individual teachers' instructional practices because it provides useful but bare-bones *markers* of quality, simple presence or absence of effective features of pedagogy and organization. For these and like purposes, qualitative methods such as supplementary narrative descriptive notes and interviews with teachers are useful. Other supplementary data can include frequency ratings of the features (rather than simple presence or absence). In this study, I used both of these supplementary methods to provide data beyond the simple presence and absence of features and for sampling of case study teachers for further in-depth study.

Note

This study is part of a 5-year research project supported under the Education Research and Development Program, PR/Award No. R306A60001, the Center for Research on Education, Diversity & Excellence (CREDE), as administered by the Office of Educational Research and Improvement (OERI), National Institute on the Education of At-Risk Students (NIEARS), U.S. Department of Education (USDOE). The contents, findings, and opinions expressed here are those of the author and do not necessarily represent the positions or policies of CREDE, OERI, NIEARS, or the USDOE.

I thank the school principals, teachers, and students who opened up their classrooms for study; Patrick Shields for critical comments on earlier drafts of this chapter; Gina Guardino and Phoumy Sayavong for assistance with data collection and management; Barbara Imhoff for assistance with graphics and database management; Geneva Haertel for statistical advice; and Maribel Hernandez, Maria Diaz, Ana Cubias, and Michele Gilkey for data entry.

References

Brookhart, S. M., & Rusnak, T. G. (1993). A pedagogy of enrichment, not poverty: Successful lessons of exemplary urban teachers. *Journal of Teacher Education, 44*(1), 17–26.

Brown, A. L., & Campione, J. C. (1994). Guided discovery in a community of learners. In K. McGilly (Ed.), *Classroom lessons: Integrating cognitive theory and classroom practice* (pp. 229–271). Boston: MIT Press.

Cohen, E. G. (1994). Restructuring the classroom: Conditions for productive small groups. *Review of Education Research, 64*(1), 1–35.

Cohen, E. G., & Lotan, R. A. (1997). *Working for equity in heterogeneous classrooms.* New York: Teachers College Press.

Cummins, J., & Sayers, D. (1990). Education 2001: Learning networks and educational reform. *Computers in the Schools, 7*(1/2), 1–29.

Dalton, S. S. (1998). *Pedagogy matters: Standards for effective teaching practice* (Research Report No. 4). Santa Cruz: Center for Research on Education, Diversity & Excellence, University of California.

David, J. D., & Shields, P. M. (2001). *When theory hits reality: Standards-based reform in action*. Menlo Park, CA: SRI International.

Estrada, P. (1997). *Patterns of social organization in a sample of nine culturally and linguistically diverse schools* (Technical Report No. 1, Project 5.8). Santa Cruz: Center for Research on Education, Diversity & Excellence, University of California.

Estrada, P., & Imhoff, B. D. (2001a, April). One road to reform: Professional development, pedagogy, and student achievement in the context of state reform of literacy instruction. Symposium paper presented at the annual meeting of the American Educational Research Association, Seattle.

Estrada, P., & Imhoff, B. D. (2001b, April). *Patterns of language arts instructional activity: Excellence, inclusion, fairness, and harmony in six first-grade classrooms*. Roundtable paper presented at the annual meeting of the American Educational Research Association, Seattle.

Garcia, E. E. (1990). Instructional discourse in effective Hispanic classrooms. In R. Jacobson & C. Faltis (Eds.), *Language distribution issues in bilingual schooling* (pp. 104–117). Clevedon, U.K.: Multilingual Matters.

Genesee, F. (1999). *Program alternatives for linguistically diverse students* (Research Report No. 1). Santa Cruz: Center for Research on Education, Diversity & Excellence, University of California.

Goertz, M., & Duffy, M. (2000). *Variations on a theme: What is performance-based accountability?* Paper presented at the annual meeting of the American Educational Research Association, New Orleans.

Goldenberg, C. N., Gallimore, R., Reese, L. J., & Garnier, H. (1998). *Cause or effect? A longitudinal study of immigrant Latinos' educational aspirations and expectations and their children's school performance*. Unpublished manuscript, Department of Psychiatry, University of California at Los Angeles.

Haberman, M. (1991). The pedagogy of poverty versus good teaching. *Phi Delta Kappan, 73*(4), 290–294.

Hallinan, M. T. (1976). Friendship patterns in open and traditional classrooms. *Sociology of Education, 49*(4), 254–265.

Knapp, M. S., & Shields, P. M. (1990). Reconceiving academic instruction for the children of poverty. *Phi Delta Kappan, 71*(10), 753–758.

Langer, J. A. (1995). *Envisioning literature: Literary understanding and literature instruction*. New York: Teachers College Press.

Lemke, J. L. (1990). *Talking science: Language, learning, and values*. Norwood, NJ: Ablex.

Leont'ev, D. A. (1981). The problem of activity in psychology. In J. V. Wertsch (Ed.), *The concept of activity in Soviet psychology* (pp. 37–71). Armonk, NY: Sharpe.

Lipka, J. (1994). Culturally negotiating schooling: Toward a Yup'ik mathematics. *Journal of American Indian Education, 33*(3), 14–20.

Moll, L. C., Amanti, C., Neff, D., & Gonzalez, N. (1992). Funds of knowledge for teaching: Using a qualitative approach to connect homes and classrooms. *Theory into Practice, 31*, 132–141.

Nystrand, M., & Gamoran, A. (1991). Instructional discourse, student engagement, and literature achievement. *Research in the Teaching of English, 25*(3), 261–290.

Padrón, Y. N., & Waxman, H. C. (1993). Teaching and learning risks associated with limited cognitive mastery in science and mathematics for limited proficient students. In Office of Bilingual Education and Minority Language Affairs (Ed.), *Proceedings of the third national research symposium on limited English proficient students: Focus on middle and high school issues* (Vol. 2, pp. 511–547). Washington, DC: National Clearinghouse for Bilingual Education.

Padrón, Y. N., & Waxman, H. C. (1999). Effective instructional practices for English language learners. In H. C. Waxman & H. J. Walberg (Eds.), *New directions for teaching practice and research* (pp. 171–203). Berkeley, CA: McCutchan.

Rivera, H. (1998). *Activity settings: Training and observer reliability of a new observational system.* Paper presented at the annual meeting of the American Educational Research Association, San Diego, CA.

Rivera, H., Tharp, R. G., Youpa, D., Dalton, S., Guardino, G., & Lasky, S. (1999). *ASOS: Activity Setting Observation System coding and rule-book.* Santa Cruz: Center for Research on Education, Diversity & Excellence, University of California.

Rogoff, B. (1990). *Apprenticeships in thinking: Cognitive development in social context.* New York: Oxford University Press.

Saunders, W. M., & Goldenberg, C. (1999). *The effects of instructional conversations and literature logs on the story comprehension and thematic understanding of English proficient and limited English proficient students.* Santa Cruz: Center for Research on Education, Diversity & Excellence, University of California.

Siegel, S. (1956). *Nonparametric statistics.* New York: McGraw-Hill.

Slavin, R. E. (1996). Research on cooperative learning and achievement: What we need to know, what we need to do. *Contemporary Educational Psychology, 21*(1), 43–69.

Speidel, G. E. (1987). Conversation and language learning in the classroom. In K. E. Nelson & A. Van Kleeck (Eds.), *Child language* (pp. 99–135). Hillsdale, NJ: Erlbaum.

Stephen, V. P., Varble, M. E., & Taitt, H. (1993). Instructional strategies for minority youth. *The Clearing House, 67*(2), 116–120.

Tharp, R. G., Estrada, P., Dalton, S. S., & Yamauchi, L. (2000). *Teaching transformed: Achieving excellence, fairness, inclusion, and harmony.* Boulder, CO: Westview Press.

Tharp, R. G., & Gallimore, R. (1988). *Rousing minds to life: Teaching, learning, and schooling in social context.* Cambridge, MA: Harvard University Press.

Vygotsky, L. S. (1978). *Mind and society: The development of higher psychological processes* (M. Cole, V. John-Steiner, S. Scribner, & E. Souberman, Trans.). Cambridge, MA: Harvard University Press.

Waxman, H. C., Huang, S. L., & Padrón, Y. N. (1995). Investigating the pedagogy of poverty in inner-city middle level schools. *Research in Middle Level Education, 18*(2), 1–22.

Weisner, T. S. (1984). Ecocultural niches of middle childhood: A cross-cultural perspective. In W. A. Collins (Ed.), *Development during middle childhood: The years from six to twelve* (pp. 335–369). Washington, DC: National Academy of Science.

Wells, G. (1999). *Dialogic inquiry: Toward a sociocultural practice and theory of education*. New York: Cambridge University Press.

Wertsch, J. V. (Ed.). (1981). *The concept of activity in Soviet psychology*. Armonk, NY: Sharpe.

Wertsch, J. V. (1985). *Vygotsky and the social formation of mind*. Cambridge, MA: Harvard University Press.

7

Using Classroom Observation as a Research and Formative Evaluation Tool in Educational Reform

The School Observation Measure

Steven M. Ross, Lana J. Smith, Marty Alberg, and Deborah Lowther

Through the Comprehensive School Reform Demonstration (CSRD) program (Public Law 105-78; see Doherty, 2000) and Title I School-Wide programs (Natriello & McDill, 1999), there is currently considerable impetus for reforming education using whole-school change models. Implementing comprehensive school reform (CSR) programs requires tremendous commitment and effort by school districts and their individual schools. As the literature on school reform indicates, it also takes time (Bodilly, 1996). What the public, media, and school boards sometimes fail to understand is that programs by themselves are not what improve student learning. Rather, the critical factor is the positive changes that the reforms engender in school climate, resources, and, most critically, the quality of classroom teaching and learning. But whether achievement effects are evidenced in a relatively short period, as occurred after 2 years in Memphis (Ross et al., 2001) or, more typically, after 5 or more years (Herman & Stringfield, 1995; Levin, 1993), key stakeholders (e.g., the public and school boards) want fairly immediate information about what is happening in the schools to justify the reform effort. At the same time, teachers and administrators within schools need formative evaluation data to know whether their efforts are producing the tangible changes desired.

These considerations prompted our development of the School Observation Measure (SOM; Ross, Smith, & Alberg, 1999), the instrument to be described in this chapter. A major part of our rationale was that "black box" studies focusing on student achievement outcomes offer only limited information for decision making by failing to increase understanding of whether the factors most likely to affect achievement directly, namely, classroom teaching strategies and learner activities, are being impacted. Although *process* data on implementation, school climate, and participants' attitudes are routinely collected in program evaluation and research, observations of teaching and learning are rarely incorporated. Obvious barriers are the practical demands of conducting observations and concerns about the validity of the data collected.

As will be described in this chapter, SOM was developed with these two criteria in mind. Practicality was addressed by creating a process that could be readily taught to observers who, once trained, could collect useful and accurate observation data within a half-day (3-hour) period. Validity was addressed by (a) identifying strategies that different groups of educators (teachers, administrators, researchers) would universally associate with positive educational reform and effective teaching for diverse schools and students; (b) operationalizing the strategies for observers so that recorded data would have high reliability; and (c) orienting the focus to capture the degree to which the target strategies are prevalent in an entire school (rather than in isolated lessons or classes), using data from as many as 60 to 100 classrooms over the course of the year. Despite the advantages of practicality and high reliability, SOM has the associated disadvantages of being unable to (a) capture specific practices that comprise an overall classroom strategy (e.g., establishment of individual student accountability in cooperative learning) and (b) assess the quality or effectiveness of observed practices. To address these limitations in various projects, we have attached to SOM supplementary Expanded Rubrics that focus on effective use of targeted strategies.

In general, SOM differs from most other observation instruments by taking a whole-school perspective in capturing the methodologies that are most and least prevalent. We view this as a logical first step in gaining an impression of what instruction is like at a given site and whether teaching methods conform to school or program goals. Another unique aspect of SOM is the relative ease with which observers can be trained to conduct reliable assessments. As of this writing, we have trained hundreds of observers from groups such as retired teachers, graduate students, university faculty, principals, teachers, and school administrators. This chapter provides the complete story of SOM, starting with its origin, contents and procedures, reliability and validity support, and recent illustrative uses in a large multistate formative evaluation process and three applied quasi-experimental research studies.

DEVELOPMENT OF SOM

The Classroom Observation Measure

SOM evolved out of the authors' earlier observational research with at-risk learners (Ross, Smith, Lohr, & McNelis, 1994). The Elementary Classroom Observation Measure (ECOM) was developed from review of observation instruments used in previous studies (e.g., Good & Brophy, 1987) and from the need to have systematic and relatively objective data recording multiple classroom events and teacher/student behaviors. ECOM was later refined and broadened to incorporate additional elements reflective of high school environments and was retitled the Classroom Observation Measure (COM).

COM consisted of six major components: (1) Classroom Ecology and Resources, (2) Classroom Makeup and Physical Environment, (3) Interval Coding (of the subject taught, teaching orientation, student engagement, teacher activities, and student behavior), (4) Session Teacher Behaviors (e.g., praises good performance, motivates students, maintains a positive climate, and keeps students' attention), (5) Session Teaching Methods (e.g., uses cooperative learning, direct instruction, tutoring, ability grouping, and seatwork), and (6) Field Notes. Each COM observer remained in one classroom for approximately 1 hour. The interval coding consisted of nine intervals of 5 minutes for a total of 45 minutes. During this time, the observers watched and listened for 1 minute and then recorded for 4 minutes until the nine cycles and 45 minutes were completed. The additional 15 minutes were used for noting details of the classroom and for general field notes.

A detailed manual was developed for the COM that described the observation procedures, operationally defined categories, and types of teacher–student behaviors and gave examples. Observers were trained by thoroughly reviewing the manual and practicing with videotaped teaching sessions, followed by observing and rating at least three full "live" sessions in groups of three to five at a nearby school. In these initial sessions, observations were interrupted after the completion of each coding interval to permit observers to compare and discuss responses. Once observers produced reliable ratings (typically in the first practice session), they were certified to observe classrooms individually and to collect data. Quantitative reliability measures (percentage of interobserver agreement and interobserver correlations) and qualitative reliability checks (member checking) showed high consistency of ratings (see Ross et al., 1994).

Following validation, COM was used extensively as a research tool in examining school programs. Exemplary applications were (a) comparing teaching methods in regular versus reduced-sized, ability-grouped elementary classes (Ross et al., 1994), (b) describing teaching methods used in culturally diverse schools using CSR models (Stringfield, Datnow, & Ross, 1998), and (c) comparing teaching methods used in CSR versus matched control schools receiving funding for Title I schoolwide programs (Ross, Alberg, & Wang, 1998). A second category of COM application was to observe and evaluate formatively the classroom practices of preservice teachers participating in student teaching at the University of Memphis.

Despite these varied beneficial uses of COM, we felt that for expanded application to school program research, the instrument was limited by the complexity of its recording procedures and the associated data analysis, and by the extensive time (1 hour) spent with individual teachers, thus severely limiting the sampling in a typical study. These considerations led us, in the fall of 1997, to create the SOM, using the Session Teaching Behaviors and Methods section from the COM as a foundation.

SOM Contents

A copy of the SOM instrument is provided in Appendix A. The main content of the SOM is a listing of 24 teaching strategies/events that may be used separately or in combination with others at a given time in a classroom. Examples are cooperative learning, direct instruction, project-based learning, and student discussion. As the instrument shows, the strategies are classified into the following six categories:

Instructional Orientation ($n = 4$)
Classroom Organization ($n = 3$)
Instructional Strategies ($n = 6$)
Student Activities ($n = 7$)
Technology Use ($n = 2$)
Assessment ($n = 2$)

These categories were derived subjectively for the purpose of facilitating discussion and interpretation of the data, but they are not formally used in the data analysis.

The 24 strategies were selected through an extended process directed to the goal of addressing (a) national teaching standards in core subjects, (b) teaching methods associated in the literature with improved academic achievement, (c) teaching methods associated with contemporary educational reforms, and (d) usage of ability and multiage grouping structures that might be used (effectively or inappropriately) in accommodating student diversity. The first step in our approach was to start with the 12 global strategies incorporated in the COM (see the previous discussion). Second, we refined and extended the list based on current national performance standards in math, science, and language arts (see, e.g., International Reading Association and National Council of Teachers of English, 1996, and, for effective pedagogy, Dalton, 1998). These standards explicitly or indirectly encourage the use of such strategies as cooperative learning, higher-level questioning and feedback, subject integration, teachers acting as a coach/facilitator, experiential learning, work centers, student discussion, sustained reading and writing, independent inquiry, performance assessment, student self-assessment, and technology use for instructional delivery and as a learning tool. Third, we invited reviewers representing different potential user groups to examine the listing and suggest additions and deletions in view of the preceding four goals. Specific groups represented were school district Title I staff, teachers, principals, educational researchers, and regional educational laboratory staff, particularly AEL and South Eastern Regional Vision for Education (SERVE), with whom we were collaborating in CSRD research projects.

Using the feedback and suggestions provided, we developed the final listing shown in Appendix A. In addition to the 24 classroom strategies/events, we added two "summary items" based on the extensive literature showing student achievement to be positively correlated with "academically focused class time" and "student interest and engagement" (Good & Brophy, 1987).

Drawing from our experiences and suggestions from the reviewers, we identified a half-day observation (3 hours) as a practical but suitably long period of assessment for an individual school visit. One perceived advantage was that an observer could remain at a given school for a full day or visit two schools in close geographic proximity to complete, if desired, two SOM visits a day. Alternatively, an observer with a tighter time schedule could very comfortably complete a single SOM, even with extensive travel or the unanticipated disruptions that occur while visiting classes. During the 3 hours, we wanted observers to visit a large enough sample of classes to obtain an accurate impression of how prevalent each of the 24 strategies was in the entire school. After considering the advantages and disadvantages of different time intervals per class, we decided on 15 minutes as the standard. This interval was judged to give the observer sufficient time to become settled in the class and see enough to comprehend the basic goals and associated teaching strategies. The 3-hour visit would also allow 10–12 different classes to be viewed, thereby providing a reasonably large sampling from which to form holistic impressions.

At the end of the 3-hour visit, the observer rates each of the 24 strategies/events using the five-point rubric shown at the bottom of Appendix A. As can be seen, the rubric categories consist of Not Observed, Rarely, Occasionally, Frequently, and Extensively. Judgments depend on two factors: the number of classrooms in which the particular strategy was observed and the perceived emphasis on or prevalence of the strategy as a form of instruction. These two factors need to be evaluated in combination based on a qualitative holistic impression. Thus, for example, it is possible that an observer might see cooperative learning in 6 out of 10 classes at one school, yet rate that usage as less prevalent (e.g., Occasionally) than at another school (e.g., Frequently) in which the strategy is seen in only 5 classes. In the former case, the six classes might use cooperative learning activities in a brief and very limited way, whereas in the latter case, the five classes might feature very rich and extensive applications. Note, however, that the rubric requests only a descriptive assessment of strategy *use*, not a judgment about quality. Supplementary instruments (and observers having specific expertise in the targeted teaching strategies) would need to be employed to address quality issues.

For the two summary items, a 3-point rating scale is used: low, moderate, high. In trial runs, we found observer confidence and reliability to be higher using this number of categories as opposed to a 5-point scale.

Observation Procedure

In preparation for the visit, we recommend that the observer obtain (a) a map of the school showing the location of each classroom, (b) a listing of all certified staff by grade level and room number, (c) a schedule of the school day (e.g., when different classes go to special subjects, to lunch, etc.), (d) a name badge, and (e) a letter from the district (or other appropriate organization) authorizing the visitations and assuring school personnel that no individual data will be recorded or provided to anyone.

Prior to arriving at the school, the observer selects 10–12 classrooms to visit and schedules them in some predetermined order. The selection of classrooms should be random in nature while attempting to include different grades and classrooms that the observer has visited the fewest number of times in any prior SOM visits. The goal is to observe different classrooms/teachers a fairly equivalent number of times over the course of the year (or program period).

Observers are instructed to call the schools a few days before the planned visit to ensure that no unusual events (e.g., parent meetings, school carnival) are scheduled. When the observer arrives at the school, he or she checks in at the front office, determines whether there are any unanticipated events or conflicts, and then begins the first observation as scheduled. For example, if the prearranged schedule lists Room 201 as Observation 1, the observer would start by finding that room. Should students not be present or something unusual happening (e.g., a Halloween party), the closest available classroom (say, Room 202) should be substituted. The observer would then complete the 15-minute observation and then attempt to follow the prescribed schedule for the subsequent observations.

In scheduling and visiting classes, observers typically restrict choices to those focusing on core or other subjects (e.g., foreign language) that tend to be taught by conventional rather than highly specialized teaching methods (as typically are employed in music, art, or physical education). Similarly, special classes (e.g., special education, English as a Second Language, or small-group tutoring) that may involve small numbers of selected students are generally avoided. If particular contexts differ greatly from those of the regular classes, it may not make sense to mix them all together in an attempt to capture a holistic perspective. On the other hand, classes taught by substitute teachers generally *are* observed. The rationale is to reinforce the preparation of substitutes, through professional development support and making appropriate lesson plans available for them, to use teaching orientations consistent with school emphases and philosophies. However, the types of classes included or excluded will ultimately be determined by the needs of the particular study.

Once in a classroom, the observer tries to be as unobtrusive as possible, finding a chair or an area in which to stand toward the back of the room. If student-centered activities are taking place, it is usually appropriate to move around the classroom to see as much as possible. If the lesson is teacher-directed (e.g., lecture presentation), the observer will most likely have to remain at a stationary location. Several items on the SOM may not be possible to ascertain without information from the teacher or an administrator. These include ability grouping, multiage grouping, and often the status and role of any other adult that may be in the classroom. Where feasible, the observer may ask the teacher for clarification during the classroom visit. Where such questions would be disruptive, the observer may try to find the teacher later in the day, ask an administrator who might know the answers, or, if unable to make a determination (which is rare), base the holistic impression on other classrooms.

In each of the classes, the observer uses a Notes form to record impressions. The form includes spaces to record information about the classroom visit (date, school, time in, time out, subject, grade, SOM number, etc.) but never anything that could possibly identify the teacher (e.g., name or room number). The Notes form lists each of the 24 strategies/events, with a place to check whether or not it was observed during the 15 minutes and adjacent space to record comments about what took place. The primary purpose of the Notes is to provide a written record of each class to support an accurate holistic rating at the end of the school visit. Another purpose in some projects is to record qualitative feedback about teaching methods (not about individual teachers) that may be communicated to the school as a supplement to the formal data summary to be described.

Data Summary Form

Once the 3-hour visit is completed, the observer is expected to complete the SOM Data Summary Form (Appendix A) as soon as possible. The more time that elapses between the observations and the ratings, the less accurate will be the impressions and recollections of what was seen. As previously indicated, the 3-hour visit should generally yield at least 10 different classroom observations. If, for any reason, the observer has not seen at least eight classes, the visit needs to be extended until that minimum number is attained.

Over the course of the school year, observers will typically make at least 6 visits to a school, although 8–10 are strongly encouraged. The visits should be equally divided between morning and afternoon, and reasonably distributed across different days of the week and times of the year. Each school should be visited by at least two different individuals to reduce the effects of any observer bias, as well as to avoid a situation where the school's final results can be attributed to a single identified observer.

In formative evaluation contexts and where appropriate in research studies, the school receives a summary report once the prescribed number of visits is completed. Typically, the report is received toward the end of the school year. However, in some projects, such as one currently being implemented in Memphis with low-performing schools, intermittent reports are prepared so that results can be discussed and changes made during the year. Appendix B shows a sample report for a school having the pseudonym Clover Valley Elementary. Clover Valley was in the first year of implementing a CSR model that stressed placing greater emphasis on constructivist and learner-centered strategies such as teacher coaching, student discussion, project-based learning, and cooperative learning. As can be seen at the top of Appendix B, 10 total SOM visits were made to Clover Valley. The values indicated in the data matrix show the percentage of times that the individual strategies were classified into each rubric category (frequency/amount of use). For example, upon receiving the report, Clover Valley staff may be disappointed to learn that they are still employing teacher-centered (direct) instruction fairly frequently. Projects were rarely observed in 40% of the visits and occasionally observed in 60%. Hopefully, the school faculty will discuss the results for each item, make decisions, set goals, seek needed professional development in targeted areas, and examine progress when they receive the next report. For research studies, of course, the data will be treated as frequencies or ordinal scores in descriptive and inferential analyses.

Training Program

Permission or license to use SOM is granted only for observers who have successfully completed formal training provided by the Center for Research in Educational Policy (CREP) at the University of Memphis. The training lasts 1 whole day using the following illustrative structure:

8:30–9:30:	Overview, observation/rating procedures
9:30–11:15:	Definition of SOM strategies/events
11:15–12:15:	Video simulation practice
1:15–2:45:	Practice at a school
2:45–3:15:	Review

At the beginning of the training session, each participant receives a detailed training manual that reviews all procedures and strategy definitions. Observers are told to bring the manual on all school visits, regardless of their experience and expertise in using SOM. The school practice session consists of dividing the trainees into groups of two to four individuals and the total time into five 15-minute observations. After completing the fifth observation, each group is given the opportunity to compare impressions and receive clarification and feedback from the trainer in a whole-group review session. An additional requirement in most projects is that trainees complete their first actual SOM with a partner, filling out the ratings forms separately, comparing ratings, and then completing a *consensual* form to turn in as the results. If any questions arise at that session or subsequently, the observers can receive feedback or information from CREP trainers by phone or e-mail. The independent ratings also allow interrater reliability to be formally determined where desired. The process will be described in the next section.

Interrater Reliability

A study of interrater reliability was conducted by Lewis, Ross, and Alberg (1999). Ten pairs of trained observers participated. Each pair consisted of a faculty researcher and one of four experts in SOM from CREP. At least one member of each pair had extensive experience in using the COM (Ross et al., 1994) to record classroom observations.

Pairs conducted joint observations of approximately 10 classrooms in Memphis City schools, independently completing the Notes forms and subsequently the Data Summary form. After completing the summary, the observers discussed areas where they disagreed and then completed a consensual summary form for actual use by the school. The original, independently completed summaries were collected unchanged by the experienced member of the pair and submitted for the reliability analysis.

Difference score analyses were performed to determine the percentage of times that the two observers agreed with one another or demonstrated disagreement by one, two, or more rubric categories. Results indicated that there was perfect agreement on 67.7% of the ratings. Agreement within one category occurred 93.8% of the time and within two categories 100% of the time. In addition, a simple bivariate correlation was run for each pair of observers across all items. The resultant correlations ranged from .679 to .968, with a median of .762.

Individual item analyses showed high interobserver agreement on all items except five: (a) cooperative learning (seemingly due to definitional confusion); (b) ability grouping (due to the difficulty of recognizing such structures; (c) higher-level instructional feedback (due to confusing routine feedback with higher-level feedback); (d) sustained writing (due to confusion about routine vs. true sustained writing); and (e) teacher acting as coach or facilitator (due to the difficulty of distinguishing between routine monitoring and active coaching and support). Training in these and other selected areas was then strengthened to provide more examples and clarification. Based on the overall results and the judgments of the review panel regarding content, SOM was considered to have sufficiently high reliability and validity for use as a research and evaluation tool.

ILLUSTRATIVE APPLICATIONS

In this section, we review four recent projects in which the SOM was used to collect data about classroom teaching strategies. We present actual results from some studies to illustrate the type of information obtained. First, we describe a large-scale formative evaluation process intended to provide information to individual schools implementing CSR designs.

CSRD Formative Evaluation Process

Starting in the fall of 1999, approximately 2,000 schools nationwide received federal funding of at least $50,000 per year for 3 years to implement CSR designs (see Doherty, 2000). In collaboration with a regional educational laboratory (AEL), CREP developed a formative evaluation process designed to provide schools with information to help them assess and improve their design implementation. Table 7.1. shows summary data from the first full year of evaluation for 103 elementary CSRD schools (totaling 819 SOM visits) in five states: Georgia, Kentucky, Tennessee, Virginia, and West Virginia.

Although each school received an individual report comparable to that shown in Appendix B, the summary results reveal the degree to which the different strategies were evidenced in the population. For the vast majority of these schools, the adopted CSR designs stressed placing greater emphasis on student-centered teaching and higher-order learning. However, the results reveal that many of these methodologies were observed relatively infrequently, whereas direct instruction, a traditional teaching strategy, was seen frequently or extensively in 75% of the school visits. Strategies that many of the schools might want to attend to more often as their design implementations continue include project-based learning (73% not observed), independent inquiry (80%), parent/community involvement (74%), student discussion (58%), performance assessment (65%), and technology as a learning tool (59%). It is encouraging that the majority of classes (57%) were rated as having high academically focused class time, and 95% were perceived to have moderate to high student interest.

The high school results presented in Table 7.2. are a summary of data from 167 visits to 21 schools. Contrary to expectations, the findings indicated that direct instruction (69% frequently or extensively observed) was not more prevalent than in the elementary schools (75%). Nor was independent seatwork (both levels = 46%). Relative to elementary schools, high schools were somewhat less likely to feature work centers, parent/community involvement, and sustained reading but slightly more likely to include project-based learning and independent inquiry. Overall, high schools were not rated as highly as elementary schools in maintaining student interest and attention (26% vs. 43% high interest).

The important use of the data, as previously emphasized, is at the individual school level. Each school has its own design and goals for curriculum and instruction. The expectation is that each school leadership team will compare the SOM results to those goals and share their perceptions and the data with faculty. The culminating product will hopefully be a data-driven plan for professional development and changes in instructional strategy use.

Co-nect Evaluation Study

SOM was employed as a primary data source in an evaluation of uses of the Co-nect design in five Memphis elementary schools (Ross, Lowther, & Plants, 2000b). Co-nect is one of eight CSR designs sponsored by New American Schools (Stringfield, Ross, & Smith, 1996). Key instructional emphases of Co-nect are extensive technology use and integration with the curriculum, project-based learning, and engagement of students in active learning experiences. The research design grouped the Co-nect schools into two socioeconomic (SES) strata, one ($n = 3$) that served very high percentages (86–94%) of disadvantaged children and another ($n = 2$) serving relatively low percentages (39–40%). Within each

TABLE 7.1. *SOM Data Summary (103 CSRD Elementary Schools), 1999–2000 (N = 819)*

The extent to which each of the following was used or present in the school . . .	Percentage None	Percentage Rarely	Percentage Occasionally	Percentage Frequently	Percentage Extensively
Instructional Orientation					
Direct instruction (lecture)	0%	5%	18%	43%	32%
Team teaching	47%	36%	11%	3%	0%
Cooperative/collaborative learning	34%	35%	19%	7%	2%
Individual tutoring (teacher, peer, aide, adult volunteer)	43%	33%	13%	6%	1%
Classroom Organization					
Ability groups	33%	23%	16%	16%	8%
Multiage grouping	51%	19%	12%	9%	4%
Work centers (for individuals or groups)	31%	36%	20%	7%	1%
Instructional Strategies					
Higher-level instructional feedback (written or verbal) to enhance student learning	13%	17%	23%	27%	17%
Integration of subject areas (interdisciplinary/ thematic units)	57%	29%	8%	2%	1%
Project-based learning	73%	18%	5%	0%	0%
Use of higher-level questioning strategies	28%	34%	23%	9%	2%
Teacher acting as a coach/facilitator	16%	25%	26%	19%	10%
Parent/community involvement in learning activities	74%	19%	2%	1%	0%

Student Activities					
Independent seatwork (self-paced worksheets, individual assignments)	2%	14%	34%	33%	13%
Experiential, hands-on learning	31%	41%	19%	5%	1%
Systematic individual instruction (differential assignments geared to individual needs)	67%	23%	6%	1%	0%
Sustained writing/composition (self-selected or teacher-generated topics)	52%	36%	8%	1%	0%
Sustained reading	40%	37%	13%	5%	1%
Independent inquiry/research on the part of students	80%	14%	2%	0%	0%
Student discussion	58%	24%	8%	3%	3%
Technology Use					
Computer for instructional delivery (e.g., CAI, drill & practice)	49%	33%	11%	2%	0%
Technology as a learning tool or resource (e.g., Internet research, spreadsheet or database creation, multimedia, CD ROM, Laser disk)	59%	28%	9%	1%	0%
Assessment					
Performance assessment strategies	65%	20%	7%	4%	0%
Student self-assessment (portfolios, individual record books)	74%	14%	6%	1%	0%

Summary Items	Low	Moderate	High
Academically focused class time	2%	39%	57%
Level of student attention/interest/engagement	3%	52%	43%

TABLE 7.2. *SOM Data Summary (21 CSRD High Schools), 1999–2000 (N = 167)*

The extent to which each of the following was used or present in the school …	Percentage None	Percentage Rarely	Percentage Occasionally	Percentage Frequently	Percentage Extensively
Instructional Orientation					
Direct instruction (lecture)	0%	9%	19%	50%	19%
Team teaching	87%	11%	0%	0%	0%
Cooperative/collaborative learning	29%	47%	16%	6%	0%
Individual tutoring (teacher, peer, aide, adult volunteer)	48%	29%	16%	5%	0%
Classroom Organization					
Ability groups	41%	24%	9%	12%	9%
Multiage grouping	29%	18%	22%	25%	4%
Work centers (for individuals or groups)	51%	36%	10%	1%	0%
Instructional Strategies					
Higher-level instructional feedback (written or verbal) to enhance student learning	10%	22%	31%	26%	8%
Integration of subject areas (interdisciplinary/thematic units)	60%	33%	4%	0%	0%
Project-based learning	49%	35%	11%	1%	0%
Use of higher-level questioning strategies	21%	50%	23%	3%	0%
Teacher acting as a coach/facilitator	14%	26%	37%	18%	3%
Parent/community involvement in learning activities	93%	5%	0%	0%	0%

Student Activities					
Independent seatwork (self-paced worksheets, individual assignments)	3%	16%	34%	37%	9%
Experiential, hands-on learning	24%	48%	22%	3%	1%
Systematic individual instruction (differential assignments geared to individual needs)	76%	21%	1%	0%	0%
Sustained writing/composition (self-selected or teacher-generated topics)	61%	29%	6%	1%	0%
Sustained reading	59%	34%	4%	1%	0%
Independent inquiry/research on the part of students	61%	29%	7%	0%	0%
Student discussion	47%	32%	15%	3%	0%
Technology Use					
Computer for instructional delivery (e.g., CAI, drill & practice)	47%	44%	7%	0%	0%
Technology as a learning tool or resource (e.g., Internet research, spreadsheet or database creation, multimedia, CD ROM, Laser disk)	32%	43%	22%	1%	0%
Assessment					
Performance assessment strategies	55%	35%	7%	0%	0%
Student self-assessment (portfolios, individual record books)	77%	19%	2%	0%	0%

	Low	Moderate	High
Summary Items			
Academically focused class time	6%	48%	44%
Level of student attention/interest/engagement	6%	65%	26%

stratum, two Control schools were matched to the Co-nect schools for comparison purposes. Outcome data consisted of SOM, a supplementary computer observation form (see the following discussion), school climate, and a teacher questionnaire.

In the Co-nect study, eight SOM visits were made to each school by unbiased observers. As an illustration of one type of analysis performed, Table 7.3 presents the percentage of times that each of the SOM strategies was observed or not observed (rating categories 1–4 collapsed) in Co-nect versus Control schools. Significant differences favored Co-nect schools over the Control schools on project-based learning (75% observed vs. 44%), computer as a learning tool (75% vs. 31%), and use of the computer for instruction (45% vs. 16%). In subsequent analyses using the full five-category rubric, the significant differences were extended to sustained writing and independent inquiry. Control classes, however, were significantly higher on team teaching and the more traditional strategies of direct instruction and seatwork. These results helped to substantiate the impacts of the design on changing classroom instruction in the directions desired, outcomes that had previously been supported only through anecdotal evidence.

Two additional aspects of the study merit special attention. One is that when analyses were performed separately by SES stratum, the differences favoring Co-nect were much stronger for the low-SES grouping, including a significant advantage in student interest and engagement. These schools face many challenges including high student and teacher mobility, low parent involvement, and lack of educational resources for students outside of school. Apparently, the Co-nect teachers in the low-SES schools were taking the design implementation quite seriously and changing the ways they were teaching and managing their classrooms to increase learner involvement and activity.

A second special feature of the study was combining SOM with a companion instrument, the Survey of Computer Use (SCU; Lowther & Ross, 1999). The SCU is designed to capture specifically student access to and use of computers with regard to activities, type of technology, software use, student skills and engagement, and meaningfulness of the experience for enhancing learning. Not surprisingly, given the focus of Co-nect and the overall SOM findings on the two technology items, SCU results showed Co-nect students to be more active computer users than Control students on a variety of SCU indicators. This application, along with others to be described, illustrates how SOM can be supplemented to focus more specifically on teaching strategies or events of interest using the same classroom visitation schedule and identical time commitment.

TABLE 7.3. *Percentage of Times an Event Was Observed (1–4) versus Not Observed (0) in the Co-nect Study*

	Co-nect		Control	
Strategies	Observed	Not Observed	Observed	Not Observed
Direct instruction*	95.0%	5.0%	100.0%	0.0%
Independent seatwork*	85.0%	15.0%	100.0%	0.0%
Use of higher-level questioning	80.0%	20.0%	68.8%	31.3%
Higher-level instructional feedback	77.5%	22.5%	78.1%	21.9%
Hands-on learning	77.5%	22.5%	65.6%	34.4%
Teacher as facilitator	77.5%	22.5%	84.4%	15.6%
Computer as a tool***	75.0%	25.0%	31.3%	68.8%
Project-based learning**	75.0%	25.0%	43.8%	56.3%
Cooperative learning	72.5%	27.5%	65.6%	34.4%
Sustained writing/ composition	67.5%	32.5%	46.9%	53.1%
Work centers	60.0%	40.0%	43.8%	56.3%
Student discussion	60.0%	40.0%	46.9%	53.1%
Sustained reading	55.0%	45.0%	56.3%	43.8%
Computer for instructional delivery**	45.0%	55.0%	15.6%	84.4%
Integration of subject areas	42.5%	57.5%	37.5%	62.5%
Independent inquiry/ research	35.0%	65.0%	15.6%	84.4%
Performance assessment	27.5%	72.5%	43.8%	56.3%
Individual tutoring	15.0%	85.0%	18.8%	81.3%
Ability groups	15.0%	85.0%	21.9%	78.1%
Student self-assessment	15.0%	85.0%	18.8%	81.3%
Parent/community involvement	12.5%	87.5%	18.8%	81.3%
Systematic individual instruction	5.0%	95.0%	3.1%	96.9%
Multiage grouping	5.0%	95.0%	0.0%	100.0%
Team teaching*	2.5%	97.5%	15.6%	84.4%

*$p < .05$. **$p < .01$. ***$p < .001$.

Schools for Thought Study

The focus of the next illustrative study was outcomes of the Schools for Thought (SFT) model that was implemented at 21 schools in the Metropolitan Nashville School District (Ross, Lowther, & Plants, 2000a). SFT is part of an international project that emphasizes teaching and learning based on deep disciplinary knowledge, skill development, authentic problems, feedback and reflection, and social structures that encourage learning.

The school district was exploring the use of SFT for teacher professional development to engender learning activities such as higher-order thinking, reflection, inquiry, and technology use. A key question was whether SFT classrooms would actually reflect such processes and look different than conventional classrooms. As in the Co-nect study just described, the SCU was employed in combination with SOM to assess technology applications in more detail.

Two other features were unique to the SFT study. First, an additional supplement to SOM – the Extended Rubric – was developed to provide more explicit data regarding the following six classroom practices emphasized by SFT: cooperative learning, project-based learning, higher-level questioning, experiential learning, independent inquiry/research, and discussion. Each of the six rubric items was written as a 5-point scale, with 1 indicating a very low level of application and 5 representing a high level of application (both with corresponding verbal descriptions). The second special study feature was using SOM in targeted SFT versus Control classrooms rather than surveying a random sample of classrooms within the school. For this purpose, observers remained in the selected classrooms for a full 90 minutes and completed a slightly modified form of the SOM rubric for each classroom. The modification basically involved judging the degree to which the particular classroom employed each SOM strategy. Therefore, classroom rather then school visits served as the units of analysis. The SCU and the Extended Rubric were also used to provide targeted classroom observations as part of the 90-minute SOM visit.

SOM results depicted SFT classrooms as much more active places than Control classrooms, characterized by greater use of technology and strategies that engendered higher-order learning through questioning and feedback. Specifically, 15 out of 26 comparisons yielded statistically significant differences. Of these, only one – independent seatwork – favored the Control group. Those associated with effect sizes of +.40 or higher (suggesting educationally meaningful differences) were student engagement, higher-level questioning, higher-level instructional feedback, technology as a tool, independent inquiry, and teacher as a facilitator. The strongest effect for all comparisons was that favoring SFT in student attention/interest/engagement. Results on the Extended Rubric further showed significant and strong advantages of four out of the six strategies, especially cooperative learning and higher-order questioning.

Program monitors from the United States Department of Education, who provided funding for the SFT project, were naturally interested in the degree to which SFT might have raised student achievement relative to that attained with traditional teaching. Unfortunately, there were too few SFT and Control classes to perform a valid test of achievement effects. The classroom observation data thus served a highly important function by showing that apparently positive changes in teaching and learning were in fact occurring. The very positive assessment given to the evaluation (and to the project overall) by the sponsors corroborated the credibility and importance of using observation data to assess program impacts.

Laptop Study

A fourth recent application of SOM was in a research study (Ross, Lowther, Plants, & Morrison, 2000) to determine the impacts of a student laptop project on classroom instruction and learning. The program involved providing fifth- and sixth-grade students with continual access to laptop computers to use at school and at home. Altogether, 32 Laptop classrooms and 18 Control classrooms were examined. The Laptop classrooms were equipped with wireless access to the Internet and printers. Laptop teachers received 10 full days of professional development prior to the academic year and six half-day sessions during the year. Students and parents also had the opportunity to receive training in basic computer skills.

As in the Challenge Grant study just described, SOM was used, following the targeted classroom procedure (this time for 60 minutes per class) rather than the whole-school survey approach. Another similarity was combining SOM with the SCU to obtain more specific data regarding computer applications. Other measures included a writing sample for Laptop and Control students, as well as interviews and questionnaires administered to students, teachers, and parents.

Results showed significant differences favoring Laptop over Control teachers on project-based learning (65% observed vs. 22%), independent inquiry/research (58% vs. 24%), computer use for instructional delivery (22% vs. 0%), higher-level instructional feedback (61% vs. 39%), and computer as a learning tool (88% vs. 17%). In general, strategies promoting learner activity, such as cooperative learning, inquiry, sustained writing, and computer use, were more prevalent and emphasized in Laptop classrooms. Complementary SCU results further revealed that Laptop classes provided significantly greater access to computers and associated peripheral equipment to develop higher skill levels in students, to engage students and teachers more extensively in computer applications, to use computers more for research and production in writing and design, to make greater use of word processing and Internet software, and to make more meaningful use of computers for learning.

Significant differences favoring Laptop students were also found in the writing sample. This result is important, suggesting a learning advantage of the Laptop program. The credibility of this finding is further supported by SOM and SCU ratings, by qualitative data, and by increased and intensive engagement in writing activity among Laptop students.

IMPLICATIONS OF PRESENT WORK AND FUTURE DIRECTIONS

As illustrated in the preceding examples, although SOM is a relatively new instrument, it is currently receiving extensive and varied use in school-based evaluations and research studies. As a formative evaluation tool, it provides schools and districts with descriptive information about the degree to which various teaching strategies are being employed in typical classrooms. The validity and usefulness of such information has been supported in two ways: (a) the formal reliability testing process (see the preceding description and Lewis et al., 1999) and (b) client feedback, which has been extremely positive and accepting even when results have not confirmed schools' expectations. We feel confident that SOM effectively provides the information that schools need to determine how closely actual practices conform to improvement goals. As a consequence, informed decisions can be made regarding the need for professional development and other types of support for teachers having difficulty using certain strategies. We are less certain at this time, however, about how well the majority of schools will actually engage in reflective analyses of the data and associated improvement planning. If the latter processes prove more challenging than anticipated, an important extension of SOM will be the development of support material and training to guide schools through data interpretation and decision-making processes.

As the described evaluations are intended to illustrate, SOM can be a critical source of data regarding the impacts of school programs. At the time that each study was conducted, it was not reasonable to assess student achievement effects due to the unavailability of appropriate test data, the inability to conduct valid program-control group comparisons, and/or the lack of opportunity for the program to impact student learning to a measurable degree. To maintain support at their present schools and expand to others, all three programs (Co-nect, SFT, and Laptop) will need to demonstrate convincingly that they improve student learning noticeably and substantively. In the meantime, the SOM results, where they occur in the desired directions, can be presented to stakeholders as supportive information that the programs are favorably impacting classroom teaching. Specifically, in the case of Co-nect, the evaluation study will prove valuable as positive evidence in national syntheses of CSR design outcomes and benefits (e.g., see Herman, 1999). For SFT, as previously described, the observation data made a positive impression on Office of Educational Research and Improvement (OERI) program sponsors at a culminating project review. Of equal importance, local school board members were sufficiently impressed by SOM's documentation of active teaching methods to promote the expansion of SFT in the district and its central role in future professional development programs. The Laptop study report was disseminated publicly to the school board and local media in October 2000. The result was favorable national and local publicity highlighting the classroom observation findings and a decision by the school board to expand the program for the following year.

Extending beyond the implications of individual studies are the collective perspectives that SOM is providing about teaching and learning in America's classrooms. For over 3,000 classrooms in a single year, our ratings data and observers' qualitative impressions reveal an overwhelming reliance on teacher-centered methods involving lecture and recitation. These impressions are fairly consistent across all grades and core subjects. The key question, of course, is how these methods affect student achievement. Some of the schools that predominantly use traditional methods show very positive results, but other schools perform poorly. Whether increasing reliance on other methods (such as cooperative learning, projects, etc.) will raise student achievement remains to be determined both globally and site by site.

As Tables 7.1 and 7.2 reveal, merely implementing a CSR design that emphasizes alternative strategies may not guarantee a quick

TABLE 7.4. *Percentage of Times an Event Was Observed Frequently or Extensively in Three Studies*

	SFT Study		Co-nect Study		Laptop Study	
Strategy	Treatment (36)	Control (36)	Co-nect (40)	Control (32)	Laptop (32)	Control (18)
Direct instruction	29.8%	37.9%	17.5%	50.0%	43.0%	50.0%
Cooperative learning	20.9%	5.6%	10.0%	0.0%	24.1%	11.0%
Higher-level questioning	24.4%	4.2%	7.5%	6.5%	37.5%	22.3%
Computer as a tool	4.2%	1.4%	5.0%	0.0%	65.6%	0.0%
Project-based learning	11.8%	4.9%	17.5%	0.0%	54.9%	16.7%

change from traditional practices. Our recent findings suggest that targeted programs may achieve more success in this regard. Table 7.4 presents a summary of results from the SFT, Co-nect, and Laptop studies, comparing the percentage of times five selected strategies (direct instruction, cooperative learning, higher-level questioning, use of the computer as a tool, and project-based learning) were observed frequently or extensively at program schools versus Control schools. Whereas direct instruction remains fairly common in all contexts (although less so in program schools), the remaining strategies were prevalent only in program schools.

Do classroom practices differ across varied school contexts? Our preliminary findings from the aforementioned research, including a recent study of 38 CSRD schools in SERVE's six-state region (Lowther, Smith, Ross, & Alberg, 2000), suggested that more diversified usage of teaching strategies tended to occur in (a) elementary schools more than middle and high schools, (b) schools having fewer minority students, (c) in schools serving 51–75% disadvantaged students (free or reduced-price lunch), and (d) rural schools. Still, these effects tend to be weak and inconsistent compared to the effects of programs that promote particular practices.

Usage of the SOM to observe teaching in culturally diverse classrooms has several advantages. First, SOM is a survey-type measure that is not biased toward particular strategies or judgmental regarding which interventions are more or less desirable than others for certain types of students. Consequently, an accurate picture can be obtained about what types of teaching take place in typical classroom contexts and the degree to which changes occur over time. Second, using SOM to provide first impressions in formative (or pilot summative) evaluation studies gives researchers and practitioners a clearer sense of the "playing field" prior to designing more targeted evaluation measures. Such is the approach that we directly employed in several of the studies described earlier in this chapter, that is, start with overall SOM observations, learn about the schools and programs of interest, and then determine what to examine more closely using more refined instruments (e.g., the Extended Rubrics and the Survey of Computer Use). For example, we could easily envision researchers in culturally diverse classrooms developing companion instruments that examine in conjunction with SOM visits how cultural differences are addressed in areas such as language, examples and illustrations used, projects, and/or ability groupings. SOM, therefore, provides a useful starting point for developing innovative, targeted observation tools for culturally and linguistically diverse settings. An important result will be increasing understanding of practices that best and least serve the needs of such students, and how to engender appropriate positive changes in the usage of each type.

The planned expansion of our work involves three areas. One is to correlate SOM data with student achievement scores in different districts to determine whether certain practices and changes in teaching orientations are associated with improved student learning. A second is to develop additional supplementary instruments (like the SCU) so that selected strategies can be described in more detail. A third is to develop supportive guidelines and materials to help school faculty and administrators use SOM data for improvement planning. It remains our fundamental belief that there is no simple formula for identifying which collection of teaching strategies will work at a particular school. What we do know is that the *effective* strategies will tend to be those that best foster learner engagement in academically relevant events. School staff need to have the central roles in (a) determining which instructional approaches are most consistent with their goals and talents, (b) evaluating their success in using those strategies, and (c) making decisions for improvement based on reliable and meaningful data. SOM has thus far shown strong potential to support these purposes.

Suggestions for Use

Based on the preceding descriptions of SOM's development, validation, and usage, we would like to conclude by reinforcing appropriate
applications. SOM should be employed where there is an interest in de-
picting *to what degree* or *how frequently* the targeted classroom strategies
are used across an entire school. Although it is possible to employ SOM
in a single classroom (i.e., making the teacher rather than the school the
unit of study), such applications still pertain only to frequency of usage,
not to effectiveness or quality. If teachers feel they are being evaluated in
the latter ways, it will change their receptivity to observation and willingness to display routine behaviors. Another possible misuse of SOM is
violating the need to visit random classrooms rather than ones selected
for convenience or by the schools. A third and perhaps most critical
misuse is to employ individuals who have not been certified as trained
observers. The value of SOM and of any other observation instrument
strongly depends on obtaining meaningful and reliable data.

References

Bodilly, S. J. (1996). *Lessons from New American Schools Development Corporation's
demonstration phase*. Santa Monica, CA: RAND Corp.

Dalton, S. S. (1998). *Pedagogy matters: Standards for effective teaching practice*
(Research Report No. 4). Santa Cruz: Center for Research on Education,
Diversity & Excellence, University of California.

Doherty, K. M. (2000). *Early implementation of the Comprehensive School Reform
Demonstration (CSRD) program* (Summary Report). Washington, DC: U.S.
Department of Education, Office of Under Secretary, Planning and Evalua-
tion Service, Elementary and Secondary Division.

Good, T., & Brophy, J. (1987). *Looking in classrooms* (4th ed.). New York: Harper &
Row.

Herman, R. (1999). *An educators' guide to schoolwide reform*. Arlington, VA: Educational Research Service.

Herman, R., & Stringfield, S. (1995). *The promising programs for educating disadvantaged students: Evidence of impact*. Paper presented at the annual meeting of
the American Educational Research Association, San Francisco.

International Reading Association and National Council of Teachers of English.
(1996). *Standards for the English language arts*. Newark, DE: International Reading Association.

Levin, H. (1993). *Learning from accelerated schools*. Unpublished paper, Stanford
University.

Lewis, E. M., Ross, S. M., & Alberg, M. (1999). *School Observation Measure:
Reliability analysis*. Memphis, TN: Center for Research in Educational Policy,
University of Memphis.

Lowther, D. L., & Ross, S. M. (1999). *Survey of computer use*. Memphis, TN: Center for Research in Educational Policy, University of Memphis.

Lowther, D. L., Smith, L. J., Ross, S. M., & Alberg, M. J. (2000). *SERVE Intensive research study of comprehensive school reform implementation for the southeast region* (Summary Report Year 1). Memphis, TN: Center for Research in Educational Policy, University of Memphis.

Natriello, G., & McDill, E. L. (1999). Title I: From funding mechanism to educational reform. In G. Orfield & E. H. DeBray (Eds.), *Hard work for good schools: Facts not fads in Title I reform* (pp. 31–45). Cambridge, MA: The Civil Rights Project, Harvard University.

Ross, S. M., Alberg, M., & Wang, L. W. (1998). *The impacts of alternative school restructuring designs on at-risk learners: A longitudinal study* (Progress Report to U.S. Department of Education of At-Risk Students). Memphis, TN: Center for Research in Educational Policy, University of Memphis.

Ross, S. M., Lowther, D. L., & Plants, R. T. (2000a). *Challenge grant evaluation: Final report*. Memphis, TN: Center for Research in Educational Policy, University of Memphis.

Ross, S. M., Lowther, D. L., & Plants, R. T. (2000b). *The impact of the Co-nect design on classroom instruction and school climate in five Memphis schools*. Memphis, TN: Center for Research in Educational Policy, University of Memphis.

Ross, S. M., Lowther, D. L., Plants, R. T., & Morrison, G. R. (2000). *Final evaluation of the Anytime, Anywhere Learning Laptop program*. Memphis, TN: Center for Research in Educational Policy, University of Memphis.

Ross, S. M., Sanders, W. L., Wright, S. P., Stringfield, S., Wang, L. W., & Alberg, M. (2001). Two- and three-year achievement results from the Memphis restructuring initiative. *School Effectiveness and School Improvement, 12,* 323–346.

Ross, S. M., Smith, L. J., & Alberg, M. (1999). *The School Observation Measure*. Memphis, TN: Center for Research in Educational Policy, University of Memphis.

Ross, S. M., Smith, L. J., Lohr, L. L., & McNelis, M. J. (1994). Math and reading instruction in tracked first-grade classes. *The Elementary School Journal, 95*(1), 105–109.

Stringfield, S., Datnow, A., & Ross, S. (1998). *Scaling up school restructuring in multicultural, multilingual contexts: Early observations from Sunland County* (Research Report No. 2). Santa Cruz: Center for Research on Education, Diversity & Excellence, University of California.

Stringfield, S. C., Ross, S. M., & Smith, L. J. (1996). *Bold plans for school restructuring: The New American Schools designs*. Mahwah, NJ: Erlbaum.

APPENDIX A: The School Observation Measure (SOM) Data
Summary Form

School Name: _____ Observer Name: _____

Date of Observation: _____ SOM # _____ Observer Role/Affiliation: _____

Number of classroom observations comprising this SOM: _____

Directions: Use your class-specific notes to reflect upon the extent to which each of the following is present in the school:

	0 - Not observed	1 - Rarely	2 - Occasionally	3 - Frequently	4 - Extensively
Instructional Orientation					
Direct instruction (lecture)	O	O	O	O	O
Team teaching	O	O	O	O	O
Cooperative/collaborative learning	O	O	O	O	O
Individual tutoring (teacher, peer, aide, adult volunteer)	O	O	O	O	O
Classroom Organization					
Ability groups	O	O	O	O	O
Multiage grouping	O	O	O	O	O
Work centers (for individuals or groups)	O	O	O	O	O
Instructional Strategies					
Higher-level instructional feedback (written or verbal) to enhance student learning	O	O	O	O	O
Integration of subject areas (interdisciplinary/thematic units)	O	O	O	O	O
Project-based learning	O	O	O	O	O
Use of higher-level questioning strategies	O	O	O	O	O
Teacher acting as a coach/facilitator	O	O	O	O	O
Parent/community involvement in learning activities	O	O	O	O	O
Student Activities					
Independent seatwork (self-paced worksheets, individual assignments)	O	O	O	O	O
Experiential, hands-on learning	O	O	O	O	O
Systematic individual instruction (differential assignments geared to individual needs)	O	O	O	O	O
Sustained writing/composition (self-selected or teacher-generated topics)	O	O	O	O	O
Sustained reading	O	O	O	O	O
Independent inquiry/research on the part of students	O	O	O	O	O
Student discussion	O	O	O	O	O

Technology Use

Computer for instructional delivery (e.g., CAI, drill & practice)	O	O	O	O	O
Technology as a learning tool or resource (e.g., Internet research, spreadsheet or database creation, multimedia, CD ROM, Laser disk)	O	O	O	O	O

Assessment

Performance assessment strategies	O	O	O	O	O
Student self-assessment (portfolios, individual record books)	O	O	O	O	O

Summary Items $1 = Low, 2 = Moderate, 3 = High$

Academically focused class time	O	O	O
Level of student attention/interest/engagement	O	O	O

Rubric for SOM Scoring

(0) Not Observed:	Strategy was never observed.
(1) Rarely:	Observed in only one or two classes. Receives isolated use and/or little time in classes.
	Clearly not a prevalent/emphasized component of teaching and learning across classes.
(2) Occasionally:	Observed in some classes. Receives minimal or modest time or emphasis in classes.
	Not a prevalent/emphasized component of teaching and learning across classes.
(3) Frequently:	Observed in many but not all classes. Receives substantive time or emphasis in classes.
	A prevalent component of teaching and learning across classes.
(4) Extensively:	Observed in most or all classes. Receives substantive time and/or emphasis in classes.
	A highly prevalent component of teaching and learning across classes.

APPENDIX B: Sample SOM Summary Report

SOM Data Summary: Clover Valley Elementary School (N = 10), 1999– 2000

The extent to which each of the following was used or present in the school . . .	Percentage None	Percentage Rarely	Percentage Occasionally	Percentage Frequently	Percentage Extensively
Instruction Orientation					
Direct instruction (lecture)	0%	0%	10%	40%	50%
Team teaching	100%	0%	0%	0%	0%
Cooperative/collaborative learning	0%	20%	80%	0%	0%
Individual tutoring (teacher, peer, aide, adult volunteer)	60%	40%	0%	0%	0%
Classroom Organization					
Ability groups	80%	20%	0%	0%	0%
Multiage grouping	20%	60%	20%	0%	0%
Work centers (for individuals or groups)	0%	70%	30%	0%	0%
Instructional Strategies					
Instructional feedback (written or verbal) to enhance student learning	20%	0%	80%	0%	0%
Integration of subject areas (interdisciplinary/ thematic units	80%	20%	0%	0%	0%
Project-based learning	0%	40%	60%	0%	0%
Use of higher-level questioning strategies	0%	30%	60%	10%	0%
Teacher acting as a coach/ facilitator	0%	60%	40%	0%	0%
Parent/community involvement in learning activities	100%	0%	0%	0%	0%
Student Activities					
Independent seatwork (self-paced worksheets, individual assignments)	0%	0%	80%	20%	0%
Experiential, hands-on learning	0%	100%	0%	0%	0%
Systematic individual instruction (differential assignments geared to individual needs)	100%	0%	0%	0%	0%

The extent to which each of the following was used or present in the school ...	Percentage None	Percentage Rarely	Percentage Occasionally	Percentage Frequently	Percentage Extensively
Sustained writing/ composition (self-selected or teacher-generated topics)	0%	100%	0%	0%	0%
Sustained reading	20%	60%	20%	0%	0%
Independent inquiry/ research on the part of students	75%	25%	0%	0%	0%
Student discussion	80%	20%	0%	0%	0%
Technology Use					
Computer for instructional delivery (e.g., CAI, drill & practice)	100%	0%	0%	0%	0%
Technology as a learning tool or resource (e.g., Internet research, spreadsheet or database creation, multimedia, CD ROM, Laser disk)	20%	20%	60%	0%	0%
Assessment					
Performance assessment strategies	100%	0%	0%	0%	0%
Student self-assessment (portfolios, individual record books)	100%	0%	0%	0%	0%

Summary Items	Low	Moderate	High
Academically focused class time	0%	100%	0%
Level of student attention/ interest/engagement	0%	100%	0%

8

Observing School Restructuring in Multilingual, Multicultural Classrooms

Balancing Ethnographic and Evaluative Approaches

Amanda Datnow and Susan Yonezawa

The goal of this chapter is to discuss a methodology for conducting classroom observations in culturally and linguistically diverse schools implementing externally developed reform designs. The classroom observation strategy discussed in this chapter was developed for a study entitled *Scaling Up School Restructuring in Multicultural, Multilingual Contexts*.[1] In this study, we conducted longitudinal case studies of 13 elementary schools in Sunland County Public Schools (SCPS),[2] each of which was implementing one or more nationally regarded school reform designs.

Assessments of such reform models have become particularly important as the number of schools implementing these models has increased dramatically in the past few years. The passage of the Obey–Porter law, a bipartisan initiative that allocated 150 million federal dollars in the fall of 1998 (and additional funds in subsequent years) to schools willing to adopt research-based reform programs, is evidence of the growing enthusiasm for external models. This was spurred in part by research suggesting that scaling up externally developed school reform models or *promising programs* may be the best way to systematically raise students' academic achievement (Stringfield et al., 1997).

However, we know little about how these reforms can be implemented successfully in districts serving linguistically and culturally diverse student populations. Many externally developed school reform models were developed mindful of schools serving students who speak English as a first language. None of the models was developed specifically for multicultural, multilingual student populations. Exito para

174

Todos, the Spanish version of *Success for All*, is the only reform model designed specifically for non-English-speaking students.

Yet children of color currently constitute the majority in 25 of the largest school districts in the country. Many of these students have pan-ethnic backgrounds and do not speak English as their first language. The majority of these students are from Hispanic and Asian countries that produce a steady flow of immigrants each year; however, immigration from Africa, South America, and the Middle East is also on the rise. Collectively, these groups are changing the face of American education (*Here They Come*, 1986, in Davidson & Phelan, 1993; President's Initiative on Race, 1997). The question is: Can the externally developed reform models being proposed serve these students effectively? If so, how? Our study fills an important gap in the literature by examining the implementation and effects of scaling up reform models in schools currently serving linguistically and culturally diverse student populations.

Most prior studies of externally developed school reform models or programs have used an approach to conducting classroom observations that is grounded in the methods of program evaluation and/or educational psychology. These studies, conducted in the objectivist paradigm, have employed data collection instruments that allow the observer to both assess the fidelity of implementation and measure the effects of a program on students at the classroom level. For example, the Dissemination Efforts Supporting School Improvement (DESSI) study comparing four school change strategies used a *practice profile* that listed the program elements as intended and allowed for assessment of the extent to which those elements were present in the observed setting (Loucks & Crandall, 1981; Scheirer, 1996). The DESSI researchers also conducted limited ethnographic observations of classrooms. The Follow Through Classroom Observation Evaluation (Stallings & Kaslowitz, 1974), which compared several innovative programs through a quasi-experimental design, employed low-inference classroom observations in their attempt to assess whether models were in accordance with design specification and what their effects were on children. The Urban and Suburban/Rural Special Strategies study of promising programs for disadvantaged students used both low-inference observations and *whole school day* shadowing of students to determine the relative effectiveness of externally versus locally developed reform efforts (Stringfield et al., 1997). These studies have contributed significantly to our understanding of the implementation and effects of various school reform models or programs.

At the same time, ethnographic studies (e.g., Fine, 1991; Heath, 1983; Metz, 1978; Rose, 1989) of schools or classrooms composed of students from diverse racial, ethnic, and linguistic groups have contributed to an understanding of the schooling experiences of these students. Ethnographic methods in sociology are often allied with the interpretive theoretical traditions of symbolic interactionism and ethnomethodology. Ethnographic studies have urged researchers to look at schools and classrooms as lived cultures and to see teachers and students as active agents negotiating interaction. Evaluations of school programs often now include narrative accounts based on intensive observations (Fetterman, 1984).[3] Moreover, ethnographic studies in the interpretivist tradition have made contributions to theories that attempt to account for social inequality by introducing cultural elements and human agency into these theories and by revealing the reflexive relationship between institutional practices and students' lives in schools (Mehan, 1992).

In understanding the success or failure of school reforms, program evaluators would identify the factors that inhibit or facilitate successful reform implementation. On the other hand, anthropologist or sociologist ethnographers would likely see reform failure or success as located in the sets of relationships that characterize school settings. Second, program evaluators would focus on identifying *best practices* and how efficiently educational reforms meet the goals of improving student achievement. At the same time, ethnographers would focus on what the reforms mean to the participants in the setting or their impact on social life (Smith, 1992).

In our study of school reform in multicultural, multilingual contexts, we drew upon both anthropological approaches and program evaluation/educational psychology approaches as we conducted classroom observations. As we will explain, our eclectic observational methodology is four-pronged and covers the range of observational structures from ethnographic to low-inference. By drawing on multiple paradigms and methodological tools, our classroom observation methodology is distinct. It is also unique in the comprehensive assessment it provides of any individual classroom (which, of course, also means that the various observation instruments take considerable time to complete and analyze) and in its explicit focus on observing school reform activities.

The multimodal method we describe in this chapter, which was informed by the aforementioned methodological research and research on best practices for diverse students (to be discussed later), was designed to gather a variety of observational data so that we could report to the policy community on the effects of the school reform models, as well as illuminate the lived realities of students and educators engaged in reform. We think this is particularly important, given that the students (and, to some extent, the educators) in our study represent racial and linguistic minority groups whose voices may not otherwise be heard in studies of school change (Weis & Fine, 1993).

THE STUDY

The *Scaling Up School Restructuring in Multicultural, Multilingual Contexts* study focused on understanding the effectiveness of various school restructuring designs in improving the achievement of students in schools serving linguistic and ethnic minority students in a multicultural context. In assessing broader issues of the effectiveness of the reforms, the study focused on implementation, curriculum and pedagogy, classroom dynamics, and the impact of reform on the lives of educators, students, and the community. In doing so, we also focused on the broader policy and social and political contexts in which each school was located.

In almost all of the schools, the majority of students were from contexts traditionally regarded as placing the students at risk of educational failure. SCPS provides education to students from a richly diverse set of cultures and language groups. Sunland County has one of the largest second-language populations of any district in the country, with Spanish and Haitian Creole being the most common of over 100 languages and dialects.

Several most commonly used school restructuring models were represented in SCPS. The district received special support from New American Schools (NAS) Corporation to implement several of the NAS designs in multiple sites.[4] The NAS designs we studied in SCPS include (1) Success for All/Roots and Wings, which organizes school resources to ensure that students learn to read and provides detailed descriptions of both how to organize schools and classrooms and what and how to teach (Slavin, Madden, & Wasik, 1996); (2) Modern Red Schoolhouse, which aims to extend and deepen the educational assets embodied in the classic "little red schoolhouse" through an individually paced approach to learning established between a student and his or her parents and teacher, and specific organizational and curricular elements (Heady & Kilgore, 1996); and (3) the Audrey Cohen College System of Education, which redesigns the entire school setting, including its curriculum, to achieve meaningful purposes using a transdisciplinary approach (Cohen & Jordan, 1996). (For detailed descriptions of these designs, see Stringfield, Ross, & Smith, 1996.)

We also studied three independently developed designs (not part of NAS): (1) Core Knowledge Sequence, which provides a detailed curriculum in language arts, history, math, science, and fine arts while leaving issues of pedagogy and school organization to the judgment of the principal and faculty (Core Knowledge Foundation, 1995; Hirsch, 1993); (2) Coalition of Essential Schools (CES), which advocates a total restructuring of traditional school organization, practices, and beliefs through the adoption of nine common principles (Sizer, 1992); and (3) Comer School Development Program, a schoolwide restructuring process to address the needs of the whole child (Comer & Haynes, 1996). Like CES, the Comer model emphasizes organizational processes and guiding principles but does not specify curriculum content.

The SCPS study employed a combination of quantitative and qualitative methods. The quantitative component of the study examined the relationships between implementation level of the restructuring design and academic gains and experimental–control differences in achievement gains over 4 years. The qualitative component involved longitudinal case studies of 13 restructuring elementary schools, which we followed over a 4-year period from 1996 to 2000.

The case study data we gathered at each school included interviews with principals, teachers, parents, and students. We also interviewed district administrators and representatives of the various design teams regarding their perceptions of the conditions affecting successful implementation, as well as parents and students to ascertain their perceptions of the reform models. In addition, we conducted observations of key meetings that related in some way to the reform.

A key component of the case studies was classroom observations. Through observations, we were able to better understand if and how the restructuring models were being implemented and adapted by teachers for use with diverse student populations. They also helped us gather data on the effects of the various models on student engagement, the interaction of students and teachers in the classroom, and, more generally, what characterized classroom instruction and organization in the 13 restructuring schools. It is this simultaneity, or "I was there" quality, that makes these observation data powerful (Guba & Lincoln, 1989, p. 192). In sum, classroom observations allowed us to see inside the black box of schooling (Mehan, 1978) and school reform.

OUR WORKING ASSUMPTIONS

We entered the field with notions of what constituted worthwhile school change efforts and ideas on where and how the process of change might manifest itself. We did so with the intention of giving the study direction and guiding data collection (Bogdan & Biklen, 1982; Greene, 1993; Miles & Huberman, 1984; Yin, 1984). These working assumptions shaped the observational methods we chose and what we looked for in classrooms:

- We believe that classroom events (and reform implementation) are dialectically related to the larger social, political, and policy contexts in which they are located. For example, we looked at the way in which a state-testing mandate shaped instruction.
- Our protocol allowed us to look at the "program as intended" versus the "program as delivered" in a manner that was free of the judgment that the reform is right and any other classroom practice is wrong.
- We made some informed decisions about what constitutes sensible practice based on research on effective practice in culturally and linguistically diverse classrooms and on what we know about the local context of each school.
- We believe in the promotion of modified cultural plurality as opposed to cultural uniformity. We feel that students from linguistically and culturally diverse backgrounds should be encouraged to maintain the integrity and viability of their group identities, but we also believe that students should be encouraged to develop bicultural and bilingual abilities.
- We believe that the most valuable educational changes are those that, in addition to sharpening educational knowledge of teaching and learning, strive for a more equitable, just, and ethical society.

Of course, we recognize that stating our theoretical orientations up front does not relieve us from the weight of our subjectivity throughout the entire research process (Peshkin, 1988). It merely allows us to be systemically aware of its capacity to shape what we see and do not see in classrooms.

OUR ROLE AS RESEARCHERS

Gold's (1958) classic typology of naturalistic observer roles includes the complete participant, the participant-as-observer, the observer-as-participant, and the complete observer (in Adler & Adler, 1994, p. 379). Reflecting more active forms of participation in the research setting, Adler and Adler (1994) outline a more recent typology, which includes the complete-member-researcher, the active-member-researcher, and the peripheral-member-researcher.

We consider ourselves somewhere between complete observers and peripheral-member-researchers. We were not complete observers in the pure sense because we were noticeable in the classroom settings, not observing from the outside. We were also not true peripheral-member-researchers because we did not have an insider's identity in the classroom. Participants in the setting saw us as researchers, not as peripheral members such as parents, coaches, and so on. In this sense, we were akin to what Lofland and Lofland (1995) refer to as *known investigators* – researchers familiar to the participants and free to move about the settings in this capacity as long as standards of common courtesy are observed (i.e., no "snooping or prying") (p. 73).

Our position as known investigators occasionally placed us in a quandary during classroom observations, as our presence could influence the behaviors of teachers and students. Some teachers (and students) viewed us as evaluators and "performed" in our presence. In the case of students, this occasionally meant intentionally "not performing" (e.g., being extra shy) or performing poorly (e.g., acting out). Occasionally, teachers called upon us to interact directly with students by exchanging introductions or participating in impromptu question-and-answer sessions. Teachers used our presence as a reward: "We have someone special here visiting who wants to see all the beautiful work you've been doing." They also used us to impart nebulous threats: "We have visitors today, so you better behave yourself . . . they're here to watch you." In some cases, these interactions had a powerful effect: Students (particularly in elementary schools) often sat up, with hands folded and seats tucked in, and watched us watch them out of the corner of their eyes.

In an effort to minimize the impact of our presence in the classroom, we provided guidance to our research team members on how the classroom observations were to be conducted under ideal circumstances: Enter, introduce yourself quietly to the teacher, ask to observe, position yourself in the room where you can see but are not obvious, take notes, walk around if necessary to verify what is happening in the room, ask clarification questions if needed, issue thanks, and excuse yourself. However, we could not anticipate every possible interaction that might occur. As such, we realize that it would be disingenuous to claim that we had no effect (Sanger, 1996).

The individual members of our research team interpreted the researcher role in various ways, despite attempts to standardize it. At times, the members of our team were confronted with situations that placed their identities as human and research participant observers at cross purposes (Peshkin, 1988), and they were forced to make decisions that corresponded with their individual conscience and commitments, training or background, understanding of the study, and so on. We asked observers to include such interactions in their field notes. For instance, the following is an excerpt from the field notes of an observation in a second-grade classroom:

Manuel recently joined the class several days ago, having just emigrated from Ecuador. The teacher told me that she doesn't think Manuel can communicate in either Spanish or English, and therefore she did not supply him with a book or any of the worksheets that the other students have. She seemed content to just have him sit in his chair doing nothing. She even told one of the other students not to give him one of the worksheets because he won't be able to understand. I felt very bad for this child, who was seated next to me, so I shared my worksheet with him, despite the fact that I knew this may not go over very well with the teacher.

When the teacher held up cards with English words on them for other children (such as the word *number*), he actually read them aloud. The teacher did not take any notice. It is also apparent that Manuel can speak Spanish. When there was a break in the activity, I asked one of his classmates if she ever spoke Spanish with him, and she said no. She then said a few things to Manuel in Spanish and he responds, also in Spanish. It seemed as though the students were mimicking the teacher's exclusionary behavior of Manuel.

This excerpt shows that there are instances in which our observation data were enriched by the observers' decisions to be "human." By taking the risk of working directly with Manuel, the researcher learned a great deal more about him as a student – and about the teacher. (For the purposes of our study, it is also worth noting that the teacher's behavior was not in keeping with the particular reform design's notion of *teacher as facilitator*.)

OUR OBSERVATIONAL DESIGN STRATEGY

During 2-day school site visits annually or biannually over the 4 years of the study, we conducted intensive classroom observations at the first-through fourth-grade levels at each school undertaking reform efforts.

Our study design involved two to three researchers visiting the school each time, each observing in a different classroom for approximately 90 minutes at a time.[5] We deliberately observed academic subjects (reading, math, etc.), as opposed to music, art, or physical education. At schools implementing designs that are subject specific (e.g., *Success for All* for reading), we made sure to observe the subject area(s) targeted by the reform.

Just as there is a range of structure in interviews from questionnaire-driven interviews to unstructured conversations, there is also a range of structure in observations (Merriam, 1988). Usually, researchers elect to conduct all their observations in a similar way, depending on their skills, background, or preference.

Our eclectic observational methodology was four-pronged and covered the range of observational structure: ethnographic to low-inference. This multimodal method was designed to help us gather a variety of observation data within individual classrooms.

Ethnographic Description

This first part of our observational design strategy involved running notes of the classroom activities. This strategy approached a more ethnographic, traditional field note method. Through rich, thick description or *verisimilitude*, we tried to give life to what happened in the classrooms we observed. Our emphasis here was on documenting the sequence of activities (reform-related and otherwise) in the classrooms we observed and paying particular attention to how teachers and students interacted with one another and the meanings they derived from their interactions. We specifically attended to how the cultural and linguistic identities of the participants in the classroom (both teacher and students) affected their interactions. Thus, the skills of the observer were critical in this type of observation, as it was up to her or him to focus on the most important aspects of the class at hand.

The following excerpt from field notes gathered in a *Success for All* classroom (using the English version of the Reading Roots curriculum with a class of mostly second-grade students) is illustrative of this observational strategy:

About 25 minutes into the Roots and Wings reading period, Ms. Berger told the students that today they are going to read a tall tale. She talked to the students about exaggeration and relates the example, "You know, sometimes you say that you're so hungry you could eat a horse." She said the story is about Paul

Bunyan's pancakes. She asked students to define pancakes and discuss what they eat on their pancakes at home. She then handed out copies of the story entitled, "Paul Bunyan's Pancakes," and she asked students to preview it for a few minutes.

[Later in the lesson . . .]

Ms. Berger led the students in reading aloud the "green" words (new vocabulary) from the story, which were listed on a poster. She used the "my turn, your turn" Roots and Wings technique for doing this, soliciting whole group responses. She discussed what these words meant with the students, giving them many opportunities to give their input. One of the words was "sawmill." Ms. Berger asked students if they often saw sawmills in their city. Most students did not. She also asked them to define "boots." This was not a word that the students were very familiar with, as they do not wear boots in this part of the country. These were all vocabulary words from the Paul Bunyan book.

[Later in the lesson . . .]

Ms. Berger then went over the Roots and Wings Treasure Hunt with students. She did the first two questions with them (e.g., "What was Paul Bunyan's job?"). She wrote the answers on the board after soliciting students' responses and then asked students to do the remaining questions in their partner pairs. Some students worked independently even though they were supposed to be working together. The teacher tried hard to circulate and get students working together properly, but she was not successful in all cases. Students then "partner read." Again, this was not effective for all pairs. Some students did not read to each other.

The use of ethnographic description allowed us to see how the reform design was enacted through the interaction between the teacher and students. By recording the sequence of classroom events, we documented the evidence of implementation and captured a sense of what it looked like. We also documented how the interaction between participants in the setting affected implementation. For example, in the preceding field notes, it is evident that although cooperative learning (a key feature of the *Success for All* design) was present, this did not mean that all students actually worked cooperatively in this classroom.

We also saw how, within the course of interaction, the experiences and identities of the people involved were also continually constructed. These identities and experiences of the participants thus shaped the manifestation of the reform design. For instance, the teacher asked students to define the word *boots*. This was clearly a contextually bound adaptation made by the teacher to tailor the instruction to the students' local knowledge. The city in which this school is located has mild weather, and thus students were not familiar with the word *boots*. Overall, the ethnographic descriptions were helpful in giving us a sense of how teachers and students contributed to the social organization of the classroom within the context of the reform (Mehan, 1978).

Reform Design Implementation

The second part of our observation strategy involved an observer's assessment of the reform design's implementation. Here, through a series of directed questions that focused on the key classroom elements of the reform design, we used a template approach to compare the teacher's actual implementation of the design to what is intended by the developers (Scheirer, 1996). This approach helped us avoid erroneous judgments about a design's impact in schools where the design is a nonevent (Charters & Jones, 1973). It helped us discern which aspects of the reform are more or less likely to be implemented across multiple sites, and it allowed for expeditious cross-case comparisons. Most importantly, however, it helped us better understand how some of the philosophical aspects of the designs were manifested within the classroom. These forms were, for obvious reasons, design-specific and were designed with the aid of descriptive reports and articles about each reform.

The reform-specific observation forms varied in length and, in some cases, format, depending on the specificity of the design at the classroom level. In highly specified designs such as *Success for All*, we used a combination of checklists and short-answer, directed items to determine classroom fidelity to the reading program. When observing less specific, more philosophically driven reforms such as Coalition of Essential Schools (CES), we used directed, short-answer questions that asked the researcher to note evidence for or against stated aspects of the design. We also included a section where the observer could record his or her interpretations as to why the observed activities deviated from the model (see the Appendix for an example of the form we used for observations in CES schools).

What follows is an excerpt of reform-design implementation data collected from a CES school. This example shows how one aspect of the CES design, *tone of decency*, was observed in multiple second-grade classrooms at a single school, Cedars Elementary. The classroom data were collected individually and were subsequently collapsed for analysis within schools and across schools implementing the same design.

Was There Evidence That a "Tone of Decency" (Fairness, Generosity, and Tolerance) Existed Among the Students and Between the Teachers and Students?

Cedars – Second-Grade Classroom #1

Morton is fair, generous, and tolerant with the students. However, this modeling does not translate into these traits being exhibited between students. Morton told the children that they should, for example, listen when other students read their journal entries aloud. However, I didn't see anything in Morton that I haven't seen in kind teachers in non-CES classrooms. Moreover, most students did not listen as classmates read their journal entries aloud.

Cedars – Second-Grade Classroom #2

The teacher exhibited fairness, generosity, and tolerance. There was very little interaction between the children however. During the science lesson, in which the students drew the four parts of a plant and then pasted crepe paper on their drawings, there were many opportunities for conversations between the children. There simply were not many exchanges.

Cedars – Second-Grade Classroom #3

Among the students – when a student needed glue, a number of students offered theirs to share. The teacher reminded students that they were there not to criticize one another but to help one another. The teacher was fair in her interactions from what I saw and she provided a good deal of praise to students.

Cedars – Second-Grade Classroom #4

Not really. The class had a flat affect. Students did not really interact with one another nor did the teacher really interact with any of the students.

Cedars – Second-Grade Classroom #5

Students seemed very respectful to one another. They did not laugh at a student who mispronounced words when reading out loud. The teacher helped two students facilitate a problem they were having. The students were told to go to the back of the room and work things out until they could agree on a solution. The students told the teacher they could not reach an agreement so she helped them.

These data show that tone of decency, an element of the CES design, was exhibited in four of the five classrooms between teacher and students but less often among students. In four of the classes, the teacher's actions caused observers to conclude that the class was a decent environment. In two classes, the students behaved in ways that were perceived by the researchers as showing respect and generosity. Yet, interestingly, it was the lack of indecent or ill-mannered acts by students (not teasing or criticizing one another) that suggested to observers that the element was present rather than the presence of new relationships. Also notable was one observer's comment that the actions of teachers encouraging a tone of decency often resembled the actions of educators in non-CES schools, leading us to question the impact of this design element over and above customary teaching practices.

Effective Practices in Culturally Diverse Classrooms

In addition to assessing whether the restructuring model (or some adaptation thereof) was present in the classrooms we observed, we assessed whether the classroom was characterized by effective instructional practices. Here, we used a series of directed questions that were guided by theory and research on what constitutes effective classroom practice for culturally and linguistically diverse students. We answered these questions for all classrooms we observed. This was both a means for us to see whether the design features contributed to these effective practices and a way to see whether teachers incorporated other activities to serve their diverse student populations.

The theory and research that guided these questions were drawn primarily from the work of Cummins (1989), from the principles for effective teaching and learning that guide the Center for Research on Education, Diversity & Excellence (Tharp, 1997), and from Newmann and Wehlage's (1995) research on authentic pedagogy. After conducting an extensive review of the literature, Cummins (1989) concluded that effective programs for linguistically and culturally diverse students have the following process characteristics:

- Allow for the development of students' native linguistic talents
- Foster a sense of personal and cultural identity
- Promote multiculturalism rather than assimilation
- Employ materials relevant for minority students
- Engage students in cooperative learning
- Maintain high expectations for minority and White students
- Promote confidence in ability to learn

What also makes Cummins's research distinctive is that he focuses on student empowerment through cultural pluralism (Fillmore & Meyer, 1992). He is attentive to the need for students of color to have their histories and experiences confirmed by schools rather than disconfirmed (Giroux, 1984). Because we believe this to be a goal of schooling, we were attentive to these issues in our research. However, the tenets that Cummins outlines are effective practices not just for students of color, but for all students.

Tharp's (1997) principles for the effective education of at-risk students focus more directly on pedagogical strategies rooted in sociocultural theory. Tharp characterizes effective classroom instruction as (a) facilitating learning through joint productive activity between teachers and students; (b) developing competence in the language and literacy of instruction throughout all instructional activities; (c) contextualizing teaching and curriculum in the experiences and skills of home and community; (d) challenging students to achieve cognitive complexity; and (e) engaging students through dialogue. Newmann and Wehlage's (1995) definition of authentic pedagogy overlaps considerably with Tharp's principles. They emphasize the importance of involving students in higher-order thinking and substantive conversational exchange, producing complex understandings, and helping students connect substantive knowledge with public problems or personal experiences.

We used the research by Cummins, Tharp, and Newmann and Wehlage to develop a set of questions which noted the designs' overall sensitivity to culturally and linguistically diverse students. These same questions appeared on the form we used for observations with each type of reform (see the Appendix). For example, the following excerpt from collapsed data for one school, Nautilus Elementary, explores the extent to which students were encouraged to use language to understanding the concepts presented:

Did the Teacher(s) Employ a Pedagogy That Motivated Students to Use Language (Either Native or English) to Generate Their Own Understandings? If Yes, Give an Example

Nautilus – Second-Grade Classroom #1
No. Students worked independently on a paper and pencil test, which required them to silently read stories and answer questions about them. No opportunities for students to generate understandings through language were provided.

Nautilus – Second-Grade Classroom #2
Not really. Occasionally, Mr. Smith called on students to say their answers aloud, but this was not a frequent occurrence. However, it is notable that Mr. Smith used a methodology of employing math manipulatives that was helpful for this group of LEP students. Unfortunately, his monitoring of student work was not

very good, and therefore students ended up using the manipulatives as toys rather than learning tools.

Nautilus – Second-Grade Classroom #3

No. Students were called upon to share their answers to the math problems, but they just stated numbers and were not required to explain how they arrived at those answers.

Nautilus – Second-Grade Classroom #4

Yes. Students worked in pairs to use both oral and written language (English) to answer the following questions: What did Paul Bunyan see in the snow? Why did Paul Bunyan cut down trees? This provided a chance for students to dialogue about their own understandings of the story they just read.

These observational data were gathered in four different second-grade classrooms in one school. From these data, we could conclude that second-grade students at this school were often *not* given opportunities to use language to generate their own understandings. In only one of the four classrooms were students provided with such opportunities. This suggests that the generation of understanding through language may not have been an approach used frequently by the teachers at this school. As such, students from culturally and linguistically diverse backgrounds may not have been receiving the most effective forms of instruction, as determined by the research literature.

The Low-Inference Observation

In addition to using the aforementioned strategies, we employed a low-inference classroom observation instrument called the Classroom Observation Measure (COM). We used the COM in order to reduce classroom events to a set of variables so that we could more easily compare classroom practices, extent of implementation, and time on task across designs and schools. The COM allowed us to measure frequencies of teacher and student behaviors.

The COM was developed at the University of Memphis and has been validated using interobserver correlations in extensive pilot research and other studies of elementary school classroom instruction (Ross, Smith, Lohr, & McNelis, 1994). The COM was developed based on a review of observation instruments used in previous studies and includes both interval coding, obtained through systematic and relatively objective data recording, and holistic ratings and descriptions that reflect more global, subjective impressions of the classroom activities observed (Ross et al., 1994). A detailed manual describing the observation procedures and operationally defined categories accompanies the COM, and all observers for the study received training in its use. We modified the COM slightly for the purposes of this study. The COM took about an hour to complete and consisted of the following parts:

> *Parts I and II: Classroom Makeup and Physical Environment.* This section was used to record demographic information about the classroom (class size, racial and gender composition, number of teachers and aides), seating arrangements, and classroom resources.
>
> *Part III: Interval Coding.* This section was used to record observations from nine 1-minute segments coded at 5-minute intervals in the areas of academic subject(s) taught, teacher orientation (e.g., teacher-led, small group), teacher behaviors (e.g., lecturing, facilitating discussion), and student behaviors (e.g., listening, reading). This section also included a measure of time on task, where the observer was asked to estimate the percentage of the students showing interest or focus (all, mostly all, half, very few, none). Finally, this section included a measure of opportunity to learn, where the observer was asked to estimate the percentage of interval time used for an academic (instructional) activity.
>
> *Part IV: Overall Observation.* This section was used to record the extent to which different teaching and learning approaches (e.g., cooperative learning, direct instruction, seatwork, use of a computer) were evident during the overall observation. In order to customize the COM for use in this study of school reform, we added a category to this section, which asked the observer to rate the extent to which there was evidence of the reform design in the observed lesson.
>
> *Part V: Comments.* This section provided space for the observer to record notes of clarification of the observed classroom events.

Results from the COM analysis for *first-grade* classrooms only are presented here, with an emphasis on identifying some of the issues salient to our study. These issues include (a) evidence of reform design observed and (b) teaching and learning approaches observed. The data reported here were collected in 1997, when all of the schools in our study were ostensibly implementing reforms.

Figure 8.1 shows the extent of reform design implementation observed in 1997 in the schools we studied. The figure is organized according to reform design, not according to schools. Therefore, the first-grade

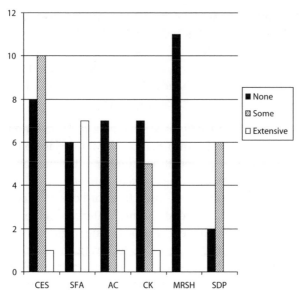

FIGURE 8.1. Extent of reform design observed. CES = Coalition of Essential Schools; SFA = *Success for All*; AC = Audrey Cohen College System of Education; CK = Core Knowledge Sequence; MRSH = Modern Red Schoolhouse; SDP = Comer School Development Program.

classrooms observed in two to three schools are represented in the data reported for each design. The *y*-axis refers to the number of classrooms, and the *x*-axis refers to the reform design type.

Figure 8.1 shows that, with the exception of *Success for All*, none of the designs showed extensive evidence of implementation. One of the reasons for this is that the *Success for All* model is so highly specified that it is either present or absent. Of course, it is possible that teachers could be adapting elements of the model for their classroom, but this was not the case in the schools we observed. Although there were slight modifications overall, the model was being used extensively during reading. It was not surprising to us that class time outside of reading showed no evidence of the reform.

Figure 8.1 also shows that we saw no evidence of reform design implementation in the first-grade classrooms we observed in the Modern Red Schoolhouse schools and little evidence in the Comer SDP schools in our sample. In the case of the Modern Red Schoolhouse schools, this was not surprising, as these schools were still in the reform planning stages during that year and thus the reform had not reached the classroom level (Yonezawa & Datnow, 1999). The Comer SDP schools, on

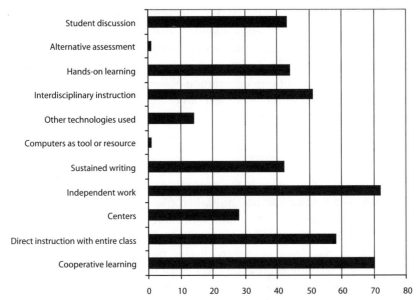

FIGURE 8.2. Percentage of classes observed in Audrey Cohen schools where there was evidence of the following instructional practices.

the other hand, were implementing the reform design at moderate to high levels (Datnow, 2001); the implementation of this reform was not obvious at the classroom level, but was more so in the schools' climate and governance structure. In general, however, these data should not be used in isolation to assess the implementation levels of the different designs in the SCPS.

Using the data gathered in Part IV of the COM (Overall Observations), we conducted a descriptive analysis of the teaching and learning approaches observed in first-grade classrooms *within* each design. Figure 8.2 shows the percentage of the first-grade classrooms in two Audrey Cohen College System of Education schools where particular instructional strategies were observed.

As Figure 8.2 shows, cooperative learning was a commonly used instructional approach by teachers, as were independent work and direct instruction. That cooperative learning was so extensively used may provide evidence for the implementation of the Audrey Cohen model, as the model stresses cooperation among students. Sustained writing/composition (either self-selected or teacher-generated topics) was observed in 43% of classrooms. This level seems quite high, considering that all the observations were conducted at the first-grade level.

Student discussion was observed in just under half of all classrooms. About half of the classrooms showed evidence of interdisciplinary instruction or an integration of two or more subject areas, and 43% of classrooms included some experiential, hands-on learning activities. This may reflect the level of implementation of the Audrey Cohen design in these SCPS schools at that time, as both of these instructional tools are characteristic of the reform.

RELIABILITY AND VALIDITY

Within quantitative research, the concept of reliability or *replicability* of methods and findings across multiple contexts is often used as an indicator of the validity or *truthfulness* of findings (Altheide & Johnson, 1994). Within qualitative research, however, each social situation or conversation is considered unique, rendering traditional definitions of reliability and validity impractical and inappropriate (Guba & Lincoln, 1989; LeCompte & Goetz, 1982; Merriam, 1988).

Qualitative researchers suggest that the primary criterion on which their work should be judged is not validity via reliability, but *understanding*: how well the methods and findings reflect a thoughtful treatment of the phenomena under study (Wolcott, 1990). Most central to qualitative research are descriptive, interpretive, and theoretical understandings (Maxwell, 1992). Triangulation, respondent review, and member checking, among others, are strategies used by qualitative researchers to ensure that their understandings cohere with the data, participants' perspectives, and larger theoretical concepts and assumptions (Guba & Lincoln, 1989; Patton, 1990; Sanger, 1996).

Our eclectic classroom observation approach allowed us to develop a deeper understanding of the nature of design implementation and effects, as it provided a complex picture of the classroom. The four-pronged approach provided a thorough description of the classrooms, both individually and collectively. It revealed how classroom participants interpret or make sense of the designs given their social context and as evidenced in their actions. It weighed theoretical assumptions (e.g., Tharp, 1997) about teaching and learning in diverse classrooms directly against classroom activities. In sum, our approach allowed us to construct the classroom in multidimensional ways and does not assume that there is one classroom reality to be measured (Merriam, 1988).

This four-pronged approach was also an excellent mechanism to triangulate the data. We did this in two ways: (a) we used multiple kinds of observation data, and (b) we used multiple observers – that is, investigator triangulation (Merriam, 1988; Patton, 1990). The blend of these two perspectives allowed us to triangulate observation data, adding strength to our findings. In any given classroom, we weighed the different kinds of observation data gathered with the others to develop a holistic understanding of the design within the classroom. We cross-checked the COM data on *evidence of implementation* and *instructional strategies used* with the data gathered through targeted questions on effective pedagogy and reform design implementation. For example, the COM asked the observer to rate whether interdisciplinary instruction was evident in the observed lesson, and one of the targeted questions asked the observer to answer a similar question – and give an example of what that interdisciplinary instruction looked like. The ethnographic notes were also used as additional triangulation for that question.

As multiple investigators visited each school, we also used the different perspectives of the researchers to enhance validity through their *pooled judgment* (Merriam, 1988, p. 169). For example, the directed-question data we presented earlier on Cedars Elementary School was collected by two different observers who visited the school that year. The following year, an additional (i.e., third) person conducted observations there.

Our multimode strategy also maximized the use of time spent at each school site by allowing us to gather a much wider range of classroom data than we might have otherwise done if we had focused solely on one strategy. Multiple case studies increase the generalizability of a case study design, but they can also place additional resource (time and money) constraints on collecting long-term, in-depth data at any one site (LeCompte & Goetz, 1982; Yin, 1984). The four-pronged approach, however, maximized the classroom observations we conducted at each site, adding to the explanatory value of the data collected. Multiple modes of collection require a trade-off in the number of each type of observation completed. Nonetheless, we believe that the triangulation across the types and the higher quality of the total data collected provided a worthwhile compromise.

ISSUES IN EMPLOYING THE METHODOLOGY

Teaming is often suggested by methodologists as a useful way to check individual bias, enhance triangulation, and maximize time in the field (Evertson & Greene, 1986; Liggett, Glesne, Johnston, Brody & Schattman, 1994; Lincoln & Guba, 1985; Lofland & Lofland 1995; Patton, 1990).

Multisite studies and studies of the public realm in particular are thought to benefit from the diversity and scope of a team perspective (Adler & Adler, 1994). Keeping a team of researchers well trained can be challenging, however. This is especially true if some members of the research team did not participate in the initial problem-definition or research-design phases of the study, as is often the case (Yin, 1984).

Over the course of our study, our team included a total of 17 observers who are regular research staff and external consultants from two geographically distant research institutions, Johns Hopkins University and the University of Memphis. Although this enhanced the soundness of our findings, we also faced some challenges.

First, offering consistent training to the observers was difficult. Yin (1984) states that in case study research, all researchers should be provided enough information about the study to make intelligent decisions about data collection while in the field. Key information, such as the study's rationale, the evidence sought, and anticipated variations, is best transmitted through dialogue with new researchers. However, because of the varied locations of our observers, such dialogues were nearly impossible to arrange with all team members simultaneously. Instead, we had to rely on written documents and relatively brief meetings to communicate. This approach was less than ideal, as it failed to allow the observers to interact with, reflect on, and ask questions or articulate concerns about the observation methods presented (Sanger, 1996).

Second, some observers were better at thick description and others were better at low inference. This happened in part because our team reflected the range of the social scientist observer: Some team members received their primary training as education psychologists; others were trained as sociologists or as curriculum and instruction specialists; and still others worked as teachers and counselors (Adler & Adler, 1994). This is not a common problem of most teams because most research designs incorporate either ethnographic or low-inference techniques and rarely attempt to integrate multiple types. We found that training observers to conduct a range of observations from quantitative to naturalistic was difficult, as it challenged the frames with which the observers generally approached their work.

Third, we all filtered what we saw through individual lenses and thus observed life in classrooms differently. Our individual lenses were influenced by our theoretical worldviews or orientations (Bogdan & Biklen, 1982; Merriam, 1988). They were also affected by our positions within the larger social structure and culture (Harding, 1993). This is because we, like all researchers, are "gendered" and "speak from a particular class, racial, cultural, and ethnic community perspective" (Denzin & Lincoln, 1994). Although the diversity of viewpoints could be an asset, as pointed out by Adler and Adler (1994), it also created the potential problem of interobserver inconsistency.

Fourth, the reform designs we studied varied tremendously in their level of specificity, causing us to seek a slightly more structured and less ethnographic approach than we would have preferred. We found that this structure was necessary because the observers had varying levels of understanding of and experience with the designs, and sometimes had difficulty recognizing elements of them. We were concerned, however, that because the majority of our techniques used targeted questions, either quantitative or short-answer, they perhaps limited the degree to which we could present a vivid account of the classrooms we observed.

Finally, using a mixed-method approach for our observations might necessitate consistency in the findings reported on one instrument with those reported on another. For example, an observer could theoretically mark on the COM that interdisciplinary instruction was used and then not describe it in the ethnographic notes. Although we did not encounter this problem in our study – and in fact found that the data from the different instruments were consistent – it is one that could potentially arise when applying this methodology to other studies or research teams.

IMPLICATIONS

Our hope is that the methods and data presented in this chapter point to the importance of using a multimodal approach to studying school reform in schools serving diverse types of students. Studies of educational reform in diverse contexts must measure academic outcomes. However, they must also examine how the context of diversity may or may not be interwoven into the reform designs themselves and the classrooms in which they are implemented. Only by incorporating both can the impact of externally developed school restructuring models on schools serving diverse student populations be adequately assessed. The model we have described is one example of how researchers might realistically incorporate both perspectives into their studies. In this way, our observational strategy provides an opportunity to understand reform through two different paradigms of educational research: the objectivist perspective of the program evaluator and the relationist perspective of the anthropologist (Smith, 1992).

Our model also helps shift the paradigm from the typical, yet narrow, definition of reform success (i.e., effectiveness as measured by higher test scores, fidelity of implementation, and popularity) to one that examines how a reform helped to improve practice (Cuban, 1998). The effectiveness standard is usually the determiner of "the usual thumbs-up or thumbs-down verdict on a reform" (p. 471). Cuban argues that we ought to move away from these measures of reform success that reflect the standards of the policy elite rather than favoring practitioner expertise anchored in schools. Expanding notions of reform success, Cuban argues for assessing the longevity of reforms and their standard for adaptiveness. A reform that is adaptable allows for inventiveness and active problem solving among teachers as they use the reform to improve their own practice and change the values, attitudes, and behavior of students. We believe that our classroom observation methodology helped us to make sense of how teachers adapt reforms for use in their classrooms and how the reforms contribute to improving practice.

Our eclectic model of classroom observation can be adapted for use in future studies to determine how well a whole-school reform model, district or state change effort, or any other innovation develops students' academic skills and enhances students' abilities to develop bilingually and biculturally. For example, researchers might wish to conduct an observational study of a state's new curriculum standards by having observers respond to a series of directed questions about whether classroom instruction fits the new standards and, importantly, whether teachers' instructional methods fit with what we know about best practice for culturally and linguistically diverse students. Such observations could be conducted in bilingual, LEP, language immersion, and regular classrooms. The COM could be used as well, as it is adaptable in almost all elementary school settings. Researchers may wish to add a couple of questions of their own that pertain to the context under study. On the other hand, researchers should be aware that using this multiple-method approach does not necessarily ensure that they will be able to capture all features of classroom life or reform effects in the same breadth or depth, particularly as the methodology calls for them to attend to multiple issues at once. Researchers should also be aware that some of the instruments can be time-consuming to complete and to analyze, depending on the extent of the data collected.

Nevertheless, by merging the objectivist and ethnographic observational approaches, researchers will be better prepared to gauge the overall effectiveness of new reforms in ways that are most suitable to the rich cultural and linguistic diversity of the student populations in American schools.

Notes

An earlier version of this chapter was presented at the annual meeting of the American Educational Research Association, April 13, 1998, San Diego, California. This work was supported under the Education Research and Development Program, PR/Award No. R306A60001, the Center for Research on Education, Diversity & Excellence (CREDE), as administered by the Office of Educational Research and Improvement (OERI), National Institute on the Education of At–Risk Students (NIEARS), U.S. Department of Education (USDOE). The contents, findings, and opinions expressed here are those of the author and do not necessarily represent the positions or policies of OERI, NIEARS, or the USDOE.

1. Sam Stringfield, Johns Hopkins University; Amanda Datnow, University of Southern California; and Steven M. Ross, University of Memphis, were coprincipal investigators on this study.
2. For the purposes of confidentiality, pseudonyms are used for all place and person names.
3. Although traditional ethnography consists of a researcher spending an extended period of time (i.e., a year or more) with the group under study, the enthusiasm for ethnography as a research method has led to the proliferation of what some call *quasi-ethnographies*, which may adopt some but not all of the methods characteristic of traditional ethnography. There are also examples of what is called *blitzkrieg* ethnography, which relies upon several days of intensive fieldwork rather than extensive time in the field. These researchers are not conducting ethnography per se, but rather are utilizing ethnographic methods or techniques for collecting data. Purists are critical of these approaches (Wolcott, 1990).
4. Created in 1991 as part of Goals 2000, New American Schools has secured financial support from foundations and corporations to fund new designs for "break-the-mold" schools. NAS design teams provide yearly on-site training and implementation assistance to schools implementing NAS reform designs.
5. In the first year of the study, we conducted whole school day observations of particular students. However, upon reflection and data analysis, we made the decision to move to 90-minute observations across each grade level, as the whole school day observations kept us confined to one classroom and did not allow us to see a broad range of implementation levels and classroom events.

References

Adler, P. A., & Adler, P. (1994). Observational techniques. In N. K. Denzin & Y. S. Lincoln (Eds.), *Handbook of qualitative research* (pp. 377–392). Thousand Oaks, CA: Sage.

Altheide, D. L., & Johnson, J. M. (1994). Criteria for assessing interpretative validity in qualitative research. In N. K. Denzin & Y. S. Lincoln (Eds.), *Handbook of qualitative research* (pp. 485–499). Thousand Oaks, CA: Sage.

Bogdan, R., & Biklen, S. K. (1982). *Qualitative research for education: An introduction to theory and methods.* Boston: Allyn & Bacon.

Charters, W. W., & Jones, J. E. (1973). On the risk of appraising non-events in program evaluation. *Educational Researcher, 2*(11), 5–7.

Cohen, A., & Jordan, J. (1996). The Audrey Cohen College System of Education: Purpose-centered education. In S. Stringfield, S. M. Ross, & L. Smith (Eds.), *Bold plans for school restructuring: The New American Schools designs* (pp. 25–51). Mahwah, NJ: Erlbaum.

Comer, J., & Haynes, N. (1996). *Rallying the whole village: The Comer process for reforming education.* New York: Teachers College Press.

Core Knowledge Foundation. (1995). *Core Knowledge Sequence.* Charlottesville, VA: Author.

Cuban, L. (1998). How schools change reforms: Redefining reform success and failure. *Teachers College Record, 99*(3), 453–477.

Cummins, J. (1989). *Empowering minority students.* Sacramento: California Association of Bilingual Education.

Datnow, A. (2001). *The sustainability of externally developed reforms in changing district and state contexts.* Paper presented at the annual meeting of the American Educational Research Association, Seattle.

Davidson, A. L., & Phelan, P. (1993). Cultural diversity and its implications for schooling: A continuing American dialogue. In P. Phelan & A. L. Davidson (Eds.), *Renegotiating cultural diversity in American schools* (pp. 1–26). New York: Teachers College Press.

Denzin, N. K., & Lincoln, Y. S. (1994). Introduction: Entering the field of qualitative research. In N. K. Denzin & Y. S. Lincoln (Eds.), *Handbook of qualitative research* (pp. 1–17). Thousand Oaks, CA: Sage.

Evertson, C., & Green, J. L. (1986). Observation as inquiry and method. In M. C. Wittrock (Ed.), *Handbook of research on teaching* (3rd ed., pp. 162–207). New York: Macmillan.

Fetterman, D. M. (1984). *Ethnography in educational evaluation.* Beverly Hills, CA: Sage.

Fillmore, L. W., & Meyer, L. M. (1992). The curriculum and linguistic minorities. In P. W. Jackson (Ed.), *Handbook of research on curriculum* (pp. 626–658). New York: Macmillan.

Fine, M. (1991). *Framing dropouts.* Albany: State University of New York Press.

Giroux, H. (1984). Ideology, agency, and the process of schooling. In L. Barton & S. Walker (Eds.), *Social crisis and educational research* (pp. 306–333). London: Croom and Helm.

Gold, R. (1958). Roles in sociological field observation. *Social Forces, 36*, 217–223.

Greene, J. C. (1993). The role of theory in qualitative program evaluation. In D. J. Flinders & G. E. Mills (Eds.), *Theory and concepts in qualitative research* (pp. 24–46). New York: Teachers College Press.

Guba, E. G., & Lincoln, Y. S. (1989). *Fourth generation evaluation.* Newbury Park, CA: Sage.

Harding, S. (1993). Rethinking standpoint epistemology: "What is strong objectivity?" In L. Alcoff & E. Potter (Eds.), *Feminist epistemologies* (pp. 49–82). New York: Routledge.

Heady, R., & Kilgore, S. (1996). The modern red schoolhouse. In S. Stringfield, S. M. Ross, & L. Smith (Eds.), *Bold plans for school restructuring: The New American Schools designs* (pp. 139–178). Mahwah, NJ: Erlbaum.

Heath, S. B. (1983). *Ways with words: Language, life, and work in communities and classrooms.* New York: Cambridge University Press.

Hirsch, E. D., Jr. (1993). *What your 5th grader needs to know: Fundamentals of a good fifth grade education.* New York: Dell.

LeCompte, M. D., & Goetz, J. P. (1982). Problems of reliability and validity in ethnographic research. *Review of Educational Research, 52*(1), 31–60.

Liggett, A. M., Glesne, C. E., Johnston, A. P., Brody, S. H., & Schattman, R. A. (1994). Teaming in qualitative research: Lessons learned. *Qualitative Studies in Education, 7*(1), 77–88.

Lincoln, Y. S., & Guba, E. G. (1985). *Naturalistic inquiry.* Beverly Hills, CA: Sage.

Lofland, J., & Lofland, L. (1995). *Analyzing social settings: A guide to qualitative observation and analysis.* London: Wadsworth.

Loucks, S. F., & Crandall, D. P. (1981). *The practice profile: An all-purpose tool for program communication, staff development, evaluation, and improvement.* Andover, MA: NETWORK.

Maxwell, J. A. (1992). Understanding and validity in qualitative research. *Harvard Educational Review, 62*(3), 279–300.

Mehan, H. (1978). *Learning lessons.* New York: Cambridge University Press.

Mehan, H. (1992). Understanding inequality in schools: The contribution of interpretive studies. *Sociology of Education, 65*(1), 1–20.

Merriam, S. B. (1988). *Case study research in education: A qualitative approach.* San Francisco: Jossey-Bass.

Metz, M. H. (1978). *Classrooms and corridors: The crisis of authority in desegregated secondary schools.* Berkeley: University of California Press.

Miles, M., & Huberman, M. (1984). *Qualitative data analysis.* Beverly Hills, CA: Sage.

Newmann, F. M., & Wehlage, G. (1995). *Successful school restructuring.* Madison, WI: Center on Organization and Restructuring of Schools.

Patton, M. Q. (1990). *Qualitative evaluation and research methods.* Newbury Park, CA: Sage.

Peshkin, A. (1988). In search of subjectivity – One's own. *Educational Researcher, 17*(7), 17–21.

President's Initiative on Race. (1997, September 30). *President's initiative on race.* Paper presented at the Advisory Board meeting, Mayflower Hotel, Washington, DC.

Rose, M. (1989). *Lives on the boundary.* New York: Penguin.

Ross, S. M., Smith, L. J., Lohr, L. L., & McNelis, M. J. (1994). Math and reading instruction in tracked first-grade classes. *The Elementary School Journal, 95*(1), 105–109.

Sanger, J. (1996). *The complete observer?: A field research guide to observation.* London: Falmer Press.

Scheirer, M. A. (1996). A template for assessing the organizational base for program implementation. In M. A. Scheirer (Ed.), *A user's guide to program templates: A new tool for evaluating program content* (pp. 61–80). San Francisco: Jossey-Bass.

Sizer, T. R. (1992). *Horace's school: Redesigning the American high school.* Boston: Houghton Mifflin.

Slavin, R. E., Madden, N. A., & Wasik, B. A. (1996). Roots and wings: Universal excellence in elementary education. In S. Stringfield, S. M. Ross, & L. Smith (Eds.), *Bold plans for school restructuring: The New American Schools designs* (pp. 207–231). Mahwah, NJ: Erlbaum.

Smith, D. M. (1992). Anthropology of education and educational research: CAE presidential address. *Anthropology and Education Quarterly, 23*, 185–198.

Stallings, J., & Kaskowitz, D. (1974). *Follow through classroom observation evaluation 1972–1973 (SRI Project URU-7370).* Menlo Park, CA: Stanford Research Institute.

Stringfield, S., Millsap, M., Yoder, N., Schaffer, E., Nesselrodt, P., Gamse, B., Brigham, N., Moss, M., Herman, R., & Bedinger, S. (1997). *Special strategies studies final report.* Washington, DC: U.S. Department of Education.

Stringfield, S. C., Ross, S. M., & Smith, L. J. (1996). *Bold plans for school restructuring: The New American Schools designs.* Mahwah, NJ: Erlbaum.

Tharp, R. G. (1997). *From at-risk to excellence: Research, theory, and principles for practice* (Research Report No. 1). Santa Cruz: Center for Research on Education, Diversity & Excellence, University of California.

Weis, L., & Fine, M. (1993). *Beyond silenced voices: Class, race, and gender in United States schools.* Albany: State University of New York Press.

Wolcott, H. F. (1990). On seeking – and rejecting – validity in qualitative research. In E. W. Eisner & A. Peshkin (Eds.), *Qualitative inquiry in education: The continuing debate* (pp. 121–152). New York: Teachers College Press.

Yin, R. K. (1984). *Case study research: Design and methods.* Newbury Park, CA: Sage.

Yonezawa, S., & Datnow, A. (1999). Supporting multiple reform designs in a culturally and linguistically diverse school district. *Journal of Education for Students Placed at Risk, 4*(1), 125–161.

APPENDIX: Sample Directed-Question Observation Form

Scaling Up School Reforms in Multicultural, Multilingual Contexts: CES Classroom Observation Form

School Name: _____ Reform: **Coalition of Essential Schools**
Observer: _____ Date: _____
Teacher: _____ Time: _____

For each classroom you observe, please answer the following questions.

If you do not see the aspect of the reform asked about, state what you saw instead. Provide *DETAILED EXAMPLES* to support your conclusions. Plenty of descriptive adjectives and specific details of the way a student looked or quotes or paraphrased recollections of a teacher's remark are always helpful. Remember: In qualitative observations it's the *details, details, details* of life in these classrooms that we want to capture. If you run out of room in the space provided, use the back of the sheet. Be *specific in your observations*, as we will code your responses during subsequent analysis.

Attach any *materials from the lesson*, such as worksheets or copies of student work, that you gathered during the observation period.

Part I: General Descriptives and Fidelity of Implementation to CES Design

1.1. General Classroom Structure

a) What *languages* were used *during instruction*? If more than one, what was the dominant language?

b) What *languages* were used *during noninstructional* conversation? Among students? Between teacher and students?

c) What evidence was there that the classroom reflected the *cultural and linguistic diversity* of the students in the class?

d) Were *block scheduling and double periods* used to provide students more time on fewer subjects? Describe. (You may not see this in the elementary schools we are studying.)

e) Were there any *scheduling variances* for particular linguistic or racial groups of students within the class? (e.g., kids getting pulled out for second language instruction during a math block.)

1.2. General Classroom Culture

a) Was there evidence that a *tone of decency* (fairness, generosity & tolerance) existed among the students and between the teachers and students?

b) Did this *tone of decency* vary by the ethnic or linguistic make-up of the students and/or teacher?

c) Was there evidence that teacher and students *trusted* one another? (e.g., anything from a teacher's willingness to let students get things out of their desk on their own to students exhibiting risk-taking behaviors in the comments they make in class or your sense as to whether or not the classroom is a safe place to read out loud if you're not a strong reader).

d) Was there evidence that this *trust existed equally* between the teacher and White and non-White students? Did it exist equally between White and minority students? (e.g., do students share things and/or secrets? Do they act as though they know that their peers won't make fun of them when they offer an answer?)

e) Was there any evidence of teachers conveying *unanxious high expectations* to their students? How?

f) Were these *high expectations conveyed equally* to White and minority students?

1.3. Curriculum

a) What evidence was there that the curriculum had an *interdisciplinary* focus?

b) What evidence was there that the curriculum had a *multicultural* focus? (Be sure to describe what parts of it were multicultural.)

c) What evidence was there that the curriculum was *guided by student interest*? (If this is unclear, it may be good to note how interested the students seemed to be. If applicable, note which *groups* of students were interested and which were not. It might also be good to ask the teacher directly after the observation if student interest played a role in the lesson's design.)

d) What evidence was there that the curriculum was *personalized* for each student? (e.g., were students working on different tasks, at different paces?)

e) What evidence was there that this "personalization" took into consideration the students' *cultural or linguistic backgrounds*?

1.4. Pedagogy

a) What evidence was there of the *student as worker* and *teacher as coach* metaphors? (e.g., did teachers assist students in figuring out the meaning of a concept v. telling them what it meant, etc.?)

b) Did this *pedagogical metaphor* work better for some groups of students than others depending on their cultural background or linguistic abilities?

c) Were there any *pedagogical adjustments* made to accommodate culturally or linguistically diverse student groups?

d) How would you characterize the *teacher-student interactions* you witnessed? (e.g., frequent, haphazard, nonexistent, friendly, consistent, etc.)

e) Were the *teacher-student interactions* you witnessed similar in quantity and quality across linguistic and cultural groups?

f) Was there any evidence throughout the day that teachers *collaborated with students' families*?

g) Was there any evidence that some *linguistic or cultural groups of families* collaborated more often or in different ways than others?

1.5. Assessment

a) Describe any *assessment strategies* you observed.

b) How were the assessments based on *student performances of real tasks*?

c) How did *teacher observation of students' work* get incorporated into assessments?

d) What opportunities (either during your observation or told to you by the teacher would happen in the future) were available to students to *demonstrate their expertise* in front of family or community members?

e) How, if at all, were assessments tailored to a *culturally and linguistically diverse class*?

Part II: Effectiveness of Classroom Instruction for Linguistically and Culturally Diverse Students

2.1. Linguistically and Culturally Sensitive Curriculum

a) Did the curriculum as planned and presented allow for the *development of students' native linguistic talents*? If not, were there times when such opportunities would have been appropriate? Explain.

b) Did the curriculum foster a sense of *personal and cultural identity*? If so, how?

c) Approximately how much class emphasis was placed on *teaching content vs. basic skills*?

d) Was there evidence that the teacher(s) encouraged development of a *"democratic character"* (e.g., did the teacher(s) encourage students to deliberate rationally on topics?)

2.2. Linguistically and Culturally Sensitive Pedagogy

a) Did the teacher(s) employ a pedagogy that motivated students to *use language (either native or English) to generate their own understandings*? If yes, give an example.

b) Did the teacher(s) use *group learning, cooperative learning, and/or peer teaching*? Describe.

2.3. Linguistically and Culturally Sensitive Assessment

a) Were the assessment strategies employed good measures of *student content knowledge* such that a student could be successful regardless of his or her level of English language fluency or American acculturation? Explain.

b) Did the curriculum and pedagogy employed *promote confidence* in students' ability to learn? Example?

Part III. Brief Descriptions

3.1. Unusual Classroom Activities Please use the space below to note any unusual classroom activities that were not captured by the above questions.

3.2. Reflections Please use this space to reflect on the classroom you observed and to note your overall perceptions. Was there something about it you found particularly attractive, disturbing, dull, or unique?

9

Sociocultural Activity Settings in the Classroom

A Study of a Classroom Observation System

Héctor H. Rivera and Roland G. Tharp

This chapter reports on the theoretical conceptualization, development, and measurement properties of an observation instrument for coding classroom instructional activities. This required the examination of several fundamental issues concerning sociocultural theory as it relates to schooling. These issues are presented through a discussion of the relationships between theory, method, and analysis used in the development of a training program for observing, analyzing, and quantifying classroom activities.

In the past two decades, we have seen many treatments of activity theory in the field of education. From the sociocultural perspective, many interesting and useful constructs have been proposed to capitalize on these ideas. However, the accumulation of empirical research has been retarded by the lack of suitable quantifying instruments. In our view, as important as all these ideas are in the field of education, they serve no one well if they don't promote active empirical research.

Most of the critical data in sociocultural theory have been qualitative, and many have been thick ethnographic and discourse analytic descriptions. Critics of sociocultural theory often object to the lack of objective, quantifiable methods that are more typical of sociologists and psychologists. In particular, much work on activity theory in education has relied on thick observation, but applications in real educational settings have been minimal because there are no instruments for broader use that allow for more studies of a different kind. Sociocultural theorists have asked: Can a thin system for observing and quantifying sociocultural activities be developed? Can these rich concepts be thinly assessed or is the field of sociocultural research doomed to expensive, impractical ways to measure its conceptual richness? The answers to these questions are unfolded later in this chapter.

The potential uses of a thinner but reliable, valid, and uniform system of description include comparison of events across (a) time and/or developmental progress, (b) institutions, communities, or cultures, and (c) student outcomes. Such studies are rarely possible at the present time because sociocultural methodology lacks a basis for description that is theoretically principled, commonly applicable, economical, and subject to precise comparison such as provided by mathematical analyses.

The Activity Setting Observation System (ASOS) is different from other instruments in that it provides a thin method of description that is (a) based on the essential principles of sociocultural theory, (b) reliable across observers, (c) practical for the live and accurate description of a typical classroom or similar setting, (d) subject to meaningful quantification, and (e) eligible for simultaneous, more detailed, thicker annotation. This chapter reports on the theoretical design and development of the ASOS, a classroom observation instrument for coding the single or multiple activities that occur in classroom settings.

UNIT OF ANALYSIS: THE ACTIVITY SETTING

The activity setting is the basic unit of analysis in sociocultural theory. Activity represents the framework society uses for communal actions and for the socialization of its members. Children engage in communal activities that are formative for their cognitive development, perceptions, motives, and values. This is accomplished through language and problem-solving activities that are culturally compatible with the values and beliefs of the participants (Rogoff, 1994).

When using the activity setting as the unit of analysis, we study individual development through changing participation in sociocultural activities. Several developmental approaches call attention to the concept of participation for understanding, learning, and development. Researchers in sociocultural theory argue that the central focus should be the study of the shifts in participation that occur within the context of the activity in which the individual participates (Rogoff, Baker-Sennett, Lacasa, & Goldsmith, 1995). The concept of development through participation in sociocultural activities has led us to consider the individual to exist not in isolation or out of cultural context; rather, participation requires a description or an explanation of how people engage in sociocultural activities that are not formed by individuals alone, but by individuals interacting with other people in the community (Rogoff et al., 1995).

Tharp and Gallimore (1988), as well as O'Donnell and Tharp (1990), suggest a strategy for analyzing the interrelated dimensions of activity by studying a basic unit of analysis: the activity setting. The name *activity setting* incorporates two essential features: the cognitive and motoric action itself (activity) and the external, environmental, and objective features of the occasion (setting). Activity settings are the who, what, when, where, and why of everyday events that take place in communities, homes, schools, and workplaces (Tharp & Gallimore, 1988; Wertsch, 1981). Activity settings are elements of everyone's daily schedule. Briefly, the "who" of activity settings refers to the individuals present. The "what" of activity settings refers to the things that are done (i.e., the operations) and the knowledge structures and scripts that guide these operations. The "when" and the "where" of activity settings involve descriptions of the time patterns and the places of their occurrence, respectively. Finally, the "why" of activity settings includes the motivations of the members and the meanings of the activities to the participants (Rivera et al., 1999).

ACTIVITY IN EDUCATIONAL SETTINGS

According to Vygotsky (1978), children's learning and development begin long before they attend school. These are interrelated processes that begin on the first day of life. The learning that a child experiences in school during classroom activities has a historic context in interpsychological processes developing from the child's involvement in community activities. Sociocultural theory provides a framework for examining these processes and practices in communities as well as in the classroom. The impact of this theory has been demonstrated by its wide applicability across disciplines. Sociocultural theory was introduced for community psychology in the areas of program development and prevention. There is also ample evidence of its impact on the development of educational theories (Forman & McPhail, 1993; Gallimore & Tharp, 1992; Moll, Amanti, Neff, & Gonzalez, 1992; O'Donnell & Tharp, 1990; Rogoff et al., 1995).

In the educational context, school can be analyzed in activity setting units, from learning centers in classrooms to independent self-study groups (Gallimore & Tharp, 1992; O'Donnell & Tharp, 1990). The study of activity settings in schools allows the disciplined analysis of instructional methods. The means of assistance can be observed and quantified as long as we have a clear picture of the beginning and end of the activity, the personnel involved in the activity, and the product individually or jointly generated during the activity. Observation of activity lays the foundation for the formation of principles for culturally compatible pedagogy, which may serve to assess and assist the teacher in delivering effective pedagogy.

THE ACTIVITY SETTING OBSERVATION SYSTEM (ASOS)

The ASOS was developed by Rivera et al. (1999) for analyzing, quantifying, and providing a thin description of activities as they occur in school settings or communities. It provides an objective description of the defining attributes of classroom activity settings. The major categories in the ASOS will now be described. They provide a context for the theoretical and empirical basis of the system under examination. Readers interested in further theoretical descriptions should also refer to Chapters 3 and 6 of this volume.

The ASOS contains the following categories: Number of Activity Settings, Activity Setting General Type (ASGT), Product of Activity (PA), Personnel, Student Initiative or Choice (SIC), Joint Productive Activity (JPA), Modeling/Demonstration (MD), Teacher/Student Dialogue (TSD), and Responsive Assistance (RA). These are the categories developed for the ASOS and scored by the trainees during reliability tests. The results of the study yielded significant levels of observer reliability using Cohen's Kappa reliability coefficient and the Spearman–Brown effective reliability formula.

The ASOS records most observed categories in a binary form, that is, "present" or "absent," during the period of observation. Although simple social systems might allow frequency counts or connoisseur-like judgments of quality, a complex, fast-paced classroom will require concentrated attention and vigorous recording merely to recognize activity settings and the presence or absence of critical features. The ASOS can be correlated with other observation or rating systems, as well as with qualitative data, but in itself the ASOS is intended to provide a quick check for important features of complex systems of human interaction.

DISTINGUISHING AMONG ACTIVITY SETTINGS

The first and basic task of the ASOS is to distinguish among activity settings, that is, to establish the boundaries between them. Determining the differences between one activity and the next is necessary for any further description or analysis within or across activity settings. Therefore, all other categories of observation are secondary to the identification and delimitation of the activity setting itself. Other categories of observation can then be employed, each identifying a characteristic of the given activity setting. Once the unit of analysis is identified, the interrelated dimensions of the activity can be recorded to quantify and describe its components. The defining criterion of an activity is its purpose, objective, object, or product. Rivera et al. (1999) state that "this is consistent with activity setting theory and socio-cultural theory foundation. Human existence is organized by coherent objectives; the meaning unit, and the basis for analysis, consists of these basic, purposeful complexes, defined by their objectives or products" (p. 12). Therefore, we adopted the product of the activity as an objective indicator of intention and motivation (Rivera et al., 1999).

DESCRIPTIONS OF CATEGORIES WITHIN ACTIVITY SETTINGS: THEORY-BASED

Joint Productive Activity

From the sociocultural perspective, teaching and learning occur best in the context of joint productive activity with peers and the teacher (Tharp, 1991; Tharp, Dalton, & Yamauchi, 1994). The social organization of traditional classrooms is primarily whole-class oriented, with a teacher who leads, instructs, or demonstrates to the whole group. Some form of individual practice follows, and learning is assessed by individual achievement (Tharp, 1993; Tharp & Yamauchi, 1994). When experts and novices work together for a common product or goal, and when they have opportunities to converse during such activity, skills, cognitive operations, and values are created. Joint productive activity provides the opportunity for academic concepts to be manipulated for the solution of practical problems during classroom activities (Forman & McPhail, 1993; Tharp, 1991; Vygotsky, 1978; Wells & Chang-Wells, 1992).

Responsive Assistance

Before children can function as independent agents, they must rely on adults or more capable peers for other-regulation of task performance

(Tharp & Gallimore, 1988; Vygotsky, 1978). The amount and kind of other-regulation or responsive assistance that a child requires depends on the nature of the task, the child's developmental level, and the level at which the child is able to perform with assistance, that is, on the zone of proximal development (ZPD) (Gallimore & Tharp, 1992; Tharp & Gallimore, 1988).

Responsive assistance also requires careful consideration of the cultural values of those being assisted, as well as the values of those providing the assistance. Rogoff et al. (1995) have addressed this issue using the concept of guided participation. From Rogoff's perspective, guided participation involves children's engagement in the activities of their community. These are challenging activities, but the communities also offer a system of support from caregivers and peers with varying degrees of skills and status. The social organization of the classroom frequently allows only individual achievement, rather than a more natural reliance on joint productive activity and responsive assistance similar to those found in the homes and communities of students (Tharp & Gallimore, 1988).

Contextualization

People who live and learn in a community create shared meanings, a common language, values, and goals through participation in joint activities (Dewey, 1944) or joint productive activities (Tharp & Gallimore, 1988). It is only by incorporating students' repertoire of familiar experience and knowledge into classroom activity settings that teachers and students can begin to understand how the other defines the words they use and thus to see how the other sees the world.

Historically, the recitation script has been the pervasive means of instruction in the classroom. The recitation script consists of a series of often unrelated teacher questions that require convergent factual answers and students' display of known information (Tharp & Gallimore, 1988). In spite of the recitation script, the effectiveness of the educational system in the majority culture can be understood through the principles of sociocultural theory. Traditional North American schools have the luxury of practicing the recitation script because the schools have been able to rely on the family and community experiences of majority-culture adults to provide the activity, the conversation, the language development, and the shared context upon which the schools depend. However, the schools must now provide the common experience, activity, language, and conversation that learners require, both for individual development and for the development of a common, shared, and mutually endorsed community (Tharp et al., 1994).

The accurate use of this category depends on the observer recognizing community-based elements in the classroom. Observers in unfamiliar communities may well underestimate these elements. Nevertheless, the coding of contextualization should not occur without some reportable evidence. Relevant outside information may be sought after an observation. However, if that is not possible, the issues should be noted in the ASOS coding sheet as part of an ethnographic record of the activity.

Understanding children's learning and development in the context of their community practices provides a useful perspective on what is required for effective instruction in the classroom. It is through examination and understanding of children's previous knowledge and experiences that we can apply and develop new competencies and skills in the classroom.

Students' repertoire of familiar experience and out-of-school knowledge is the platform from which the more abstract knowledge of schooling can be made meaningful and important to them. This has been a basic tenet of sociocultural theorists from Vygotsky on. Understanding and the ability to use schooled constructs depend on relating them to the everyday experience of the learner and incorporating community activities into classroom practices. Effective teaching can be seen as the constant weaving of schooled concepts and the everyday experience of the children during classroom activities (Tharp & Gallimore, 1988).

Connected Activity Settings

Rivera et al. (1999) define connected activity settings as a form of contextualization, the primary difference between contextualized and connected activities being that "activity settings can be connected by including students' previous school knowledge without incorporating aspects of their repertoire of everyday experience or community knowledge" (p. 37).

Teacher/Student Dialogue

A responsive teacher is able to contextualize teaching in the experience base of the learner and to individualize instruction in the same way that each learner is individualized within culture (Tharp, 1993). It is through teacher–student dialogue that tasks are defined, negotiated, and evaluated. It is also a means through which students' participation is monitored and assisted. During teacher–student dialogue, students and teachers engage in the dialogic co-construction of meaning, which is the essence of education.

Literacy foci in cognitive and educational research reveal the deep ties among language, thinking, values, and culture. Language development at all levels (vocabulary through syntax) can be advocated as an overriding goal for the entire school day, thus fostering the development of thinking skills and the ability to form, express, and exchange ideas in speech and writing. Evidence strongly suggests that language development should be fostered through purposive conversation between teacher and student rather than through drill and decontextualized rules. The critical form of assisting learners is through the questioning and sharing of ideas and knowledge during dialogue (Tharp, 1993).

It is during teacher–student dialogue that the knowledge and collective practices already available in the communities foster the development of a community of learners within the classroom (Rogoff et al., 1995; Wells & Chang-Wells, 1992). A fundamental requirement for the creation of a community of learners is the development of a shared language for academic learning in which the new (subject matter) and the familiar (community activities) are acknowledged. This classroom community best reflects the social, historical, and institutional reality of the students (Rogoff et al., 1995).

Through the *appropriation* of the classroom genre, human mental functioning is shaped in socioculturally specific ways during classroom activities. Bakhtin points out that a word in a language is half someone else's. It becomes one's own only when the speaker populates it with his or her own intentions and accent or appropriates the word, adapting it to his or her own semantic and expressive intention (Wertsch & Toma, 1995). Words become meaningful when woven into the student's system of meanings and understanding. Through dialogue, extracting the threads of information from text, and arraying and preparing them for weaving into existing cognitive systems, the basic competencies of literate societies are transmitted. Also, it is usually the role of the teacher to assess and assist students in the arrangement of their personal tapestry of knowledge by means of teacher–student dialogue.

OTHER CATEGORIES

ASOS coding categories are not limited to general categories derived from sociocultural theory. Tharp et al. (1994) discerned two additional principles (modeling and demonstration and student initiative or choice) that are present in effective programs for Native American communities. These are closely tied to basic views of children and to basic characteristics of child socialization that appear to be shared by many Native American cultures. These two categories are examples of the kind of inquiry allowed by the ASOS. Variables of interest for particular communities may be added to the basic system as additional descriptors of activity settings.

Modeling and Demonstration

According to Tharp et al. (1994), an essential factor in the learning process of Native Americans is modeling and demonstration. These authors believe that in the classroom, lessons should include performance and demonstration. For example, traditional and contemporary Native American socialization emphasizes learning by observation. This *observational learning complex* is closely tied to the well-documented visual-learning patterns of Native American children, and their holistic cognitive style of learning. The inclusion of demonstration in lessons increases the understanding of verbal and conceptual explanations, especially for students with limited proficiency in the language of instruction.

Observational learning is a fundamental aspect of the complex of Native American socialization practices. Cazden and John (1971) discuss this preference for "learning by looking more than learning through language" (p. 256) as an aspect of Native American children's superior visual abilities in the context of their every day practices. Longstreet (1978) and Deyhle (1983) state that among Native American peoples, there is also a learning system of private, imagined practice that allows "learning without public failure." Cazden and John discuss this as "competence before performance."

Thus Tharp et al. (1994) report a general consensus among educational researchers and practitioners in Native America that lessons for Native American students should include modeling and demonstration. The inclusion of demonstrations in lessons increases the understanding of verbal and conceptual explanations. Therefore, integration of this community practice into the educational experience makes classroom discourse more engaging and relevant, thus increasing the potential for learning (Tharp & Yamauchi, 1994).

Student Initiative or Choice

Classroom organization influences student participation. Native American students are comfortable and more inclined to participate in activities that they themselves generate, organize, or direct. Native American cultures are distinctive in the degree of respect accorded to youthful autonomy and decision making (Tharp et al., 1994). Perhaps all children prosper when they are allowed initiative or choice in generating, joining, or acting during classroom activities. Students are inherently motivated to understand when they are allowed to solve tasks that they value and when they are confident about their abilities.

In summary, the present study reports on the design, development, and reliability testing of a system for coding observations of single or multiple activities that occur in classroom settings. Through the examination of several fundamental facets of sociocultural theory, as well as other generic principles found in given communities, activity settings can be coded to provide meaningful quantification.

METHOD

Research Background

The effective measurement of reliability training requires researchers to calibrate observers against some valid criterion scoring of classroom activities. This method requires a more *expert other* to evaluate and code lessons using the standard coding criteria. This procedure allows determination of the degree of reliability between a particular observer and the criterion scoring.

It was determined that videotaped rather then live observations were preferable in the design of a training program to test observer reliability, as well as for training observers on ASOS rules and categories. Previous analyses of live observations conducted in classroom settings revealed a low level of occurrence of the variables targeted by the ASOS. It was also determined that the average number of activities per hour during previously observed live classrooms was 4.4. There was a need to control for the low number of activity settings in order to reach a critical number that could yield significant results.

Using videotapes allowed the training program to present many more relevant phenomena per unit of time and thus enabled us to estimate levels of reliability more efficiently. Videotaped classroom activities also provided greater diversity of classroom organization, teaching styles, and communities than could be assembled for any local group of trainees, and the videotapes could be viewed repeatedly to clarify or expand on a categorical definition that might otherwise be unclear to the trainee. Training included a seminar to address the issues relevant to the categories developed in the ASOS, and selected video segments offered opportunities for responsive teaching, which was vital for observers' development and training in the principles of sociocultural theory.

The use of videotapes also helped determine whether a disagreement in coding originated with the observer, or whether it stemmed from inconsistencies in the definition of a category, or perhaps from problems with the observation media. The need for such clarification became evident during the pilot research. Individual members of the same observation team often came up with contrasting interpretations of the same classroom event when it was observed "live." Because of this tendency, it was evident that a standard, or control measurement, such as allowed by videotape, would be necessary to allow trainees to profit from feedback.

Participants

The (videotaped) participants represent members of diverse communities, as well as a diverse group of classroom settings from first grade to eighth grade, with a range of classroom size from 18 to 27 students. Part of the purpose of the design was to expose five trainees to a variety of classroom settings to validate the potential usefulness of the observation system in diverse contexts, as well as to assess observer reliability. The students and communities represented in the videotapes included Hawaiian classrooms on the island of Oahu, Native American classrooms in New Mexico, and Latino/migrant classrooms in northern California.

Materials

The materials utilized during the training and testing for reliability included (a) a book of guidelines for observing and coding sociocultural activities in the classroom settings (see Appendix A for the ASOS Quick Reference Guide)[1]; (b) a coding sheet to record activities during classroom observations (see Appendix B); and (c) videotapes of classroom instruction for teaching, training, and testing observers' reliability and understanding of the ASOS categorical variables.

Procedures

A criterion scoring system was produced to test observers' reliability in coding the number of activity settings. This criterion scoring consisted of 35 possible codes over a period of 122 minutes of videotaped classroom activity settings. The primary objective during this phase of the training was to assess observers' reliability in identifying the activity setting boundaries. Also, to further test the reliability of trainees on the categories embedded within activity settings, 57 selected videotaped segments of classroom settings were shown, with a possible criterion scoring of 420 codes. This was done to control for the low occurrence of these categories in the multiple classroom settings that were videotaped.

Videotaped classrooms were observed and coded simultaneously by each of the five senior members of the design team. Scores on the observed activities were then compared. The criterion score was achieved through a consensus of reconciled differences, resulting in a standard criterion score for each videotaped segment used for training.

A group of one undergraduate and four graduate students participated in the ASOS training program. The students represented three different research groups interested in the development of the ASOS observation system. Through videotaped classroom lessons, observers were trained to observe and code a variety of teaching scripts typically found in classrooms.

The videotapes used for training observers were actual classroom lessons. They were produced and coded in order to develop a protocol for measuring observer reliability. Three types of training tapes were used, each corresponding to a training phase: (a) teaching tapes, (b) practice tapes, and (c) testing tapes. These videotaped classroom lessons were used to assess if, given a set of rules for coding classroom activity settings, independent observers could achieve an acceptable level of agreement with the criterion scoring.

Phase One (teaching phase) began during the last 4 weeks of the fall of 1996 and consisted of four meetings with trainees. Training materials included the coding manual and articles on sociocultural theory. Group discussions were conducted on the materials and the rules for coding activity settings. Two 45-minute videotaped lessons were shown to provide a context for the coding rules and theoretical concepts. These two lessons were watched extensively and discussed by the trainer and trainees in a group setting. During this phase, the trainees began using the rules and applying their understanding of sociocultural concepts to coding classroom activities.

Phase Two (practice phase) was composed of six sessions and was designed to address the final teaching stages of activity settings and the categories of the ASOS. The emphasis was on making the trainees comfortable with the ASOS and the coding of the videotaped classroom activities. To accomplish this, the teaching and practice sections of the training program were overlapped to provide trainees with the support and assistance they required. The data collected from the practice sessions were continuously used to assess and assist the progress of trainees on their levels of agreement on the categories, as well as to rectify errors related to the procedures for coding activity settings.

Phase Three (reliability testing) was divided into two subsections totaling 14 sessions. During the first 10 sessions, each lasting an average of $1^1/_2$ hours, trainees observed entire classroom lessons ranging from 17 to 35 minutes. Each trainee individually coded these lessons. Unresolved issues on previous observations were discussed and clarified, but no changes were made to the trainees' original coding. The prime objective of this phase was to assess the reliability of the trainees in identifying activity setting boundaries. They were also asked to identify the categorical variables observed during those activities.

During the final four sessions, trainees were shown video segments representing the different categories they had been trained to code. The total number of segments shown was 57, and their duration ranged from $1^1/_2$ to 3 minutes per segment. Each session lasted an average of $3^1/_2$ hours, with breaks between every hour of observation. Afterward, observation sheets were collected to assess reliability.

RESULTS

The first step was to determine the reliability on the number of activity settings. Activity setting is a continuous variable; therefore, reliability values were calculated using the Spearman–Brown effective reliability formula.

Effective Reliability (*R*) Values on the Number of Activity Settings

To determine the degree of relationship between the criterion and trainees' codes on activity settings, five Pearson correlations were calculated. The correlations were then transformed into the corresponding Fisher's *Z*, deriving the mean Z_{Fisher}, and then transforming the mean Z_{Fisher} back into the corresponding mean correlation. The mean Z_{Fisher} derived for these five interjudge correlations corresponded to an average correlation of $r = .92$. The Spearman–Brown effective reliability (*R*) formula was used to adjust this mean interjudge agreement as a function of the number of judges involved (Mullen, 1989). The effective reliability based on these five judges was $R = .99$, a relatively high degree of interjudge agreement. This was a theoretically important result because it demonstrated that observers could distinguish the beginnings and the ends of activity settings. Therefore, all the other categories embedded in the activities become meaningful in the unfolding and understanding of activity settings in the classroom context.

Kappa Values Between Criterion Scoring and Trainees

Observer reliability on the categories was determined using Cohen's Kappa. According to Bakeman and Gottman (1986), this statistical procedure provides a coefficient of agreement that corrects for the proportion of agreement derived by chance. $P_{(o)}$ is the observed proportion of agreement, and $P_{(c)}$ is the proportion of agreement expected by chance (Bakeman & Gottman, 1986; Hartmann, 1977).

$$K = \frac{P_o - P_c}{1 - P_c}$$

In considering different measurements of reliability, researchers need to consider Kappa as a more rigorous test of reliability. *Agreement percentage* is a more general term (Bakeman & Gottman, 1986). It describes the extent to which two observers agree with each other. *Reliability* is a more restricted term. As used in psychometrics, it determines how accurate a measure is, that is, how close it comes to the truth. Therefore, when two observers are compared to each other, only agreement can be reported. However, when an observer is compared against a criterion score assumed to be true, observer reliability can be discussed.

According to Hartmann (1977), reliability at this micro level of analysis primarily indicates the adequacy of the behavioral definitions, as

TABLE 9.1. *Effective Reliability (R) Values on the Number of Activity Settings and Kappa Values Between Criterion Scoring and Trainees*

	Step 1	Step 2	
Categories	R	Average Kappa	Range
Activity settings	.99		
Product		.73	(.73 to .74)
Personnel		.84	(.61 to 1.0)
SIC		.84	(.79 to 1.0)
JPA		.65	(.59 to .70)
M/D		.68	(.65 to .72)
TSD		.72	(.63 to .79)
RA		.82	(.79 to .87)
Contex.		.71	(.61 to .81)
Conn.		.68	(.63 to .75)

SIC = Student Initiative or Choice; JPA = Joint Productive Activity; M/D = Modeling and Demonstration; TSD = Teacher and Student Dialogue; RA = Responsive Assistance; CAS = Connected Activity Settings.

well as the thoroughness of observer training in the use of both these definitions and the observational forms such as coding sheets. Results from the observer training program provide an average of the Kappa values and the range of those values among the five observers. Gelfand and Hartmann (1975) state that Kappa should exceed .60 in order to be interpreted as an acceptable level of observer reliability. Bakeman and Gottman (1986) and Hartmann (1977) state that there is a consensus among researchers that characterizes a Kappa value of .40 to .60 as fair, .60 to .75 as good, and over .75 as excellent. Average Kappa values for ASOS categories ranged from .65 to .84 (see Table 9.1).

DISCUSSION

We now turn to the questions posed at the beginning of the chapter. First of all, can a thin system for observing and quantifying sociocultural activities be developed? The answer is "Yes." Overall, the findings from the study show that acceptable levels of observer reliability were obtained for all ASOS categories. The ASOS may effectively be used as a tool for observing and quantifying classroom activities in diverse settings. A reliable system such as the ASOS also allows observers to provide teachers with feedback as part of any teacher professional development program. Researchers can use it to highlight the absence or presence of effective strategies to be used with a diverse student population.

The ASOS contributes to the process of assessing and assisting teachers in applying the principles described in this chapter. This is of great importance because these principles are found in the communal activities in which children participate. Therefore, the application of these principles in the classroom creates a familiar context of experience and development that children can relate to as they learn new subject matter.

The results also reflect the complexity of our coding system, which requires observers to engage in the unfolding of both single and multiple activities and, within those activities, to carefully examine and record interrelated aspects of the multidimensionality of activity settings in the context of classrooms.

For any given activity, the ASOS can provide a baseline analysis that later can be correlated with other methods of classroom observation such as ethnography or discourse analysis of the same activity. The ASOS records the presence or absence of activity features. It is a quick method for providing teachers with feedback while other in-depth analysis is in progress.

Now we turn to the second question posed at the beginning of the chapter. Can the rich concepts of sociocultural theory be thinly assessed? The answer is "Yes."

The ASOS can be used for coding the presence or absence of meaning features for effective instruction. This can be done with either live or videotaped activities. The potential uses of the ASOS are shown in the following example. The example examines the meaning of scores obtained using this system, as well as the implications of the findings for teacher professional development or any other kind of activity assessment.

This example illustrates a small portion of what an observer may find in a classroom setting and how the ASOS can be used to code meaningful features of effective instruction. On the "Brief Description" section of the ASOS form, the observer noted general aspects of the classroom setting.

Example

Brief Description. The teacher and her students were discussing a recent field trip they took to the zoo. The teacher pointed to the multiple centers to show her students the upcoming activity entitled "make your own zoo." During preparation for the activity, she asked a student to show her classmates the procedure for gathering materials and getting ready for the activity.

The teacher also used this introductory lesson to help her second-grade students learn how to write the names of animals, as well as how to classify them. Together they produced a classification table on the board. She inquired about students' experiences at the zoo and the types of animals they saw. She also questioned students about which animals belong together in the same habitat.

After the introductory lesson, students were ready to move into small groups. Five centers were set for this activity. During the activity, students applied their understanding from the previous activity on the geography, climate, and habitats of different animals. The teacher moved around the classroom offering assistance to students in their small groups. The following is part of a dialogue captured by observers.

TEACHER: What were some of your favorite animals from the zoo?
LUIS: Mmmm . . . I like the lions and the polar bears.
EDGAR: I like the snakes and tropical birds.
TEACHER: So, when you design your zoo, are you going to place them together or are there differences in climate and geography you need to think about?
EDGAR: I will put them together, like in the zoo.
DANIEL: Yea.
TEACHER: Well, I guess you guys are right. They are somewhat together in the zoo. But let's think about this for a second. Do you remember when we went to visit the lions?
STUDENTS: Yes.
TEACHER: How about when we went to see the polar bears?
EDGAR: Oh, yea, I remember. It was cold. I had to put my jacket on.
TEACHER: Okay, so it was cold. Why do you think it was cold?
LUIS: Because polar bears like the cold.
TEACHER: Yea, they like the cold. And what kind of climate do you think lions like?
EDGAR: They like the sun.
TEACHER: Good! So, now you can think about what kind of habitat you need to have in your zoo for your animals. Think about it and I'll come back later to see how you are doing.

Using the ASOS, the observer noted that during this period of observation, the students and the teacher where engaged in two activities. The first activity involved an introductory lesson in which the teacher

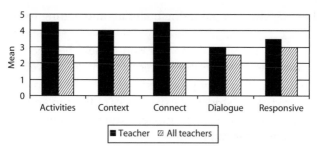

FIGURE 9.1. Mean scores on classroom activity categories observed for an individual teacher in comparison to the overall mean for the rest of the second-grade teachers in the school.

and students discussed the classification of animals and their respective habitats. In the second activity, the teacher set up five tables with materials and animal figures for an activity that she called "make your own zoo." Even though there were five tables, the observer coded the event as one activity because, in this observational system, if all groups are doing the same thing and are all working toward the same product, it is considered one activity setting.

Several observers were engaged in the research across all second-grade classrooms at this site. All second-grade teachers were observed during the first two periods in the morning. Researchers observed a variety of activities for the next 2 days. Figure 9.1 shows some of the findings from those 2 days of classroom observation. For purposes of illustration, we have separated the teacher in the preceding example from her peers. Figure 9.1 shows her mean performance in comparison to that of her peers during the 2 days of classroom observation. The findings indicate that this particular teacher has good teaching strategies and that in comparison to her peers she also tended to maintain an active atmosphere in the classroom, as shown by her greater number of activities per unit of observation, as well as other features of effective pedagogy.

The ASOS is an instrument used to assess the presence or absence of features of effective instruction. The preceding example represents a classroom environment in which effective instructional practices were used. The information gathered through the ASOS can be correlated with information collected using other instruments for the purpose of assessing and improving teaching practice. Aspects of students' community experience, history, and social practices can be incorporated into classroom activities through either formal planning (e.g., embedding the curriculum in a community activity) or impromptu actions (spontaneous references while providing responsive assistance).

The analysis of activity can be used as a basis for implementing and assessing the enactment of sound principles for teaching and learning during classroom activities. The ASOS is a commonly applicable measurement of teaching practice. It is also an economical procedure for obtaining a snapshot of classroom activities before further in-depth analysis.

To use the ASOS appropriately, we must remember that it provides a thin description of classroom activities. It can be used as a pre- and postassessment instrument in order to identify improvements in instructional practices, but it should be used in conjunction with other instruments that offer thicker descriptions of the activities observed. We encourage researchers using the ASOS to include brief descriptions and dialogical interactions between teachers and students. It is not enough to check the box indicating that there was "responsive assistance by teacher." In our experience, most observers will have enough time to describe the nature of the interaction to which they are alluding as an effective instructional practice.

CONCLUSION

All prior work in the analysis of activity settings has involved the use of qualitative data, principally ethnographic or microethnographic, providing thicker accounts of events than those typical of quantitative methods. It is clear that the potential use of a thinner but reliable, valid, and uniform system of description can facilitate comparison of events across (a) time and developmental processes; (b) institutions, communities, or cultures; and (c) student outcomes.

The ASOS is based on the essential principles of sociocultural theory; it is practical for the live and accurate description of a typical classroom or similar setting. It offers a close examination of the fundamental principles for effective pedagogy that are also the essence of everyday learning and development in all communities.

In order to bring effective education to the classroom and assist the performance of students through the zone of proximal development, school activities must be measured and assessed to determine their degree of compatibility with the cultural norms, values, and beliefs of the participants in the activity. Connecting previous knowledge, experiences, and community practices to new information is a fundamental attribute of human development and learning. For at-risk students, this attribute needs to be acknowledged, and their previous experiences and cultural practices need to be integrated into the curriculum as an effective strategy for teaching and learning.

It is through the unfolding of instructional activities that we can assess teaching and learning. Assessing whether cultural components for effective instruction are present or absent is vital in order to maximize learning, as well as to assist teachers in their professional development.

Teaching and learning, as well as any other components of classroom activities, can be assessed through this quantitative method for observing classroom activities. The use of the observational system and methods presented in this study allow for assessment as well as assistance in the process of developing, enacting, and constructing effective classroom activities for teaching and learning.

Note

1. Rivera, H., Tharp, R., Youpa, D., Dalton, S., Guardino, G., & Lasky, S. (1999). ASOS: *Activity Setting Observation System coding and rulebook*. Santa Cruz: Center for Research on Education, Diversity & Excellence, University of California.

References

Bakeman, R., & Gottman, J. M. (1986). *Observing interactions: An introduction to sequential analysis*. Cambridge, MA: Cambridge University Press.
Cazden, R. C., & John, V. P. (1971). Learning in American Indian children. In M. L. Wax, S. Diamond, & F. O. Gearing (Eds.), *Anthropological perspectives on education* (pp. 252–272). New York: Basic Books.
Dewey, J. (1944). *The sources of a science of education*. New York: Liveright.
Deyhle, D. (1983). Measuring success and failure in the classroom: Teacher communication about tests and the understanding of young Navajo students. *Peabody Journal of Education, 61*, 67–85.
Forman, E., & McPhail, J. (1993). *Contexts for learning: Sociocultural dynamics in children's development*. London: Oxford University Press.
Gallimore, R., & Tharp, R. G. (1992). Teaching mind in society: Teaching, schooling, and literature discourse. In L. C. Moll (Ed.), *Vygotsky and education: Instructional implications and applications of sociohistorical psychology* (pp. 175–205). New York: Cambridge University Press.
Gelfand, D. M., & Hartmann, D. P. (1975). *Child behavior analysis and therapy*. New York: Pergamon Press.
Hartmann, D. P. (1977). Considerations in the choice of interobserver reliability methods. *Journal of Applied Behavioral Analysis, 10*, 103–116.

Longstreet, W. S. (1978). *Aspects of ethnicity: Understanding differences in pluralistic classroom(s)*. New York: Teachers College Press.

Moll, L. C., Amanti, C., Neff, D., & Gonzalez, N. (1992). Funds of knowledge for teaching: Using a qualitative approach to connect homes and classrooms. *Theory into Practice, 31*, 132–141.

Mullen, B. (1989). *Advanced basic meta-analysis*. Hillsdale, NJ: Erlbaum.

O'Donnell, C., & Tharp, R. G. (1990). A theory model for community intervention. In A. S. Bellack, M. Hersen, & A. E. Kazdin (Eds.), *International handbook of behavior modification and therapy* (2nd ed., pp. 251–266). New York: Plenum Press.

Rivera, H., Tharp, R. G., Youpa, D., Dalton, S., Guardino, G., & Lasky, S. (1999). *ASOS: Activity Setting Observation System coding and rulebook*. Santa Cruz: Center for Research on Education, Diversity & Excellence, University of California.

Rogoff, B., Baker-Sennett, J., Lacasa, P., & Goldsmith, D. (1995). Development through participation in sociocultural activity. In J. Goodnow, P. Miller, & F. Kessel (Eds.), *Cultural practices as contexts for development* (pp. 45–65). San Francisco: Jossey-Bass.

Tharp, R. G. (1991). *Intergroup differences among Native Americans in socialization and child cognition: An ethnogenetic analysis*. Paper presented at the workshop "Continuities and discontinuities in the cognitive socialization of minority children," National Institute of Mental Health, Washington, DC.

Tharp, R. G. (1993). Research knowledge and policy issues in cultural diversity and education. In B. McLeod (Ed.), *Language and learning: Educating linguistically diverse students* (pp. 129–167). Albany: State University of New York Press.

Tharp, R. G., Dalton, S., & Yamauchi, L. (1994). Principles for culturally compatible Native American education. *Journal of Navajo Education, 11*, 21–27.

Tharp, R. G., & Gallimore, R. (1988). *Rousing minds to life: Teaching, learning, and schooling in social context*. Cambridge, MA: Harvard University Press.

Tharp, R. G., & Yamauichi, L. A. (1994). *Effective instructional conversation in Native American classrooms* (Research Report No. 10). Santa Cruz: National Center for Research on Cultural Diversity and Second Language Learning, University of California.

Vygotsky, L. S. (1978). *Mind in society: The development of higher psychological processes* (M. Cole, V. John-Steiner, S. Scribner, & E. Souberman, Trans.). Cambridge, MA: Harvard University Press.

Wells, C. G., & Chang-Wells, G. L. (1992). *Constructing knowledge together: Classrooms as centers of inquiry and literacy*. Portsmouth, NH: Heinemann.

Wertsch, J. V. (Ed.). (1981). *The concept of activity in Soviet psychology*. Armonk, NY: Sharpe.

Wertsch, J. V., & Toma, C. (1995). Discourse and learning in the classroom: A sociocultural approach. In L. Steffe & J. Gale (Eds.), *Constructivism in education* (pp. 159–174). Hillsdale, NJ: Erlbaum.

APPENDIX A: Activity Setting Observation System – Quick
Reference Guide

Activity Setting (AS)	AS is a unit of analysis encompassing the externally observable and internal, subjective features of activity. An AS is defined by its product/purpose.
Product of Activity	There are two types of products of an activity that are registered in the ASOS: 1) a *tangible* product is an externally observable outcome or artifact that integrates a series of actions, 2) an *intangible* product is some achieved physical, psychological, or social state that integrates a series of actions.
Student Initiative or Choice	Student initiative or choice is coded when it occurs between activity settings and not within an activity setting. The student must have initiated or generated the AS, or must have chosen it from other activities during classroom observation.
Joint Productive Activity (JPA)	JPA refers to any collaborative interaction that leads to a single product. Collaboration can take many forms: shared ownership, authorship, use, sharing of ideas, or responsibility for a product. It can also include division of labor as well as the creation of parallel or similar products.
JPA w/Teacher	JPA w/T occurs when the teacher is a collaborator within the AS. Both the teacher and students work jointly to produce the product.
JPA w/Peers	JPA w/Peers occurs whenever collaboration takes place only between peers. In this situation the teacher is absent during the activity setting.
JPA Both	When both events (JPA w/Teacher and w/Peers) occur in same AS.
Modeling/ Demonstration	For any action to be coded as M/D, it must be explicitly indicated as modeling/demonstration by the teacher or performer during the activity. Modeling/Demonstration is used for preparing students to learn a new skill, process, or procedure or to reinforce a previously introduced one.
M/D by Teacher	When the teacher (or aide) explicitly indicates that his/her action is for "showing how."
M/D by student	1) When the student makes a presentation which shows classmates how to do or make something or is called on by the teacher to show classmates by example how to do or make something; 2) the teacher praises or otherwise draws attention to a student's behavior, thus offering it as a model behavior for others.

Teacher/Student Dialogue	Discourse between teacher and student(s) must be extended to at least two speech turns each, and must consist of more than just providing an answer or a fact. Speech turns consisting only of "yes," "no," "uh-huh," or "I don't know" are not sufficient to earn this coding. Look for the providing of clues, the asking of open-ended questions, or sustained conversation on a single topic.
Structured	Structured T/S Dialogue is part of the plan for the AS, has time, place, and opportunity allotted for it, and is generally initiated by the teacher in order to meet an instructional objective.
Ad hoc	Ad hoc T/S Dialogue occurs spontaneously and does not have time, place, or opportunity allotted for it. It can be initiated by either the teacher or the student(s) during the activity.
Responsive Assistance (RA) by Teacher and by Student	RA consists of two parts: 1) on-the-spot, informal processes which involve monitoring, observing, or testing to discover students' current level of performance and understanding, and 2) formal processes which involve adjusting, selecting, or modulating the assistance provided to enable an advance in the learning activity. Responsive Assistance includes: 1) *Modeling*: providing a demonstration; 2) *Feeding Back*: providing information about student performance compared with a standard; 3) *Contingency Management*: rewards or punishments that are contingent on students performance; 4) *Questioning*: questions that assist students to advance their comprehension beyond their previous level; 5) *Instructions*: providing clear verbal directions for performance; 6) *Cognitive Structuring*: providing explanations or rules for proceeding; 7) *Task Structuring*: providing assistance by segmenting/sequencing portions of task.
Structured	RA is structured when time and opportunity for assistance are designed into the AS. This includes question/answer times that are built into lessons and/or centers, where opportunities for assistance from classmates or the teacher are present.

Ad hoc	RA is ad hoc when the time and opportunity for assistance are not built into the AS. The structure of the AS may allow for spontaneous RA, but the differentiating element is whether the AS specifically allocates time or opportunities for RA or whether it occurred spontaneously.
Contextualization	An activity setting is contextualized when student's knowledge from *outside the classroom or school* is actively incorporated into the activity setting. For example, the teacher solicits and/or makes an explicit statement connecting previous student knowledge and work to the activity setting. Students' statements about their previous knowledge may be elicited by the teacher or spontaneously offered by students.
Individual Experience	When the teacher, aide, or peer incorporates some aspect of the learner's everyday experience or knowledge into an AS. This category is intended to include virtually any aspects of students' experiences outside the classroom or school that are individual or personal.
Community	When the teacher, aide, or peer incorporates some aspect of community experience, history, or activities into the AS, either through formal planning or through impromptu actions. Accuracy of this category depends on the observer recognizing community-based elements in the classroom.
Connected AS	Classroom activity settings are connected when students' previous classroom/school knowledge, experience, or products are incorporated by the teacher into the present activity setting. The criterion for continuity can be satisfied by specific statements of connection made by the teacher or by using products from a previous activity setting for the completion of the current product.
To Current AS	"Current" activity settings are those that are present simultaneously or were present in the *same period of observation*.
To Previous AS	Previous activity settings refer to those that occurred prior to the current period of instruction. Since this is not subject to direct observation, observers should not use this category unless there is some specific and clear evidence for a connection of the two activity settings.

Note: This Quick Reference Guide contains guidelines on the procedures for coding activity settings using the ASOS. For a complete guide to the rules established for the ASOS, see Rivera et al. (1999).

APPENDIX B: Classroom Activity Settings

AS# _____ of _____ **Activity Setting General Type:** _____
Date (mm/dd/yy): _____ **Observer(s):** _____ : _____
Time: From _____ To _____ Resumed _____ To _____ Resumed _____ To _____
School: _____ **Grade:** _____ **Teacher:** _____
Classroom # _____ Location: Classroom Area _____ **Class Period** _____

I. General Subject (Check All That Apply): [] Math [] Science [] Soc. Studies
[] Language Arts [] Other: _____
II. Specific Subject: _____
III. Product of Activity: [] Tangible _____ [] Intangible _____
IV. Personnel: [] Teacher Continuous [] Teacher Intermittent
                [] Aide Continuous [] Teacher Not Engaged
                [] Aide Intermittent [] Other Personnel _____
V. Number of Students (R1)_____ (R2)_____ (R3)_____ (R4)_____
VI. Brief Description: _____
_____
_____
_____
_____

Student initiative or choice in generating   Notes _____
or joining the AS? []Yes [] None   _____

Joint Productive Activity?   Notes _____
[] w/Teacher [] w/Peers [] Both [] None _____

Modeling/Demonstration?   Notes _____
[] By Teacher [] By Students [] None   _____

Teacher/Student Dialogue?   Verbal Data _____
[] Structured [] Ad hoc [] None   _____

Responsive Assistance?   Verbal Data _____
By Teacher [] Structured [] Ad hoc [] None _____
By Student [] Structured [] Ad hoc [] None _____

Contextualized ?   [] Yes   [] None   **Notes** _____
[] Personal experience   _____
[] Community values, beliefs, activities   _____
[] Other_____   _____

Connected ?   **Notes** _____
[] Current AS [] Previous AS [] None   _____

[] Further Notes Attached

Note: Classroom Activity Settings coding sheet. This coding sheet is utilized during a period of observation to obtain a thin description of an activity setting. The observed activity is then quantified as a function of the presence or absence of critical elements for effective teaching and learning.

10

The Influence of School Reform on Classroom Instruction in Diverse Schools

Findings from an Observational Study of Success for All

Marisa Castellano and Amanda Datnow

Improving teaching and learning, especially for culturally and linguistically diverse students, has been a constant goal of the education community. We have learned much over the past few decades, and every new reform addresses some aspect of schooling thought to affect outcomes for students. In many states and districts, standards have been raised, teacher professional development has been expanded, and changes in school governance have given more decision-making authority to educators at the school level. But as Elmore (1996) and others have noted, for a school reform to have results, it must affect what goes on in the classroom. The classroom is the locus of teaching and learning, and yet we do not know much about what school reform looks like at the classroom level. Systematic, guided observation is the best way to explore what happens in classrooms, and whether reforms result in changes in instruction and increased student engagement and learning.

This study illustrates the use of both qualitative and quantitative classroom observation methods in a study of one model of school reform, *Success for All* (SFA), that is being implemented in hundreds of elementary schools across the United States and abroad. As will be described, SFA reorganizes time and resources to provide rich reading instruction for all children. In this chapter, we use our dual methodological approach to explore what that reorganization and a new reading curriculum mean for teachers and students: how teachers' practices change and whether those changes result in improved student engagement and learning. We report these findings in a way that allows the reader to understand the advantages and disadvantages of the observational techniques used.

Our approach differs from most others in that we used mixed observation methods in order to develop a fuller picture of classroom life. We employed multiple data collection instruments that triangulated our observations and provided a high level of confidence in the results. The classroom observation instruments used in this study were customized for the purposes of observation research on SFA and are similar to the methods described by Datnow and Yonezawa (this volume). Overall, we find that the specificity of the observational methods described herein can be useful to educational researchers in obtaining the types of findings about school reform that we report here.

LITERATURE REVIEW

For at least three decades, researchers and advocates for minority groups have decried the poor state of education for culturally and linguistically diverse students (Abrahams & Troike, 1972; Cummins, 1989; Heath, 1983; Valdes, 1996). Many studies describe "bright-eyed and bushy-tailed" first graders, entering the school system eager to please their teachers and to learn, but by third grade many of these same students are having problems reading, keeping up with classwork, and behaving properly in the classroom (Fillmore, 1990; Stringfield & Teddlie, 1991).

This transformation has been attributed to many causes, some of which are no longer tenable, such as those based on genetic or cultural deficit theories. Other researchers cite larger societal conditions, such as the need to reproduce the unequal class system in the United States (Bowles & Gintis, 1976). Still others point to teacher attitudes. For instance, many teachers expect that children will come to school with some knowledge of American English sounds, letters, and words, and they believe that such knowledge must precede any reading or writing of texts (Franklin, 1986). Thus, when children arrive at school without this background knowledge, teachers often use instructional techniques that are no longer centered on the purpose of reading – creating an understanding of an author's intent; instead, they focus exclusively on phonics and rules that are quite apart from that purpose. They drill the *building blocks* of reading and expect children to put these blocks together themselves and automatically arrive at the purpose of reading on their own. This process often becomes a downward-spiraling whirlpool of lowered expectations as culturally or linguistically nonmainstream children are labeled poor readers or slow learners and the possibility for school success becomes more remote.

Research on the education of culturally and linguistically diverse children has been qualitative for the most part; that is, small-scale, in-depth studies of classrooms make up the bulk of the research base (Foley, 1991; Gilmore & Glatthorn, 1982; Macleod, 1987; Spindler, 1982). In a review of these interpretivist studies, Mehan (1992) noted that they have helped to open up the "black box" of schooling for minority students, whereas the more positivist large-scale quantitative studies that dominated the sociology of education informed us of general trends but told us little about the daily realities of schooling.

The qualitative research base on the education of multicultural, multilingual students has significantly improved our understanding of the processes of schooling for children with different cultural or linguistic backgrounds. We now know of the importance of considering students' home discourse strategies (e.g., ways of telling stories or displaying knowledge) when trying to explain why some students may not participate or excel in middle-class American classroom activities (Heath, 1983; Philips, 1972). We now have a library of effective teacher practices for multicultural, multilingual classrooms (Cazden, 1988; Cummins, 1989; Tharp, 1997). It seems that we know what we need to improve education for all students, and now the task is to create the conditions in schools under which all children can indeed learn and document that success.

Contemporaneous with the qualitative research on classrooms of culturally and linguistically diverse students was the release of a series of commissioned reports during the 1980s and 1990s that decried a "rising tide of mediocrity" (National Commission on Excellence in Education, 1983) in American schooling (National Center on Education and the Economy, 1990). These reports warned that inattention to the education of minority students in particular, who were becoming an increasing percentage of the school-age population, would lead to a generation of underprepared adults unable to grab the helms of the U.S. economy, and the nation would lose ground economically to other developed countries (Johnston & Packer, 1987). One solution that many of the reports pointed to was serious school reform that set tougher standards for both teachers and students.

As the 1990s began, educators and policymakers realized that raising standards was not enough; schools needed to provide the support necessary to help all students meet those standards. This led to a second wave of school reforms characterized by restructuring, which has many definitions but usually includes site-based management and scheduling changes (Michaels, 1988). The past few years have seen the rise of what may be a third wave, the comprehensive school reform movement, characterized by schools adopting externally developed reform models, presumably all of which have research-based track records. These models incorporate many of the elements found in the second wave of school reform, such as changes in professional development, school governance, moral climate, and/or curricular materials. They also include such things as scheduling changes, social services delivered on the school campus, project-based learning activities, and/or team teaching. The difference between the last two waves is the institutionalization of certain reform models and the emergence of companies, universities, or foundations to represent and market these models to schools across the country, which adopt them more or less completely.

It appears that the school reform movement is poised to make a difference in the education of culturally and linguistically diverse students. Many of the reform models include practices generally considered to constitute effective teaching, and most have had some form of objective research conducted showing their efficacy (Herman, 1999). In addition, the passage of the Comprehensive School Reform Demonstration Program (CSRD) by the U.S. Congress in 1997 has helped schools pay for the adoption of research-based reform designs. In 2002, an additional $260 million was allocated to CSRD. As of August 2003, there were over 1,500 elementary schools nationwide implementing SFA. There are dozens of other school reform models, such as Accelerated Schools, the Comer School Development Program, and the New American Schools Designs, all with national support groups, most rapidly growing with hundreds if not thousands of schools involved in implementation. This scale-up of externally developed reform models is indeed shaping the next wave of school reform in the United States.

The question now is whether any of these reforms will improve teaching and learning for culturally and linguistically diverse students. In this chapter, we will address this question using qualitative and quantitative classroom observation methods to explore one such reform model, SFA. Our purpose here is not only to ascertain the effects of the reform model on classroom life, but in doing so to expose the methods we used in studying this particular reform. SFA, developed at Johns Hopkins University but now based at the nonprofit SFA Foundation, is a research-based reform model that focuses on prevention and early intervention to ensure that students succeed in reading throughout the elementary grades (Slavin, Madden, Dolan, & Wasik, 1996). Major components of SFA include a 90-minute reading period every day, the regrouping of students into smaller homogeneous groups for reading instruction, 8-week assessments, cooperative learning, and one-to-one tutoring. The SFA reading curriculum consists of an Early Learning program for prekindergarten and kindergarten students; Reading Roots, a beginning reading program; and Reading Wings, its upper-elementary counterpart (Slavin, Madden, Karweit, Donal, & Wasik, 1992). There are both English and Spanish versions of the program; the Spanish version of SFA is called *Exito Para Todos*. That the SFA developers made the effort to produce a Spanish version at all, rare among national reform models, reflects a commitment to linguistically diverse children.

SFA takes an aggressive approach to changing teaching and learning. As a result, the program is highly specified with respect to implementation guidelines and materials for students and teachers. Almost all materials for students are provided, including reading booklets and assessments for the primary grades and materials to accompany various textbook series and novels for the upper grades, as well as workbooks and activity sheets for all grade levels. Teachers are expected to closely follow SFA lesson plans, which involve an active pacing of multiple activities during the 90-minute reading period (Madden, Livingston, & Cummings, 1998).

The SFA Foundation requires that at least 80% of a school's teaching staff vote to adopt the program before they will provide the materials and technical assistance. They also ask that schools employ a full-time SFA facilitator, organize a Family Support Team, and organize bi-weekly meetings among Roots and Wings teachers. With these components, SFA attempts to be more than just a reading program. As with some other comprehensive school reform models, implementation is supported by ongoing professional development from program trainers and by local and national networks of SFA schools (Cooper, 1998a; Slavin & Madden, 1996; Slavin, Madden, Dolan, & Wasik, 1996).

Numerous quantitative studies of SFA have found consistent positive effects on student reading achievement, as well as reductions in special education placements and retention (Nunnery et al., 1997; Slavin & Madden, 1999; Slavin, Madden, Dolan, Wasik, et al., 1996). Two studies of SFA included qualitative components: the Special Strategies study (Stringfield et al., 1997), which focused on the implementation and effectiveness of SFA as well as other school reform models, and a study of the dimensions of change in SFA schools (Cooper, 1998b; Cooper, Slavin, & Madden, 1997). However, in both of these studies, the qualitative data presented on SFA constituted only one component of larger mixed-method studies with broader goals. Overall, there has been a dearth of qualitative research on SFA.

The mixed-method study upon which this chapter is based examined the SFA implementation process, the level of support for the reform, and the changes in teaching and learning at three schools in California with high percentages of English language learners (Datnow & Castellano, 2000a, 2000b, 2001). The qualitative aspect of this study is important in this era of comprehensive school reform because we need to see how different models are implemented and what are their results compared to claims made on paper. We also need to be able to determine if teaching practices are indeed changing and what effect these changes have on student learning. This calls for systematic observation of teaching and learning, using research instruments designed to discern effective practices and their effect on students, in schools that are implementing whole school reforms.

As noted in Evertson and Green's (1986) review of observation as inquiry and method in education research, observation is a multifaceted phenomenon: "It is a tacit part of the everyday functioning of individuals as they negotiate the events of daily life" (p. 163). Although we all make observations on a daily basis, observation for research purposes is more deliberate and systematic. It is mediated by the observers' training, beliefs, and biases, as well as by the instruments used.

The data for this chapter were gathered using two different observation strategies in order to gather a wide range of classroom data (cf. Datnow & Yonezawa, this volume): a low-inference instrument that involved both interval coding and holistic ratings and a higher-inference set of directed questions about the classroom practices observed. Both will be described in detail. The rationale for using such a combination of instruments was to provide a depth and breadth of understanding not possible with any single approach. These mixed methods allowed us to discern the presence of strategies of effective classroom instruction for culturally and linguistically diverse students and to describe them in detail. In this chapter, we will examine whether SFA improved teaching and learning for the culturally and linguistically diverse students at three schools that adopted the model, using data gathered in classroom observations with the multiple instruments.

METHODOLOGY

The data presented in this chapter were collected as part of a study of three SFA schools that began in January 1998 and ended in

August 1999. We used a case study approach, which enabled us to examine the process of SFA implementation in real-life contexts and allowed us to present the perspectives of those actually implementing the program (Yin, 1994).

School Sample

In keeping with the tenets of case study research, each case (school) in this study was carefully selected to ensure theoretical replication – so that it produced contrary results but for predictable reasons (Yin, 1994). In particular, we chose to conduct case studies of three SFA schools that fit the following specific criteria:

1. A school that had been implementing SFA for 2 or more years and was experiencing implementation success;
2. A school that had been implementing SFA for 2 or more years and was experiencing difficulty with implementation;
3. A new SFA school that adopted the program in 1997–1998 and began its implementation in 1998–1999.

Schools fitting these criteria were recommended to us by SFA trainers from Education Partners, an organization that disseminated SFA in five states in the western United States, including part of California. Gardena Elementary School, which received an implementation rating of "good +," was recommended as fitting the first set of criteria. Peterson Elementary School, which received an implementation rating of "fair," was recommended as fitting the second set of criteria. However, the trainers acknowledged that the differences in implementation between these two schools were not great; and indeed, we found that to be the case. The schools turned out to be quite similar in terms of level of implementation and the issues they faced. Both schools began implementation of SFA in 1996–1997. When our study began, both schools used the Spanish version of SFA, *Exito Para Todos*, with approximately half of their students.

In order to find a new SFA school fitting the third set of criteria, the trainers at Education Partners suggested that we attend an SFA Awareness Presentation that was being conducted for three schools in one district. We attended the session and approached a district administrator for a recommendation. Bayside Elementary School was recommended to us. This school voted to adopt SFA in the middle of the 1997–1998 school year, and it began implementation in the fall of 1998.

All three schools served large Hispanic and low-income student populations, and all were located in California. However, they had quite different community and school contexts, which will now be described.

Peterson Elementary School. Located in a small city, Peterson was one of six elementary schools in its district. In 1998–1999, Peterson served approximately 400 students in grades K–5, of whom over 80% were Hispanic, 10% were White, and the rest consisted of students from other racial and ethnic groups. The Hispanic population was growing, whereas the White population was decreasing. Eighty-five percent of the students were classified as limited English proficient (LEP), and 98% were eligible to receive free or reduced-price lunch. Almost all of Peterson's students, primarily from recent immigrant Hispanic families, were bused from a low-income area of the city several miles from the school. In 1998–1999, Peterson was a Title I Schoolwide Project.

Gardena Elementary School. Gardena, located in a growing agricultural community, was one of eight schools in its district. Gardena served a mix of students from low-income, Spanish-speaking, recent immigrant families, as well as some low- and middle-income White students from families who were long-time community residents. In 1998–1999, Gardena served approximately 500 students in grades K–5, of whom 46% were Hispanic, 53% were White, and 1% were other ethnicities, including African American and Asian. Forty-six percent of the students were classified as LEP, and 68% were eligible for the federal free or reduced-price lunch program. The year 1998–1999 was Gardena's third year as a Title I Schoolwide Project.

Bayside Elementary School. Located in a growing metropolitan area, Bayside was part of a large urban district of over 40 schools. In 1998–1999, Bayside served approximately 750 students in grades K–5. Some of the students lived in the surrounding neighborhood, and others were bused to the school. Seventy-two percent of the students were Hispanic, and of those, 50% were designated as LEP. The Hispanic population was mixed in terms of country of origin, length of time in the United States, and citizenship. The remainder of the student body was 15% White, 4% Asian, and 10% other ethnicities. Bayside was a Title I Schoolwide Project, and 69% of the students received free or reduced-price lunch.

Case Study Data Collection

Our two-person research team conducted a total of four 2-day site visits to Gardena and Peterson, once per semester from February 1998 to March 1999. The schedule of site visits at Bayside was somewhat different because the school began implementation of SFA in the fall of 1998. We made two visits to Bayside before it began implementing SFA and twice afterward, all between the spring of 1998 and March 1999. As part of the larger study, we conducted individual interviews with principals, SFA facilitators, and teachers at all three schools, as well as interviews with district administrators (see Datnow & Castellano, 2000a, 2000b, 2001).

Classroom Observation Protocols. We employed a three-part observation protocol, only the last two parts of which were used in the analysis for the present chapter. The first instrument, used only during SFA reading time, assessed the observed level of implementation of SFA. This form was an adaptation of those used for implementation checks by SFA facilitators; it allowed us to describe local deviations from the SFA model.

The second part of our observation protocol involved a modified version of an instrument called the Classroom Observation Measure (COM). The COM was developed at the University of Memphis to systematically study a tracked intervention model for at-risk elementary school students in one urban school system (Ross, Smith, Lohr, & McNelis, 1994). The COM includes both interval coding, obtained through systematic and relatively objective data recording, and holistic ratings and descriptions that reflect more global, subjective impressions of the classroom activities observed (Ross et al., 1994). Items on the COM were chosen after a review of the literature on observation instruments (e.g., Good & Brophy, 1987) and teaching methods considered effective for at-risk learners (e.g., Padrón, 1992).

In the present study, we used only certain parts of the COM so as not to replicate information gathered in other parts of our observation protocol. Appendix A contains this version. Briefly, the two parts we used were as follows:

The COM Part III: Interval Coding section was used to record observations from nine 1-minute segments coded at 5-minute intervals in the areas of (a) subject(s) taught, (b) teacher orientation (e.g., teacher-led, small group), (c) student attention/focus, and (d) academic engaged time, among others. All the variables were scored on a 5-point scale, where 0 = "None/close to none" and 4 = "All."

In this chapter, we focus only on the latter two variables: "Student attention/focus" is a measure of students' attention to classroom academic activity, and "academic engaged time" is an estimation of the amount of time spent on an educationally relevant activity. Both attention and academic engagement have repeatedly been found to be related to student achievement gains (e.g., Brophy & Good, 1986). Stallings (1980) and Brophy (1988) both note that measures of student engagement should not result in calls for 100% academic use of classroom time, arguing that an 80% or moderately higher engaged-time rate is consistently associated with higher achievement gains, and a rate lower than 80% is associated with lower mean achievement gains. Based on that work and our own prior research (Stringfield, Datnow, Borman, & Rachuba, 1999), we assumed that a rating greater than 3.1 but less than 3.7 out of 4 on the COM could be described as "effective use of time."

The COM Part IV: Overall Observation section was used to record the extent to which different teaching and learning approaches (e.g., cooperative learning, direct instruction, seatwork, use of computers) were used during the overall observation, noted as none, some, or extensive. Many of these approaches have been shown in prior research to be effective strategies for teaching culturally and linguistically diverse children, as detailed subsequently in the discussion of the third observation instrument.

The COM was validated in extensive pilot research and in other studies of elementary school classroom instruction (Ross et al., 1994). A detailed manual describing the observation procedures and operationally defined categories accompanies the COM. Both members of the research team read this training manual before observing classes for this study.

The COM continues to be used in studies of classrooms for at-risk elementary school students (Datnow & Yonezawa, this volume; Stringfield et al., 1999). It has provided robust, useful information on student attention and engagement, as well as on teacher pedagogical strategies. Similar combinations of data-gathering instruments have been used successfully in previous studies of school effectiveness and reform model implementation (Knapp & Adelman, 1995; Stringfield & Teddlie, 1991; Stringfield et al., 1997; Teddlie, Kirby, & Stringfield, 1989).

Finally, the third instrument was aimed at gathering rich, qualitative data about what happens in classrooms at SFA schools during reading and nonreading times. This part of the observation protocol gathered data on the nature and quality of classroom activities, the extent of constructivist teaching, and the degree to which students' individual needs appeared to be addressed by the curriculum and pedagogy employed. We developed this observation instrument because we felt that although the COM had validity, had worked well for the researchers in previous studies, and was simple to use, it was a crude measure of the kinds of teaching we were hoping to describe. We could tell from the COM how much experiential learning took place, for example, but we could not describe it. We sought a deeper texture to our data, which we achieved by supplementing the COM with a set of directed questions. Conversely, the disadvantage of the directed questions was that they were time-consuming to answer, which might have become a problem had the study been larger in scale.

The theory and research that undergirded the directed questions were drawn primarily from the principles for effective teaching and learning that guide the work of the Center for Research on Education, Diversity & Excellence (Tharp, 1997), Newmann and Wehlage's (1995) research on authentic pedagogy, and the research by Cummins (1989) on effective programs for culturally and linguistically diverse students.

Tharp's (1997) principles for the effective education of at-risk students focus on pedagogical strategies rooted in sociocultural theory. Tharp characterizes effective classroom instruction as (a) facilitating learning through joint productive activity between teachers and students; (b) developing competence in the language and literacy of instruction throughout all instructional activities; (c) contextualizing teaching and curriculum in the experiences and skills of home and community; (d) challenging students toward cognitive complexity; and (e) engaging students through dialogue. Newmann and Wehlage's (1995) definition of authentic pedagogy overlaps considerably with Tharp's principles. They emphasize the importance of involving students in higher-order thinking and substantive conversational exchange, producing complex understandings, and helping students connect substantive knowledge with public problems or personal experiences.

Consistent with these findings, Cummins (1989) concluded that effective programs for linguistically and culturally diverse students have the following process characteristics: They (a) allow for the development of students' native linguistic talents; (b) foster a sense of personal and cultural identity; (c) promote multiculturalism rather than assimilation; (d) employ materials relevant for minority students; (e) engage students in cooperative learning; (f) maintain high expectations for minority and White students; and (g) promote confidence in the ability to learn. Cummins is attentive to the need for students of color to have their histories and experiences confirmed by schools. Because we believe this to be a goal of schooling, we were attentive to these issues in our research. However, the tenets that Cummins outlines are effective practices not only for students of color, but for all students.

Based on this research, we developed a set of questions to explore effective practice, including the following (see Appendix B for complete form):

1. Did the curriculum and pedagogy used by the teacher encourage students to dialogue or use language?
2. In the course of the lesson, did students make connections between substantive knowledge and either public problems or personal experiences?
3. Did the curriculum and pedagogy foster a sense of personal and cultural identity?
4. Was there evidence that teachers had high expectations of the students?
5. Were the students engaged in meaningful and challenging learning activities?

We answered these questions for the 60 classrooms we observed, 32 of which were observed during SFA time. This instrument allowed us to see whether SFA contributed to teachers' repertoires of effective practices, and whether teachers incorporated other effective teaching strategies. Similar directed questions were used by the researchers in other studies, adapted to the particular research questions for those studies. Both researchers were very familiar with the literature that comprised the theoretical background for this instrument and with the tenets of qualitative research. We shared our observation write-ups with each other after completing them, and we discussed how we had answered the questions, often when we were unsure whether what we had observed did or did not constitute evidence of a particular instructional strategy. Apart from these activities, we did not perform other validity or reliability checks on this particular instrument.

In addition to systematically using these two instruments, in all of the classes we observed we took running notes of classroom activities, describing the actions of teachers and students and how teachers taught the SFA curriculum.

We conducted a total of 60 observations of classrooms (both English and Spanish) at all grade levels, both during the SFA 90-minute reading period and at other times of the day. Of the 60, we were able to complete the entire protocol for 58[1]: 26 at Peterson, 22 at Gardena, and 10 at Bayside. At Gardena and Bayside, we conducted observations without teachers' prior knowledge that we would be in their classrooms. Thus, they were unable to prepare for our arrival in their rooms in particular, although they knew that we would be in the school that day. However, at Peterson, the principal felt more comfortable scheduling observations with teachers, and thus the teachers knew ahead of time that we would be visiting their classrooms.

Of the 58 completed observations, 35 were conducted during SFA instructional time and 23 were conducted during non-SFA time (e.g., math, science, language arts, music). We observed a fairly even representation of Roots ($n = 15$) and Wings ($n = 17$) SFA classes overall, as well as at each school. Although we attempted to see a range of classrooms in each school, our observations during non-SFA instructional time were more often in primary grade K–2 classrooms ($n = 16$) than in grade 3–5 classrooms ($n = 8$). However, at Bayside, our only observations of non-SFA time (which were few) were in grade 3–5 classrooms. We saw many more classes in which English was the primary language ($n = 40$) as compared to Spanish ($n = 14$) or both English and Spanish ($n = 4$). This was in part because the schools reduced or eliminated Spanish bilingual classes in 1999 after the passage of Proposition 227 in California, a voter initiative to end bilingual education.

Data Analysis

For this study, we analyzed observation instruments and field notes from 60 classroom observations. We analyzed data gathered with the COM, using Microsoft Excel to calculate basic means and frequencies and using STATA version 6.0 to perform *t*-tests and analyses of variance. The qualitative classroom observation data were analyzed by compiling answers to each directed question and identifying themes in the responses.

Using three sources of data allowed us to triangulate the findings. For example, both the COM Part IV and our directed questions elicited data on effective instructional practices, one in more detail than the other.

This allowed for both a broad survey of data across many classrooms and an in-depth picture of individual classes.

With respect to the questions about effective classroom practices, we used a "yes–somewhat–no" format in determining whether a particular element (e.g., high expectations) was present in the classroom. "Yes" and "no" answers were usually straightforward and were counted as such. The following answers coded as "yes" and "no" serve as examples:

Was there evidence that the teacher had high expectations of the students? Describe how you know this. Were these expectations conveyed equally to all students?

YES: (First grade, Language Arts) – *Teacher really encourages students to write and take their writing seriously. She encourages them to think creatively and improve quality of their journal entries.*

NO: (Fourth grade, Social Studies) – *No real evidence of this. It seemed more like going through the motions.*

The "somewhat" answer reflected hedges and qualifiers by the observer (e.g., "hard to tell" accompanied by a description) or other situations that were neither "yes" nor "no." The following answers coded as "somewhat" serve as examples:

Were the students engaged in meaningful and challenging learning activities? Describe how you know this.

SFA Wings – *I think the idea of teaching prediction is important, challenging and meaningful. But I think the teacher went through it too quickly and I doubt that everyone got it.*

Kindergarten – *Given that it's kindergarten, the activities of singing, letter practice, group story reading, basic reading comprehension, seemed meaningful and challenging. Hard to tell, really. However, centers seemed somewhat unchallenging. One involved playing with dinosaurs; another was blocks. Only two centers involved academic work. Seemed like more structured activities for centers could have been better.*

The three possible answers were tallied by category. If for a given category (i.e., SFA classes) there was an equal number of "yes" and "no" answers to a given question, that was also considered "somewhat" in our overall assessment of the presence of that practice.

Given that all three schools used the Spanish version of SFA, it might seem natural that we would compare English and Spanish language classes to address the research question, namely, the effects of SFA on the teaching and learning of culturally and linguistically diverse children. However, after a preliminary analysis, we decided that such a procedure would not yield valid findings for several reasons. First of all, there were more English than Spanish classes overall at all three schools. This meant that we observed more English classes and that our attempts to compare student engagement, instructional strategies, and effective practices across language of instruction would have many more data points in English, affecting the results. Indeed, there were so few upper-level Spanish classes (because students are expected to transition to English classes by about the third grade) that we felt that this would skew the results of the Spanish classes toward an emphasis on basic skills over content instruction, when such a finding would only have been an artifact of the level of classes we observed. Second, California eliminated Spanish bilingual classes during the time of our study, which also affected the number of Spanish classes we were able to observe. Finally, we decided not to pit English classes against Spanish classes as though they were in competition. All children need to be engaged in their classwork, and they need certain instructional strategies and teacher practices in order to learn, regardless of the language of instruction. Therefore, we decided to analyze the data by SFA/non-SFA class time to discern what SFA brought to the teachers and classrooms in terms of student engagement, instructional strategies, and effective practices.

We wish to note that this study was not designed to monitor student achievement. California mandated a new state test (the Stanford Achievement Test-9) in 1998, soon after the schools in this study adopted SFA, so there was no way to compare school test scores before and after implementation. However, Peterson and Gardena reported to us that the results on SFA reading assessments were positive: More students were reading at grade level after SFA than before, including both English and Spanish native speakers. We were not able to obtain SFA reading assessment results from Bayside.

FINDINGS

Changes in Classroom Reading Activities

As described elsewhere (Datnow & Castellano, 2000a), the majority of the SFA curriculum was implemented by almost all teachers in the schools we studied. This meant that teaching and learning during reading time changed markedly for students and teachers. How markedly? The following descriptions of Roots, the beginning reading program, and Wings, its upper-elementary counterpart, show that there are very specific activities in SFA reading classes that teachers are expected to adhere to rather closely.

In Roots, the daily 90-minute reading class begins with the teacher reading a selection of quality children's literature to students and engaging them in listening comprehension and prediction activities. Then students read stories from SFA-produced small books that they can take home. These books have phonetically regular vocabulary, and the activities around them emphasize a rapid pace of instruction including shared practice, letter activities, story activities, partner reading, and a reading celebration in which two to three students read a story to their classmates. The Peabody Language Kit, which includes a carefully sequenced set of oral language development activities, is also used.

In Wings, the 90-minute reading period begins with 20 minutes of listening comprehension in which the teacher engages students in a discussion about the story and the author's craft. This is followed by a 55-minute segment of reading instruction called "Reading Together," in which there is a teacher-directed lesson and students then work in teams on follow-up activities. Basal readers, novels, or anthologies are used, depending on students' reading levels, and are accompanied by SFA-developed activities and worksheets. Depending on the day (there is a 5-day cycle), teachers will teach new vocabulary, teach how to write meaningful sentences using new words, or conduct guided practice, review, or reading comprehension exercises. Students may then engage in discussion of reading comprehension questions with their partners, write individual answers, or craft meaningful sentences using vocabulary words. Other activities include a quick editing exercise and a Book Club, in which students share books read outside of class.

We found that many teachers were smooth and pleasant in their delivery of the SFA curriculum and worked with obvious interest in the children's progress and the stories they were reading. SFA encourages teachers to spend time talking about the author, the illustrator, and the book as a physical object, which most teachers seemed to enjoy. We observed classes engaging in a meaningful dialogue as students went over predictive questions for a new story. Our observations convinced us that most children found the activities, such as beginning readers putting story events in order, to be challenging. Teachers gave students some time to connect the reading to their personal experiences. Of course, the sophistication and relevance of these discussions often depended on the age of the students. Teachers also used a lot of positive feedback and addressed different modalities of student learning. Sometimes teachers molded the SFA routine to fit the students' needs and moods, perhaps by extending the discussion time. This meant that other scheduled SFA activities were not done that day. Overall, most teachers taught solid lessons that incorporated identifiable SFA strategies, with a range of adaptations (see Datnow & Castellano, 2000a, 2000b).

Our observations also showed that students' engagement level was high. The students appeared accustomed to, but not bored by, the SFA lesson routine. The partnering of students usually worked well, both for discussion and for reading. Students had ample opportunity to dialogue with each other and with the teacher and to make some connections to their own prior knowledge and cultural experiences.

Of course, not all of the SFA classes we observed ran smoothly. At times, teachers appeared overly influenced by the pacing of activities, even cutting student discussion short in order to move on to the next activity and keep to the schedule. A few teachers used a kitchen timer to keep themselves on schedule, which was distracting and seemed stifling to us as observers. Also, we observed a number of classes where the activities (e.g., partner reading) did not go as planned, either because students were not working together well or were not being monitored closely. Most often, when we observed significant departures from the SFA curriculum, teachers engaged students in reading-related activities that seemed generally worthwhile, but did not fit with the model and thus may have compromised particular program goals.

In the subsequent sections, we use our observation data from all classrooms across the three schools to compare overall levels of student engagement in SFA and non-SFA classes and teachers' instructional strategies in both types of classes.

The Effect of SFA on Student Engagement

As described previously, the modified COM we used provided nine snapshot intervals of a classroom during every 1-hour observation. Here we focus on two of the variables measured in this section of the COM, student attention/focus and academic engaged time, which are highly correlated, as noted. Aggregating the scores on both of these variables across all intervals per school yielded a school mean for each, and averaging the two item scores produced a more reliable school-level measure of academic engagement.

We then compared the mean student attention/academic engaged times for each school. All three schools obtained schoolwide measures of student engagement that were in what might be described as the "relatively effective" range (i.e., between 3.1 and 3.7 on the 5-point scale). Gardena's mean student attention/engaged time rate was 3.16 (*SD* = 0.81), Peterson's was 3.10 (*SD* = 0.84), and Bayside's was 3.17 (*SD* = 0.88). We concluded that there were no major differences between the schools in terms of mean student attention/academic engaged time.

Because there were negligible differences between the schools, we pooled the data from all three schools to compare student attention/academic engaged time during both SFA and non-SFA classroom observation intervals. The average student attention/academic engaged time during our SFA observations was substantially higher (*M* = 3.38, *SD* = 0.69) than during our non-SFA observations (*M* = 2.71, *SD* = 0.88), and this difference was statistically significant ($p < .0001$).

Although the non-SFA class time student attention/academic engaged rate is low compared to the SFA class time and is below the range considered effective use of time, a breakdown of this time by subject explains some of the difference. Fully 38% of the non-SFA class time we observed (which was typically randomly selected, not scheduled) consisted of art, music, or no subject (transitions, directions, etc.). Student attention and academic engaged rates were predictably lower during these times. Another one-third of non-SFA class time was devoted to language arts (spelling, grammar, word games), one-quarter was spent on math, and only small amounts of writing, social studies, and science were observed. In many cases, we conducted observations of the same teachers during SFA and non-SFA time, and therefore we feel confident that our results do not reflect teacher differences.

As Figure 10.1 shows, instruction in science and math was within the effective range (i.e., above 3.1). We performed an analysis of variance (ANOVA) to determine whether there were significant differences between the means for the various subjects. Our results show that the subjects differed significantly in mean academic engagement–student attention rates, $F(8, 514) = 29.54$, $p < .00001$. Next, we performed a simple regression as a post hoc analysis to determine which of the eight subject means were significantly different from SFA (see Table 10.1). The omitted group is SFA and is the constant term in this regression equation. As Table 10.1 shows, there were no significant differences between the mean academic engaged time–student attention rates between SFA and math ($p < .213$) and SFA and science ($p < .682$); however,

TABLE 10.1. *Regression Analysis Comparing Mean of SFA Academic Engaged Time–Attention to Means for Other Subjects*

Subject	Coef.	Std. Err.
SFA (constant term)	3.38	.04
Other	−1.42***	.10
Language arts	−.30**	.096
Writing	−.92***	.21
Math	−.14	.11
Science	−.097	.24
Social studies	−.93***	.24
Music	−1.38***	.41
Art	−.94***	.18

Note: $R^2 = 0.31$; Adj $R^2 = 0.30$; root MSE $= .70$.
**$p < .001$. ***$p < .0001$.

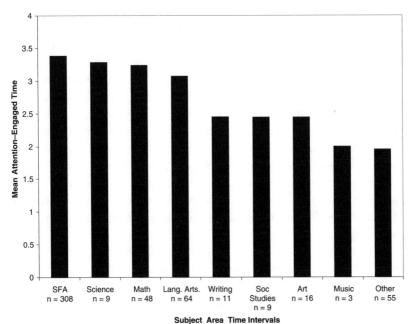

FIGURE 10.1. Mean attention–engaged time by subject.

the academic engaged time–student attention mean for SFA was significantly higher than the means for social studies ($p < .0001$), writing ($p < .0001$), other language arts ($p < .002$), music ($p < .001$), art ($p < .0001$), and other ($p < .0001$).

In sum, the mean academic engaged time–student attention rates for math and science are comparable to SFA (and in the effective range), but in the other subjects we observed, these rates are lower than SFA and no longer within the effective range.

Corroborating these classroom observation data on student engagement are anecdotal reports from principals and teachers that students mostly enjoy SFA. For example, in a 1997–1998 student survey conducted by staff at Peterson, 94% of students said that they liked to read, 82% of students reported that they liked their reading class, and 93% said they read at home. Across all three schools, the majority of teachers we interviewed noted improvement in students' interest in reading.

The Effect of SFA on Teachers' Instructional Strategies

Using data gathered in the COM, we conducted a descriptive analysis of the instructional strategies observed during SFA and non-SFA academic instructional time.[2] The data for this analysis were gleaned from the more global part of the COM that asks observers to rate whether there was none, some, or extensive evidence of a particular instructional strategy during the entire classroom observation period. Where a particular strategy was present, most ratings were skewed toward the "some" response. Only the strategy of *basic skills instruction* was skewed toward the "extensive" response. This is probably attributable to the fact that SFA instruction is by design skill-based, and, with respect to non-SFA classrooms, the skew could be attributable to the fact that we saw many more lower-grade than upper-grade classrooms, as explained previously.

We compared the instructional strategies in SFA and non-SFA academic classrooms, pooling interval data from all three schools and in both languages. Figure 10.2 shows that SFA instructional time was characterized by slightly more evidence of *direct instruction, basic skills instruction, dialogue,* and *challenging activities* and by considerably more evidence of *cooperative learning* than non-SFA academic time. These strategies, particularly the inclusion of *direct instruction* and *cooperative learning,* are consistent with the SFA curriculum. One might expect to see more evidence of *tutoring* in SFA classrooms. However, the tutoring

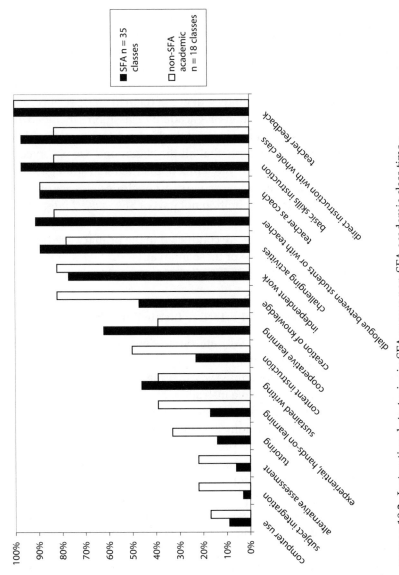

FIGURE 10.2. Instructional strategies in SFA versus non-SFA academic class time.

that is characteristic of SFA takes place outside of the 90-minute reading period, so it did not appear in our SFA class time COMs.

We found more *student creation of knowledge, content instruction,* and *experiential learning* in non-SFA academic classrooms than in SFA classrooms. These strategies are commonly accepted as good teaching practice, and we were pleased to find evidence of them in math, science, and social studies. Both SFA and non-SFA academic classrooms included extensive *teacher feedback* and instances of the *teacher acting as coach.* Taken together, this evidence suggests that all the classrooms we observed – both SFA and non-SFA – involved a mix of instructional strategies that are known to be effective. However, we saw very little evidence of other such strategies that are by definition not part of SFA: *subject integration, computer use,* and *alternative assessment.* The fact that many of our non-SFA academic observations were conducted in the primary grades may account for the low evidence of these innovative strategies, but it was disheartening to learn that they were so seldom used in these classes.

Assessment of the Degree of Effective Instructional Practices

In addition to assessing COM data on student engagement and instructional strategies, we analyzed our qualitative notes and answers to directed questions to determine whether the classrooms we observed were characterized by effective instructional practices. As noted previously, we looked to the theory and research on what constitutes effective classroom practice for culturally and linguistically diverse students to develop questions about the presence of the following five effective instructional practices: (a) encouraging students to dialogue or use language, (b) encouraging students to make connections between substantive knowledge and either public problems or personal experiences, (c) fostering a sense of personal and cultural identity, (d) holding high expectations, and (e) engaging students in meaningful and challenging learning activities.

Comparing the SFA and non-SFA academic classes yielded some interesting results (see Figures 10.3 and 10.4). In the SFA classrooms, we observed much more dialogue between students and between teachers and students. Only about half of the non-SFA academic classes were characterized by such language use. In addition, SFA classes were much stronger than non-SFA academic classes at connecting school knowledge to the world outside the school. Our analysis showed that SFA classrooms provided more meaningful and challenging activities than

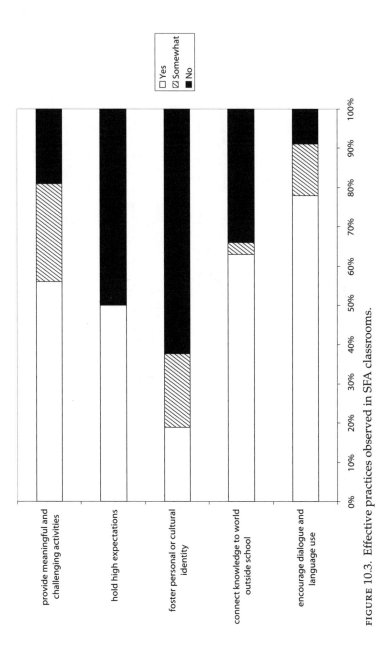

FIGURE 10.3. Effective practices observed in SFA classrooms.

254

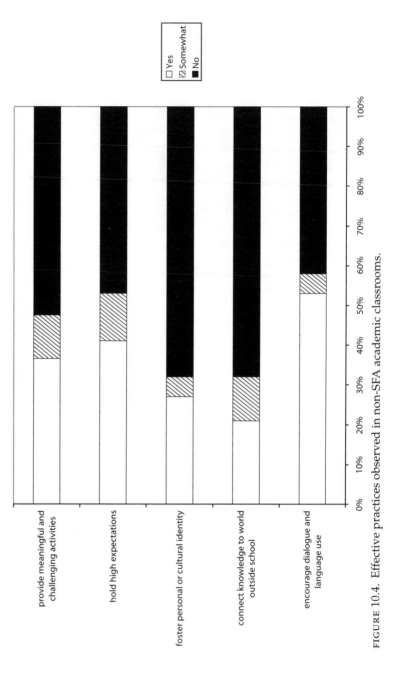

FIGURE 10.4. Effective practices observed in non-SFA academic classrooms.

the non-SFA academic classrooms. Only moderate levels of high expectations for students were found in both SFA and non-SFA academic
classes. Finally, non-SFA academic classes appeared to foster students'
personal or cultural identities more than SFA classes, although neither
did so to any considerable extent. This is problematic, given the diverse
student populations these schools serve – not just Hispanic students,
but students from other ethnicities and language groups as well.

In interpreting these results, we must recall that just as our questions come from research-based, broadly accepted principles of exemplary pedagogy for culturally diverse students, so too does SFA. The
program was designed to incorporate the best practices of reading pedagogy; therefore, it should not surprise us that it fares well in analyses of exemplary elements of classroom practice. At the same time, the
differences between SFA and non-SFA academic classes suggest that
teachers were not transferring the pedagogical practices used in SFA
to other subjects. In fact, as Figure 10.4 shows, even if we include the
"somewhat" response, only two of the practices we looked for (*high
expectations* and *encouraging dialogue*) were found in more than half of the
non-SFA academic classes. Fewer than half of the other non-SFA
academic classes appeared to be contextualizing learning for students
or challenging them with meaningful work.

CONCLUSIONS AND IMPLICATIONS

This chapter reported classroom observation data from a 2-year mixed-
method study of three SFA schools with culturally and linguistically
diverse student populations, describing the effects of SFA implementation on teaching and learning. This study has shown that systematic
observation of a comprehensive school reform model such as SFA can
illuminate changes in classroom practice resulting from implementation
of the model.

In particular, our set of classroom observations suggests that the mean
student attention and academic engaged time rates during SFA were
within the effective range on our observation measure, and in both respects were higher but did not differ significantly from those seen in
math and science instruction. The mean student attention and academic
engaged time rates during SFA were, however, significantly higher than
during our observations of other language arts, writing, social studies,
art, music, and other classes. SFA class time was characterized as being
strong in most elements of effective classroom practice and stronger

than non-SFA academic class time in most areas. In general, teachers used effective, research-proven instructional strategies more often in SFA than in other subjects. Although we do not know if student achievement improved, we can say that instruction improved, if only during reading time. Students were writing more and engaging in more cooperative learning and in more meaningful and challenging activities in SFA classrooms as compared to non-SFA classrooms – both academic and nonacademic.

This study supports the use of multiple instruments in order to gain a deeper understanding of the classroom. The quantitative components of the study confirmed the presence of pedagogical strategies known to be effective with culturally and linguistically diverse children, at least during SFA class time. The qualitative components of the study were able to address the question of whether and how these strategies changed the learning environment. This is crucial knowledge because test scores alone may not reflect the progress and achievement of students for whom English is a second language. Instead, we must look at how changes in instruction affect what goes on in classrooms.

The use of multiple methods, both a low-inference quantitative instrument and the higher-inference directed questions, provided a much broader and deeper understanding of the schools and classrooms than would have been possible with either approach alone. As we have shown, the knowledge gained from such a mixed-method study can then be used to determine whether a given reform model is likely to result in improved teaching and learning for culturally and linguistically diverse children.

At the same time, the classroom observation approach we describe has its limitations. Undoubtedly, using the exact methodology we describe requires familiarity with the SFA reading curriculum and with general elementary school methods of instruction. Training is no doubt required in order for researchers to be prepared to use these particular instruments. On the other hand, others wishing to use these methods could construct similar instruments on their own to study the classroom effects of other types of school reform initiatives. They must be careful, however, to ground their data collection in the theory and research driving their study, as well as in a good understanding of the goals of the reform and of best practices in education.

In conclusion, comprehensive school reform models such as SFA are growing in popularity across the country. Because of this growing influence, advocates for the education of culturally and linguistically diverse children must study the classroom effects of these models. Not only must the tenets of a reform model be examined, but also its implementation: how the model goes from theory to practice in specific schools. The classroom observation methods described here can help address this issue.

Notes

Note: The work reported herein was supported by a grant from the Office of Educational Research and Improvement, U.S. Department of Education, to the Center for Research on the Education of Students Placed At Risk (Grant No. R-117D-40005) and a grant to the Center for Research on Education, Diversity & Excellence under the Educational Research and Development Centers Program, PR/Award Number R306A60001. However, any opinions expressed are the authors' own and do not represent the policies or positions of the U.S. Department of Education. Please address correspondence to Marisa Castellano, Center for Social Organization of Schools, Johns Hopkins University, 3003 N. Charles St., Suite 200, Baltimore, MD 21218. E-mail: *marisa@csos.jhu.edu*

1. Due to time constraints, we did not complete the protocol in two classrooms.
2. That is, classes in which the majority of observation intervals were recorded as language arts, writing, math, science, or social studies, as opposed to art, music, or no subject. Non-SFA academic classes totaled 18 of the 23 non-SFA classes we observed across all schools, or 78%.

References

Abrahams, R. D., & Troike, R. C. (1972). *Language and cultural diversity in American education*. Englewood Cliffs, NJ: Prentice-Hall.

Bowles, S., & Gintis, H. (1976). *Schooling in capitalist America: Educational reform and the contradictions of economic life*. New York: Basic Books.

Brophy, J. E. (1988). Research on teacher effects: Uses and abuses. *Elementary School Journal, 89*, 3–22.

Brophy, J. E., & Good, T. L. (1986). Teacher behavior and student achievement. In M. C. Wittrock (Ed.), *Handbook of research on teaching* (3rd ed., pp. 328–375). New York: Macmillan.

Cazden, C. (1988). *Classroom discourse: The language of teaching and learning*. Portsmouth, NH: Heinemann.

Cooper, R. (1998a). *Socio-cultural and within-school factors that affect the quality of implementation of school-wide programs* (Report No. 28). Baltimore: Center for Research on the Education of Students Placed at Risk, Johns Hopkins University.

Cooper, R. (1998b). Success for All: Improving the quality of implementation of whole school change through local and national support networks. *Education and Urban Society, 30*(3), 385–408.

Cooper, R., Slavin, R. E., & Madden, N. A. (1997). *Success for All: Exploring the technical, normative, political, and socio-cultural dimensions of scaling up* (Report No. 16). Baltimore: Center for Research on the Education of Students Placed at Risk, Johns Hopkins University.

Cummins, J. (1989). *Empowering minority students.* Sacramento: California Association of Bilingual Education.

Datnow, A., & Castellano, M. (2000a). *An "inside" look at Success for All: A qualitative study of implementation and teaching and learning* (Report No. 45). Baltimore: Center for Research on the Education of Students Placed at Risk, Johns Hopkins University and Howard University.

Datnow, A. , & Castellano, M. (2000b). Teachers' responses to Success for All: How beliefs, experiences, and adaptations shape implementation. *American Educational Research Journal, 37*(3), 775–799.

Datnow, A. , & Castellano, M. (2001). Managing and guiding school reform: Leadership in Success for All schools. *Educational Administration Quarterly, 37*(2), 219–249.

Elmore, R. (1996). Getting to scale with good educational practice. *Harvard Educational Review, 66*(1), 1–26.

Evertson, C., & Green, J. L. (1986). Observation as inquiry and method. In M. C. Wittrock (Ed.), *Handbook of research on teaching* (3rd ed., pp. 162–207). New York: Macmillan.

Fillmore, L. W. (1990). *Latino families and schools.* Sacramento, CA: Remarks prepared for the Seminar on California's Changing Face of Race Relations: New Ethics in the 1990s.

Foley, D. E. (1991). Reconsidering anthropological explanations of ethnic school failure. *Anthropology and Education Quarterly, 22*(1), 60–86.

Franklin, E. A. (1986). Literacy instruction for LES children. *Language Arts, 63*(1), 51–60.

Gilmore, P., & Glatthorn, A. (1982). *Children in and out of school: Ethnography and education.* Washington, DC: Harcourt Brace Jovanovich and the Center for Applied Linguistics.

Good, T., & Brophy, J. (1987). *Looking in classrooms* (4th ed.). New York: Harper & Row.

Heath, S. B. (1983). *Ways with words: Language, life, and work in communities and classrooms.* New York: Cambridge University Press.

Herman, R. (1999). *An educators' guide to schoolwide reform.* Arlington, VA: Educational Research Service.

Johnston, W. B., & Packer, A. B. (1987). *Workplace 2000: Work and workers for the 21st century.* Indianapolis, IN: Hudson Institute.

Knapp, M. S., & Adelman, N. E. (1995). *Teaching for meaning in high-poverty classrooms.* New York: Teachers College Press.

Macleod, J. (1987). *Ain't no makin' it: Leveled aspirations in a low income neighborhood.* Boulder, CO: Westview Press.

Madden, N., Livingston, M., & Cummings, N. (1998). *Success for All: Roots and Wings principal's and facilitator's manual.* Baltimore: Johns Hopkins University.

Mehan, H. (1992). Understanding inequality in schools: The contribution of interpretive studies. *Sociology of Education, 65*(1), 1–20.

Michaels, K. (1988). Caution: Second-wave reform taking place. *Educational Leadership, 45*(5), 3.

National Center on Education and the Economy. (1990). *America's choice: High skills or low wages!* (The report of the Commission on the Skills of the American Work Force). Rochester, NY: Author.

National Commission on Excellence in Education. (1983). *A nation at risk: The imperative for educational reform.* Washington, DC: U.S. Government Printing Office.

Newmann, F. M., & Wehlage, G. (1995). *Successful school restructuring.* Madison, WI: Center on Organization and Restructuring of Schools.

Nunnery, J., Slavin, R. E., Madden, N. A., Ross, S. M., Smith, L. J., Hunter, P., & Stubbs, J. (1997). *Effects of full and partial implementation of Success for All on student reading achievement in English and Spanish.* Paper presented at the annual meeting of the American Educational Research Association, Chicago.

Padrón, Y. (1992). Instructional programs that improve the reading comprehension of students at risk. In H. C. Waxman, J. de Felix, J. Anderson, & J. Baptiste (Eds.), *Students at risk in at-risk schools* (pp. 222–232). Newbury Park, CA: Corwin.

Philips, S. (1972). Participant structures and communicative competence: Warm Springs children in community and classroom. In C. Cazden, V. John, & D. Hymes (Eds.), *Functions of language in the classroom* (pp. 370–394). New York: Teachers College Press.

Ross, S. M., Smith, L. J., Lohr, L. L. , & McNelis, M. J. (1994). Math and reading instruction in tracked first-grade classes. *The Elementary School Journal, 95*(1), 105–109.

Slavin, R. E., & Madden, N. A. (1996). *Scaling up: Lessons learned in the dissemination of Success for All* (Report No. 6). Baltimore: Center for Research on the Education of Students Placed at Risk.

Slavin, R. E., & Madden, N. A. (1999). Effects of bilingual and second language adaptations of Success for All on the reading achievement of students acquiring English. *Journal of Education for Students Placed At Risk, 4*(4), 393–416.

Slavin, R. E., Madden, N. A., Dolan, L. J., & Wasik, B. A. (1996). *Every child, every school: Success for All.* Newbury Park, CA: Corwin.

Slavin, R. E., Madden, N. A., Dolan, L. J., Wasik, B. A., Ross, S. M., Smith, L. J., & Dianda, M. (1996). Success for All: A summary of research. *Journal of Education for Students Placed At Risk, 1*(1), 41–76.

Slavin, R. E., Madden, N. A., Karweit, N., Dolan, L. J., & Wasik, B. A. (1992). *Success for All: A relentless approach to prevention and early intervention in elementary schools.* Arlington, VA: Educational Research Service.

Spindler, G. D. (1982). *Doing the ethnography of schooling.* New York: Holt, Rinehart & Winston.

Stallings, J. A. (1980). Allocated academic learning time revisited, or beyond time on task. *Educational Researcher, 9*(11), 11–16.

Stringfield, S., Datnow, A., Borman, G., & Rachuba, L. (1999). *National evaluation of Core Knowledge Sequence implementation: Final report.* Baltimore: Center for Social Organization of Schools, Johns Hopkins University.

Stringfield, S., Millsap, M., Yoder, N., Schaffer, E., Nesselrodt, P., Gamse, B., Brigham, N., Moss, M., Herman, R., & Bedinger, S. (1997). *Special strategies studies final report*. Washington, DC: U.S. Department of Education.

Stringfield, S., & Teddlie, C. (1991). Observers as predictors of schools' multiyear outlier status on achievement tests. *The Elementary School Journal, 91*(4), 357–376.

Teddlie, C., Kirby, P., & Stringfield, S. (1989). Effective vs. ineffective schools: Observable differences in the classroom. *American Journal of Education, 97*(3), 221–236.

Tharp, R. G. (1997). *From at-risk to excellence: Research, theory, and principles for practice* (Research Report No. 1). Santa Cruz: Center for Research on Education, Diversity & Excellence, University of California.

Valdes, G. (1996). *Con respeto: Bridging the distances between culturally diverse families and schools, an ethnographic portrait*. New York: Teachers College Press.

Yin, R. (1994). *Case study research: Design and methods* (2nd ed.). Beverly Hills, CA: Sage.

APPENDIX A: Success for All Qualitative Study: Observation Time Intervals

*Record observation in 5-minute intervals. Take 1 minute to observe activity and then record observation.

Segment	Actual Time
1	
2	
3	
4	
5	
6	
7	
8	
9	

A. Primary Subject(s)   **Time Intervals**

SFA Reading	1	2	3	4	5	6	7	8	9
Other lang. arts	1	2	3	4	5	6	7	8	9
Writing	1	2	3	4	5	6	7	8	9
Math	1	2	3	4	5	6	7	8	9
Science	1	2	3	4	5	6	7	8	9
Social Studies	1	2	3	4	5	6	7	8	9
Music	1	2	3	4	5	6	7	8	9
Art	1	2	3	4	5	6	7	8	9
Other/No subject	1	2	3	4	5	6	7	8	9

B. Orientations

Teacher led	1	2	3	4	5	6	7	8	9
Team teaching	1	2	3	4	5	6	7	8	9
Independent	1	2	3	4	5	6	7	8	9
Small Group	1	2	3	4	5	6	7	8	9
Pair/tutor	1	2	3	4	5	6	7	8	9
Student led	1	2	3	4	5	6	7	8	9
Aide led	1	2	3	4	5	6	7	8	9
Media led	1	2	3	4	5	6	7	8	9
Contest-game	1	2	3	4	5	6	7	8	9

C. Student attention-interest focus (how many students are on task?)

All	1	2	3	4	5	6	7	8	9
Mostly all	1	2	3	4	5	6	7	8	9
Half	1	2	3	4	5	6	7	8	9
Very few	1	2	3	4	5	6	7	8	9
None	1	2	3	4	5	6	7	8	9

D. Academic engaged time (how much time during interval do students have opportunity to learn?)

All	1	2	3	4	5	6	7	8	9
Mostly all	1	2	3	4	5	6	7	8	9
Half	1	2	3	4	5	6	7	8	9
Very few	1	2	3	4	5	6	7	8	9
None	1	2	3	4	5	6	7	8	9

E. Overall observation

	None	Some	Extensive
Cooperative learning	1	2	3
Direct instruction with whole class	1	2	3
Independent work	1	2	3
Tutoring	1	2	3
Teacher provided feedback (answers, info, etc.)	1	2	3
Students engaged in creation of knowledge	1	2	3
Students engaged in dialogue with each other or with teacher	1	2	3
Sustained writing	1	2	3
Computer as tool or resource	1	2	3
Integration of subject areas	1	2	3
Experiential, hands-on learning	1	2	3
Teacher acted as coach/facilitator	1	2	3
Discipline problems	1	2	3
Interruptions/outside interference	1	2	3
Content instruction	1	2	3
Basic skills instruction	1	2	3
Challenging activities	1	2	3
Alternative assessment strategies	1	2	3
Use of Success for All	1	2	3

APPENDIX B: Success for All Classroom Observation Form

School Name: _____
Observer: _____ Date:_____
Teacher: _____ Time:_____

The students (# of students, race, gender, uniforms, other distinguishing features)

The teacher (approximate age or exp. level, race, gender, demeanor)

Arrangement of space (Draw a small diagram of the classroom – are students in rows? where is the teacher? who is seated where?)

Facilities, resources, & climate (adequate space? lighting? computers? books? Is the classroom climate positive and child sensitive?)

Classroom Instruction

1. Classroom structure for linguistic and cultural diversity

a) What *language* was used during *instruction?* If more than one, what was the dominant language?

b) What *languages* were used during *non-instructional* conversation? Among students? Between teacher and students?

c) Were there any *scheduling variances* for particular linguistic or racial groups of students within the class? (e.g., kids getting pulled out for second language instruction during the reading block, etc.)

d) How even is *student participation*? Do some students participate more than others? Are some students called on more often? (e.g., boys/girls, students of different racial and ethnic groups).

2. Linguistically and Culturally Sensitive and "Authentic" Curriculum and Pedagogy

a) Did the curriculum and pedagogy used by the teacher encourage *students to dialogue or use language*? If not, were there times when such opportunities would have been appropriate? Explain.

b) In the course of the lesson, do students make *connections* between substantive knowledge and either public problems or personal experiences? Explain.

c) Was *equal access* to the curriculum provided for all students? (Or, were some students presented a version that was reduced in content or scope? Were some students excluded altogether?)

d) Did the curriculum and pedagogy foster a sense of *personal and cultural identity*? How do you know?

e) Were the curriculum, pedagogy, and assessments the teachers used able to measure *students' content knowledge* (i.e., what the students learned from the lesson) regardless of students' level of reading or language development? Explain.

f) Was there evidence that teachers had *high expectations* of the students? Describe how you know this. Were these high expectations conveyed equally to all students?

g) Were the students engaged in *meaningful and challenging* learning activities? Describe how you know this.

Summary

Description of the lesson

Attach your own running notes for this section.

Unusual Classroom Activities. Please use the space below to note any unusual classroom activities that were not captured by the above questions. This can mean anything from disciplinary policies you found particularly lax or harsh to a surprise ice cream party at the end of the period.

Overall, how would you describe **the engagement of the students?** Did they appear interested and excited?

Overall, how would you describe the **engagement of the teacher?** Did the teacher appear interested and excited, or did she/he appear bored and un-interested or contrived by curriculum?

Reflections. Please use this space to reflect on the classroom you observed and to note your overall perceptions.

(You can attach notes if you prefer.)

11

Future Directions for Classroom Observation Research

Hersh C. Waxman, R. Soleste Hilberg,
and Roland G. Tharp

This chapter summarizes the work presented in the book, reviews some of the ways classroom observation has contributed to the research knowledge in the field of teacher effectiveness, and discusses some of the important implications of the book for the improvement of teaching and student learning in culturally diverse settings. Some of the criticisms and cautions related to the use of structured observation and techniques are also summarized. Finally, some future directions for observational research are reported and three specific views are described: (a) using instruments that reflect best practices or educational standards, (b) instruments that focus on student behaviors as well as teachers, and (c) combining qualitative and quantitative methods in observation instruments.

LIMITATIONS OF SYSTEMATIC CLASSROOM OBSERVATION

Although previous chapters have highlighted some of the important purposes of classroom observation, there have also been several criticisms and cautions related to the use of structured observation techniques (Delamont & Hamilton, 1986; Evertson & Green, 1986; Galton, 1988; McIntyre & Macleod, 1986). The criticisms and limitations of using structured observation techniques are categorized into three subsections: (a) Theoretical and Epistemological Criticisms, (b) Methodological Concerns, and (c) Pragmatic Concerns. This section also includes a brief discussion of the implications of classroom observation and some future directions.

Theoretical and Epistemological Criticisms

Although observational research has produced a substantial body of important findings that can lead to improved teaching practices, there is still a lack of consensus or lack of confidence regarding the research (Nuthall & Alton-Lee, 1990). There have been many theoretical and epistemological criticisms of classroom observational, process-product research (Doyle, 1977; Evertson & Green, 1986; Fenstermacher, 1978; Galton, 1988; Popkewitz, Tabachnick, & Zeichner, 1979; Winne, 1987; Winne & Marx, 1977). Several critics, for example, have argued that this research is devoid of theory and consequently cannot explain why some instructional behaviors impact student outcomes. There are also related concerns about why some variables are selected to be observed and others are excluded. Because there is no model or theory behind the research, the critics argue that there is no justification for the selection of variables or meaningfulness associated with the interpretation of results. They further argue that the selection of events or behaviors may not be clear to anyone except the observer or instrument developer. In other words, these critics argue that classroom observation research has not dealt with the theoretical assumptions of why a particular style of teaching or set of instructional variables influences student learning.

Popkewitz et al. (1979) argue that this research approach has a behaviorist orientation that maintains that "it is possible to identify, control, and manipulate specific outcomes of teaching by altering selected aspects of a teacher's overt behavior" (p. 52). They further contend that teaching is viewed "as the sum of discrete behaviors and a change in one or several of these behaviors is assumed to affect the quality of teaching as a whole" (p. 52). Their most strenuous argument, however, concerns the notion that these teaching behaviors "are often viewed independent of the curricular context with which the techniques are associated" (p. 52). In other words, they are concerned that observers generally focus on isolated behaviors without concern for the preceding and subsequent behaviors that they feel provide the context and meaning of the behavior. Some other issues related to these concerns focus on the fact that most observational systems are generally limited in that they can only be used to observe covert behavior that can be quantitatively measured. Furthermore, these observational systems cannot adequately record complex instructional behaviors.

Methodological Concerns

Most observational techniques have limitations. Some of these concerns or limitations are related to methodological issues that can interfere with the drawing of valid conclusions. One of the primary methodological concerns or source of invalidity that needs to be addressed regarding the use of systematic observational methods relates to the obtrusiveness of the technique. Observer effects may occur because teachers and students are aware that their behaviors are being observed. In other words, the presence of an observer may change teacher or student behaviors. This may result in reactive effects such as teacher anxiety or teachers performing less well than usual, thus interfering with the drawing of valid inferences about what normally occurs in the classroom. On the other hand, there is some evidence indicating that teachers' instruction may be slightly better than usual when they are being observed (Samph, 1976). Although some researchers, like Medley, Coker, and Soar (1984), maintain that observer effects are not serious concerns, the possibility that these effects threaten the validity and reliability of data collected does exist.

There are a number of methodological concerns that similarly need to be addressed. The reliability and validity of observational systems are primary concerns. Although many systems report interrater agreement or observer accuracy, they do not specify the reliability as it pertains to stability of teacher behavior or the internal consistency of the scale (Hoge, 1985; Medley, 1992). Validity is another important concern that needs to be addressed. Construct validity, for example, which focuses on the *theoretical integrity* of the measures, is particularly important (Hoge, 1985). Criterion-related validity, or the extent to which the observational measures relate to a criterion measure, is rarely reported, and concurrent validity, or the extent to which a particular instrument is related to other instruments, is also generally neglected.

There are other methodological concerns that are related to the actual amount of time that is necessary to obtain a valid observation, as well as the appropriate number of observations required to obtain reliable and valid measures of instruction. Similarly, there are a number of methodological concerns related to the analysis of data. Most of these concerns address the issue of what the appropriate level of analysis (e.g., the student, the class, the school, or students within the class) should be used when analyzing observation data. Students are nested within classrooms, whereas classrooms are nested within schools. Prior teacher effectiveness research has often aggregated data to classroom-level analyses. This may underestimate the importance of processes within classes because all the within-class variation is lost. Recent analytic developments, such as hierarchical linear modeling (HLM), allow researchers to disentangle these nested effects and investigate hypotheses about the effects of within- and between-school or class factors on classroom instruction or students' perceptions of their learning environments (Bryk & Raudenbush, 1989; Raudenbush & Bryk, 1989; Raudenbush & Willms, 1991). Advanced statistical models such as HLM allow researchers to identify and separate individual effects from group effects after statistically controlling for other explanatory variables (Morgenstein & Keeves, 1994). Such multilevel models can estimate how group-level variables (e.g., characteristics of the classroom or school) influence the way in which individual-level variables (e.g., students' classroom behavior) affect student achievement (Stockard, 1993).

Another concern related to prior classroom observation research is that it has typically been generic (i.e., generalizing across grade levels and content areas) rather than focusing on a given grade level and/or subject area (Anderson & Burns, 1989; Gage, 1985; Gage & Needels, 1989; Needels & Gage, 1991). Similarly, the content of the lesson is often neglected, as is the quality of the interaction that is being recorded (Anderson & Burns, 1989).

Pragmatic Concerns

The final category of limitations related to classroom observation is pragmatic concerns that focus on the practicality of conducting observational research. One of the primary pragmatic concerns of observation research is that it is costly to do because it requires extensive training as well as time for someone to actually do the observations. Some training programs for observers, for example, require as much as 7 full days of intensive training before the observations are conducted in classrooms (Stallings & Freiberg, 1991). Gaining access to schools and classrooms to conduct observations is another serious concern. Many school districts are reluctant to allow researchers to observe in their schools because they feel it would be too disruptive to the learning environment. Teachers have also been known to alter their instruction dramatically when observers are present in the classroom.

Another pragmatic concern relates to the misuse of classroom observation data. Classroom observation can be very useful as a formative evaluation procedure, but it is not useful and should not be used as a basis for summative decisions such as whether or not a teacher should be dismissed or rehired. Nor should classroom observations be tied to summative decisions like salary increases. Unfortunately, several school districts and state departments of education have misused observational research and translated findings into specific rules or standards that they have used in developing evaluation instruments (Ornstein, 1991). These misuses are more accidents of the research, however, rather than problems associated with the essence of the research (Needels & Gage, 1991).

The previously mentioned criticisms and limitations, however, do not necessarily detract from the value and utility of the observational method. As previously discussed, many of these criticisms are accidents or incidental aspects of some observational research. Gage and Needels (1989), Needels and Gage (1991), and others, for example, have refuted many of these criticisms and have provided several examples of how observational research has contributed to instructional theories. Medley (1992) has also argued that the previous methodological limitations of observational research have been greatly reduced in recent years. He points out, for example, the impact that the laptop computer will have on classroom observational research. In addition to replacing traditional clipboards and stopwatches, the laptop computer will increase the precision and accuracy of researchers in recording events, as well as provide a detailed account of contextual items that occur during the observation.

Many of the chapters in this volume also illustrate how classroom observation can be done more appropriately. Many of the authors, for example, describe the theoretical/conceptual framework that their instrument is based on. Most of the instruments described in the book similarly address concerns like focusing on context (e.g., grade level or content area), and many have dramatically reduced the amount of training time required for observers. Some of the student-centered instruments also have been found to be less threatening to classroom teachers. Although research on classroom observation has made significant progress over the past several decades, there are still additional areas where the research paradigm can be strengthened. The next section addresses these future directions for observational research.

FUTURE DIRECTIONS FOR OBSERVATIONAL RESEARCH

The chapters in this book point out several future directions for class-room observation research. The following subsections briefly summarize six major themes that are derived from the work in this volume: (a) the use of best practice or standards-based observation instruments, (b) instruments that focus on student behaviors, (c) instruments that focus on effective teaching for linguistically and culturally diverse students, (d) observing technology use, (e) combining qualitative and quantitative methods, and (f) focusing on students' higher-level thinking.

Best Practice or Standards-Based Observation Instruments

One important trend in classroom observation research is the development of new observation instruments that are based on the best research knowledge available in the field of effective teaching practices. The chapters by (a) Hilberg, Doherty, Epaloose and Tharp, (b) Rivera and Tharp, (c) Estrada, and (d) Datnow and Yonezawa all describe instruments based on the Five Standards for Effective Pedagogy (Dalton, 1998; Tharp, 1997; Tharp, Estrada, Dalton, & Yamauchi, 2000), which were developed and used in the National Center for Research on Education, Diversity & Excellence. The five standards are (a) Joint Productive Activity: Teacher and Students Producing Together, (b) Developing Language and Literacy Across the Curriculum, (c) Making Meaning: Connecting School to Students' Lives, (d) Teaching Complex Thinking, and (e) Teaching Through Conversation, and there is a substantive research base that supports these teaching standards (Tharp, 1999). Several of the instruments described in the book are based on these pedagogy standards, which are very different from traditional observation instruments that have been primarily generic and descriptive in nature. These instruments have great potential for improving teachers' classroom practices because they focus on established standards of teaching excellence.

Instruments Focusing on Student Behaviors

Classroom observations that focus on students are unusual; most observation instruments focus on the teacher or the class as a whole. Student-centered observation instruments emphasize the student-mediating paradigm, which argues that the way students perceive and react to their learning tasks and classroom instruction may be more important in influencing student outcomes than the observed quality of teaching behaviors. Furthermore, student-centered observation instruments allow for comparisons between groups of students within the class (e.g., boys vs. girls, monolingual vs. bilingual, or African American vs. Anglo) that are important for many types of research studies. The chapter by Waxman and Padrón describes a student-centered classroom observation instrument (i.e., the Classroom Observation Schedule [COS]) that is very different from traditional instruments, and their research illustrates how important subgroup differences can be found when using the COS.

Effective Teaching for Linguistically and Culturally Diverse Students

Many of the instruments described in this book are based on current research on effective teaching for linguistically and culturally diverse students. This is substantially different from prior research that has traditionally focused on generic, correlational research. The chapter by Echevarria and Short, for example, is based on the model of sheltered instruction, a new instructional approach that has only recently been implemented widely for second-language learners.

Technology Use in the Classroom

Several of the instruments described in this book reflect other recent trends in classroom instruction, such as the use of instructional technology. The chapters by Ross, Smith, Alberg, and Lowther and by Waxman and Padrón, for example, include the observation of instructional technology in the classroom. This is especially important because technology-enhanced instruction has been found to be an effective teaching practice for students who are English language learners and students who attend schools in high-poverty neighborhoods (Waxman & Padrón, 2002; Waxman, Padrón, & Arnold, 2001).

Combining Qualitative and Quantitative Methods

The study of classroom instruction often requires us to collect quantitative information on the frequency, duration, and intensity of instructional behaviors, but it also needs to include qualitative information that provides rich, detailed, meaning-centered accounts (Foster,

1996). Several of the chapters in this book advocate the use of both qualitative and quantitative methods (e.g., those by Knight & Smith, Datnow & Yonezawa, and Castellano & Datnow). Knight and Smith (Chapter 5), for example, described the use of the Teaching for Meaning (TFM) Classroom Observation Form (Knight & Ackerman, 1997) that was developed to examine several projects that focused on changing teaching practices to incorporate more higher-order thinking skills and knowledge. The TFM instrument includes three components: (a) a quantitative assessment of student engagement rates, (b) qualitative reports of classroom processes and events, and (c) ratings of seven indicators of teaching behaviors. This research clearly illustrates the importance of combining multiple measures of classroom observation in order to examine changes in teaching processes. This multimethod or triangulation approach is very different from prior observational research that has traditionally been either qualitative or quantitative but *not* both. Illustrating the simultaneous use of both qualitative and quantitative classroom observation research is an important aspect of this book.

A Focus on Higher-Level Learning

Finally, many of the instruments described in this book focus on teaching practices that are geared to promote students' higher-level learning. Most of the classroom observation instruments widely used today (e.g., Stallings and Flanders's observation instrument) were developed in the 1960s and 1970s based on process-product research that focused on correlates of teaching behaviors that were positively related to achievement on basic-skills tests (i.e., low-level skills). Many of the chapters in this book focus on students' higher-level outcomes (e.g., those by Knight & Smith, Rivera & Tharp, and Hilberg, Doherty, Tharp, & Epaloose), and the authors have developed instruments that assess more authentic, interactive instructional practices that have been found to relate to student gains on higher-level cognitive outcomes.

SUMMARY

In summary, systematic classroom observations are useful for a variety of educational purposes, including describing instructional practices, investigating instructional inequities for different groups of students, improving teacher education programs, and improving teachers' classroom instruction based on feedback from individual classroom profiles. In addition, the substantive findings from this research have significantly contributed to our knowledge base about effective teaching practices. Classroom observation, however, also has some limitations. It may be costly to do because it requires training as well as time for someone to actually do the observations. Furthermore, there are some validity concerns related to the obtrusiveness of the technique, as well as the amount of time and the number of observations required to obtain a valid measure of instruction. Finally, there are concerns related to the instrumentation involved in classroom observations. Do the classroom observation instruments currently used in the field, for example, capture the important instructional variables that we should be looking at? There have been other theoretical and epistemological criticisms of classroom observational research, but these concerns appear to focus on accidental or incidental features of the research rather than the true essence of the research.

Although the findings summarized by the current observational research in the field suggest several consistent relationships between classroom instruction and students' outcomes, further correlational, longitudinal, and especially experimental research is needed to verify these results. Other research issues that still need to be investigated in this area include (a) the ideal or optimum levels and ranges of student and teacher behaviors that should exist in various classrooms, (b) whether there are other contextual variables that influence student or teacher behaviors, (c) whether there are different teaching practices used among student subgroups characterized by sex, ethnicity, grade, and achievement level, (d) whether teacher characteristics such as training and experience influence classroom instruction, and (e) what other variables or factors influence classroom teaching. More observation instruments that emphasize inquiry-based or constructivist learning environments need to be developed and validated. Because observational research has not been able to explain how students interact cognitively with process variables (Winne, 1987), further research may need to focus specifically on students' cognitive operations and observations of students' responses. Finally, observational studies are needed to address some of the substantive issues that are currently facing educators in the United States, such as (a) how reducing class size impacts student and teacher behaviors in the classroom, (b) the impact of high-stakes testing on classroom instruction, and (c) how teaching practices differ when students' primary or second language is used in the classroom.

It is important to point out again that no one data source or methodology will sufficiently answer all of our critical educational questions. Multiple measures or indicators of instruction are needed to help us capture a more comprehensive picture of what goes on in classrooms. In conclusion, classroom observation is a powerful research methodology that can be used for several important educational purposes. Combined with some of the other research methods previously described, it can be used to help us improve educational processes.

References

Anderson, L. W., & Burns, R. B. (1989). *Research in classrooms: The study of teachers, teaching, and instruction.* Oxford: Pergamon Press.

Bryk, A. S., & Raudenbush, S. W. (1989). Toward a more appropriate conceptualization of research on school effects: A three-level hierarchical linear model. In R. D. Bock (Ed.), *Multilevel analysis of educational data* (pp. 159–204). San Diego, CA: Academic Press.

Dalton, S. S. (1998). *Pedagogy matters: Standards for effective teaching practice* (Research Report No. 4). Santa Cruz: Center for Research on Education, Diversity & Excellence, University of California.

Delamont, S., & Hamilton, D. (1986). Revisiting classroom research: A cautionary tale. In M. Hammersley (Ed.), *Controversies in classroom research* (pp. 25–43). Philidelphia: Open University Press.

Doyle, W. (1977). Paradigms for research on teacher effectiveness. In L. S. Shulman (Ed.), *Review of research in education* (Vol. 5, pp. 163–198). Itasca, IL: Peacock.

Evertson, C., & Green, J. L. (1986). Observation as inquiry and method. In M. C. Wittrock (Ed.), *Handbook of research on teaching* (3rd ed., pp. 162–207). New York: Macmillan.

Fenstermacher, G. (1978). A philosophical consideration of recent research on teacher effectiveness. In L. S. Shulman (Ed.), *Review of research in education* (Vol. 6, pp. 157–185). Itasca, IL: Peacock.

Foster, P. (1996). *Observing schools: A methodological guide.* London: Paul Chapman.

Gage, N. L. (1985). *Hard gains in the soft science: The case of pedagogy.* Bloomington, IN: Phi Delta Kappa.

Gage, N. L., & Needels, M. C. (1989). Process-product research on teaching? A review of criticisms. *Elementary School Journal, 89,* 253–300.

Galton, M. (1988). Structured observation techniques. In J. P. Keeves (Ed.), *Educational research, methodology and measurement: An international handbook* (pp. 474–478). Oxford: Pergamon Press.

Hoge, R. D. (1985). The validity of direct observation measures of pupil classroom behavior. *Review of Educational Research, 55,* 469–483.

Knight, S. L., & Ackerman, C. (1997). *Teaching for Meaning (TFM) classroom observation manual.* College Station: Texas A&M University.

McIntyre, D., & Macleod, G. (1986). The characteristics and uses of systematic classroom observation. In M. Hammersley (Ed.), *Controversies in classroom research* (pp. 10–24). Philidephia: Open University Press.

Medley, D. M. (1992). Structured observation. In M. C. Alkin (Ed.), *Encyclopedia of educational research* (6th ed., pp. 1310–1315). New York: Macmillan.

Medley, D. M., Coker, H., & Soar, R. S. (1984). *Measurement-based evaluation of teacher performance: An empirical approach.* New York: Longman.

Morgenstern, C., & Keeves, J. P. (1994). Descriptive scales for measuring educational climate. In T. Husen & T. N. Postlewaite (Eds.), *International encyclopedia of education* (2nd ed., pp. 1475–1483). Oxford: Pergamon Press.

Needels, M. C., & Gage, N. L. (1991). Essence and accident in process-product research on teaching. In H. C. Waxman & H. J. Walberg (Eds.), *Effective teaching: Current research* (pp. 3–31). Berkeley, CA: McCutchan.

Nuthall, G., & Alton-Lee, A. (1990). Research on teaching and learning: Thirty years of change. *The Elementary School Journal, 90,* 546–570.

Ornstein, A. C. (1991). Teacher effectiveness research: Theoretical consideration. In H. C. Waxman & H. J. Walberg (Eds.), *Effective teaching: Current research* (pp. 63–80). Berkeley, CA: McCutchan.

Popkewitz, T. S., Tabachnick, R., & Zeichner, K. (1979). Dulling the senses: Research in teacher education. *Journal of Teacher Education, 30,* 52–60.

Raudenbush, S. W., & Bryk, A. S. (1989). Quantitative models for estimating teacher and school effectiveness. In R. D. Bock (Ed.), *Multilevel analysis of educational data* (pp. 205–232). San Diego, CA: Academic Press.

Raudenbush, S. W., & Willms, J. D. (1991). *Schools, classrooms, and pupils: International studies of schooling from a multilevel perspective.* San Diego, CA: Academic Press.

Samph, T. (1976). Observer effects on teacher behavior. *Journal of Educational Psychology, 68,* 736–741.

Stallings, J. A., & Freiberg, H. J. (1991). Observation for the improvement of teaching. In H. C. Waxman & H. J. Walberg (Eds.), *Effective teaching: Current research* (pp. 107–133). Berkeley, CA: McCutchan.

Stockard, J. (1993). Methodological issues in the multi-level analysis of school environments. In S. B. Bacharach & R. T. Ogawa (Eds.), *Advances in research and theories of school management and educational policy* (Vol. 2, pp. 217–240). Greenwich, CT: JAI.

Tharp, R. G. (1997). *From at-risk to excellence: Research, theory, and principles for practice* (Research Report No. 1). Santa Cruz: Center for Research on Education, Diversity & Excellence, University of California.

Tharp, R. G. (1999). *Proofs and evidence: Effectiveness of the five standards for effective teaching* (Effective Teaching Document Series No. 2). Santa Cruz: Center for Research on Education, Diversity & Excellence, University of California.

Tharp, R. G., Estrada, P., Dalton, S. S., & Yamauchi, L. (2000). *Teaching transformed: Achieving excellence, fairness, inclusion, and harmony.* Boulder, CO: Westview Press.

Waxman, H. C., & Padrón, Y. N. (2002). Research-based teaching practices that improve the education of English language learners. In L. Minaya-Rowe

(Ed.), *Teacher training and effective pedagogy in the context of student diversity* (pp. 3–38). Greenwich, CT: Information Age.

Waxman, H. C., Padrón, Y. N., & Arnold, K. A. (2001). Effective instructional practices for students placed at risk of failure. In G. D. Borman, S. C. Stringfield, & R. E. Slavin (Eds.), *Title I: Compensatory education at the crossroads* (pp. 137–170). Mahwah, NJ: Erlbaum.

Winne, P. H. (1987). Why process-product research cannot explain process-product findings and a proposed remedy: The cognitive mediational paradigm. *Teaching and Teacher Education, 3,* 333–356.

Winne, P. H., & Marx, R. W. (1977). Reconceptualizing research on teaching. *Journal of Educational Psychology, 69,* 668–678.

Index